ABE SAPIEN™

**CREATED BY
MIKE MIGNOLA**

THE SHAPE OF
THINGS TO COME

Ever since he was discovered in a glass tube in 1978, Abe Sapien has served as a field agent for the Bureau for Paranormal Research and Defense. His origins remained a secret for most of that time, until he found evidence of a former life as a scientist named Langdon Everett Caul. In 1865, Caul unearthed an egglike object amid ruins at the bottom of the Atlantic Ocean, leading to his disappearance, his wife's suicide, and his slow transformation into Abe Sapien.

A second transformation came recently for Abe when a young psychic named Fenix shot him in a border town in Texas, believing that he played a part in the events currently bringing mankind to its knees. Abe fell into a coma, from which he recently awoke. Now a mutated Abe Sapien has left the B.P.R.D., on the run at the end of the world . . .

ABE SAPIEN™

The SHAPE OF THINGS TO COME

STORY BY
Mike Mignola and Scott Allie

*The Shape of
Things to Come*

To the Last Man

ART BY
**Sebastián Fiumara
with Max Fiumara**

ART BY
Max Fiumara

COLORS BY
Dave Stewart

LETTERS BY
Clem Robins

COVER ART BY
Mike Mignola with Dave Stewart

SERIES COVERS BY
Max Fiumara with Dave Stewart

EDITOR **Scott Allie**
ASSOCIATE EDITOR **Daniel Chabon**
ASSISTANT EDITOR **Shantel LaRocque**
COLLECTION DESIGNER **Amy Arendts**
PUBLISHER **Mike Richardson**

DARK HORSE BOOKS®

Special thanks to Carmen Melendez, Iain McCaig, Dave Palumbo, Tim Seeley, and Michael Alexander of RimCountry.com.

Published by Dark Horse Books
A division of Dark Horse Comics, Inc.
10956 SE Main Street
Milwaukie, OR 97222

First edition: July 2014
ISBN 978-1-61655-443-9

1 3 5 7 9 10 8 6 4 2
Printed in China

Abe Sapien™ Volume 4: The Shape of Things to Come

This book collects *Abe Sapien* #6–#7 and #9–#11.

THE SHAPE OF THINGS TO COME

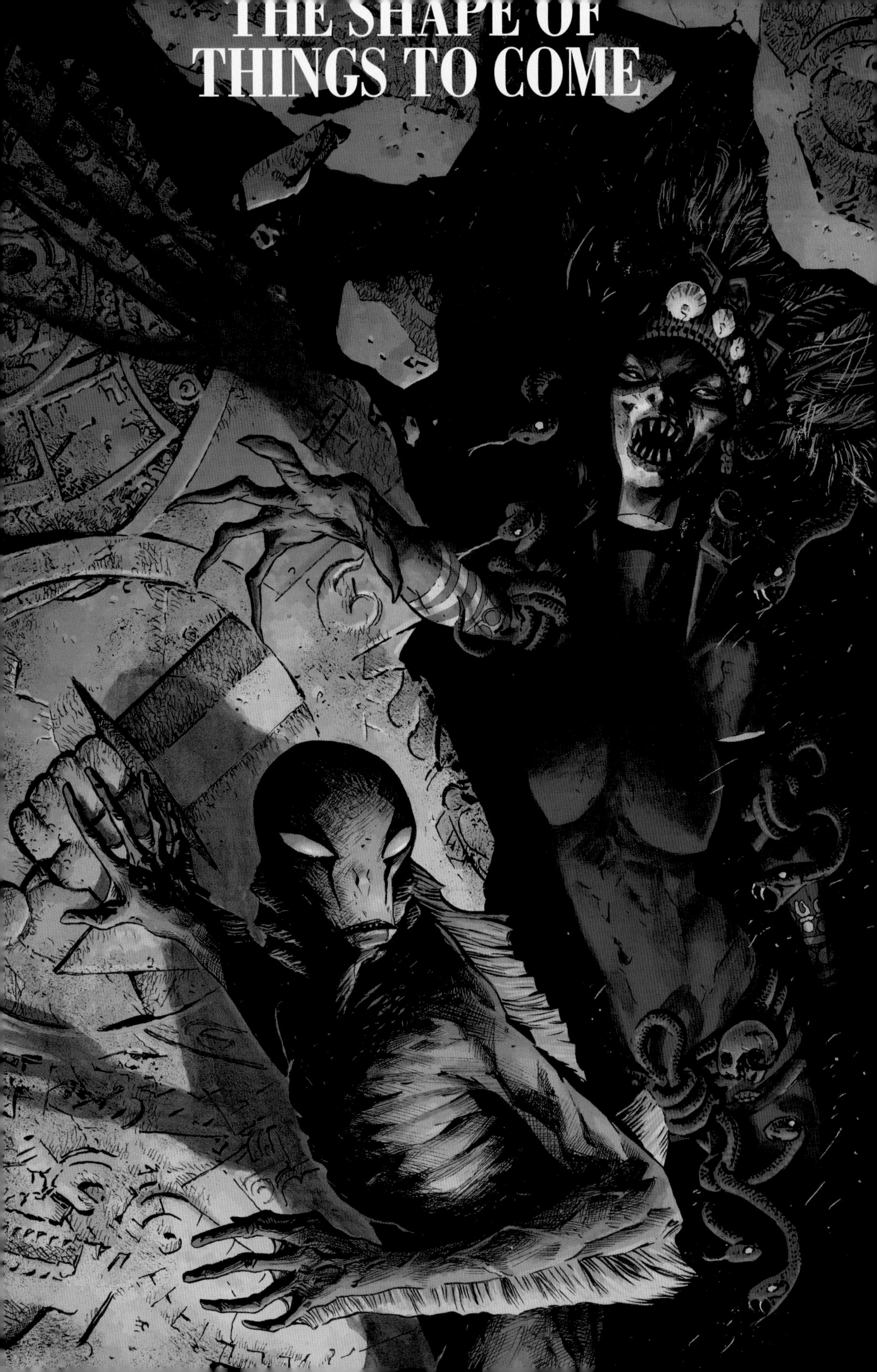

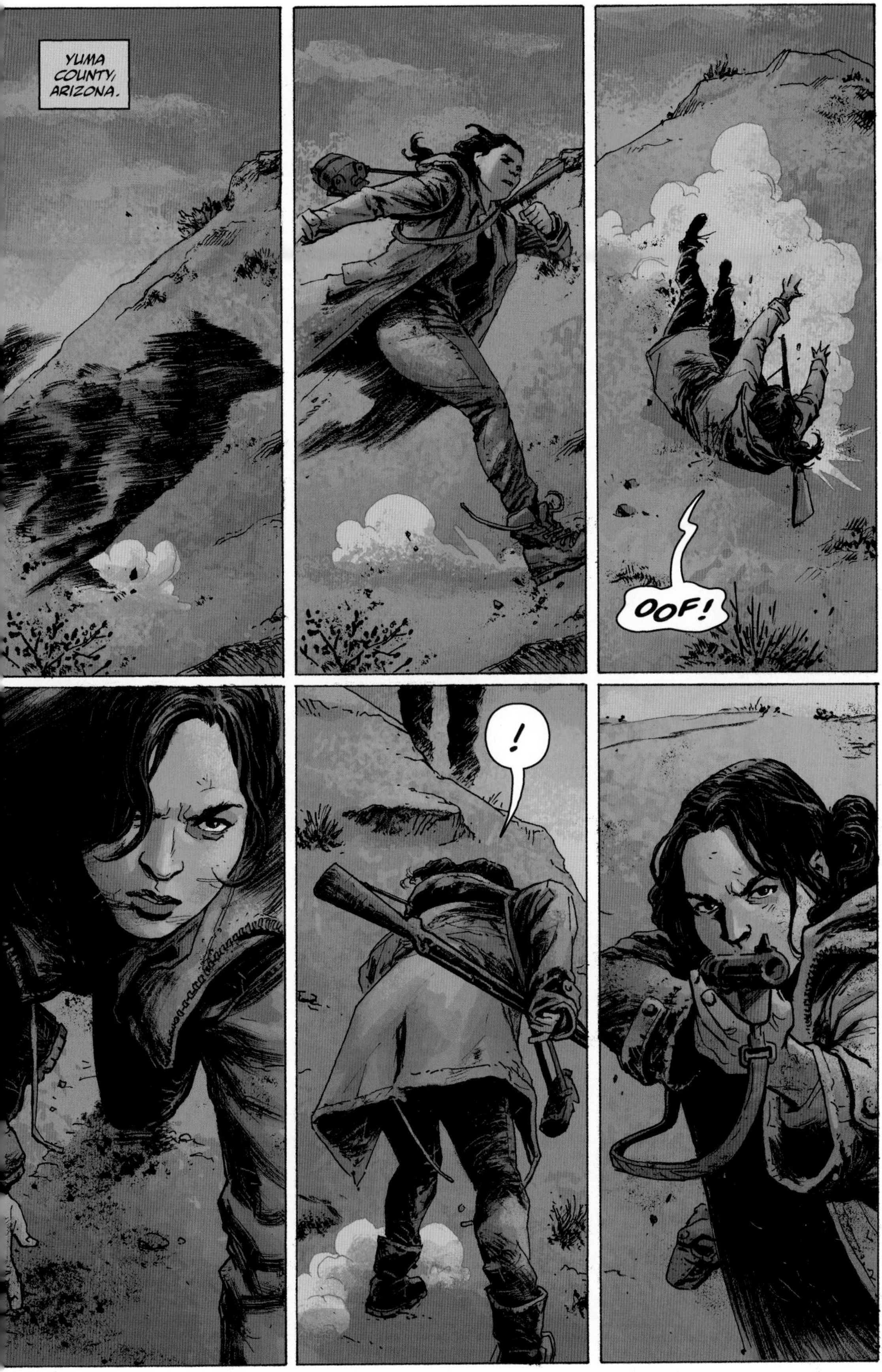

YUMA COUNTY, ARIZONA.
OOF!
!

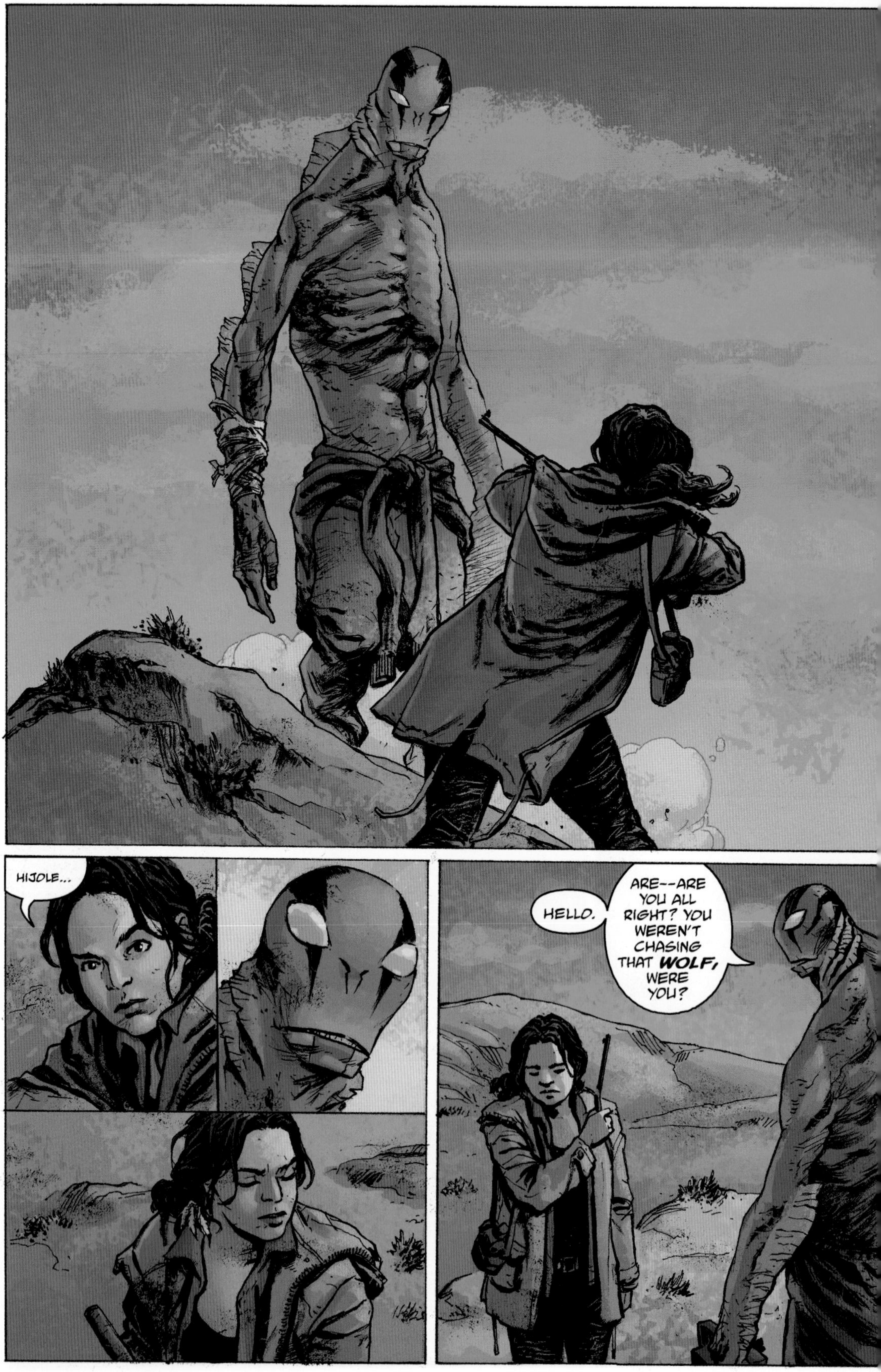
HIJOLE...
HELLO.
ARE--ARE YOU ALL RIGHT? YOU WEREN'T CHASING THAT WOLF, WERE YOU?

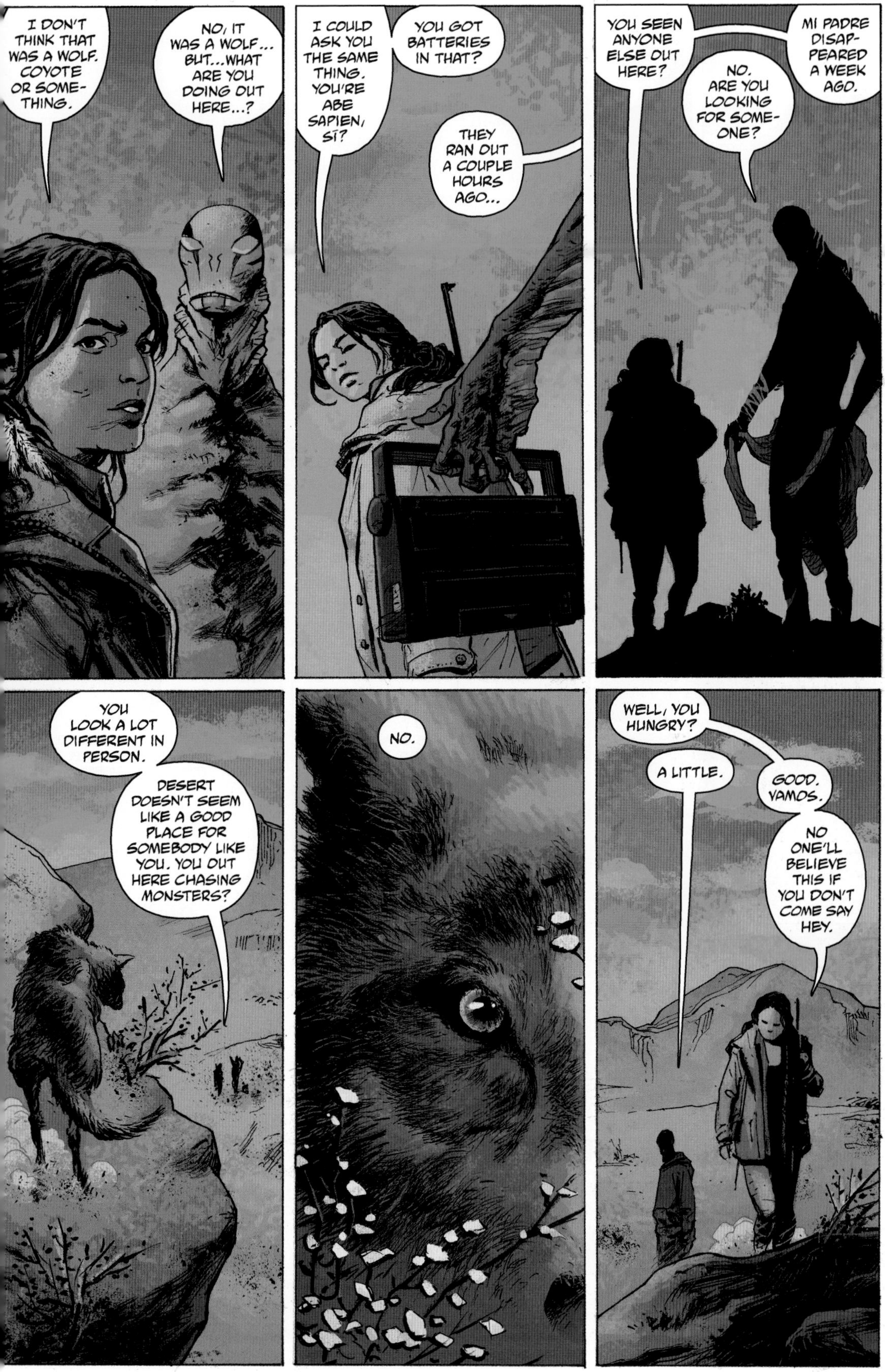
I DON'T THINK THAT WAS A WOLF. COYOTE OR SOMETHING.
NO, IT WAS A WOLF... BUT...WHAT ARE YOU DOING OUT HERE...?
I COULD ASK YOU THE SAME THING. YOU'RE ABE SAPIEN, SÍ?
YOU GOT BATTERIES IN THAT?
THEY RAN OUT A COUPLE HOURS AGO...
YOU SEEN ANYONE ELSE OUT HERE?
NO. ARE YOU LOOKING FOR SOMEONE?
MI PADRE DISAPPEARED A WEEK AGO.
YOU LOOK A LOT DIFFERENT IN PERSON.
DESERT DOESN'T SEEM LIKE A GOOD PLACE FOR SOMEBODY LIKE YOU. YOU OUT HERE CHASING MONSTERS?
NO.
WELL, YOU HUNGRY?
A LITTLE.
GOOD. VAMOS.
NO ONE'LL BELIEVE THIS IF YOU DON'T COME SAY HEY.

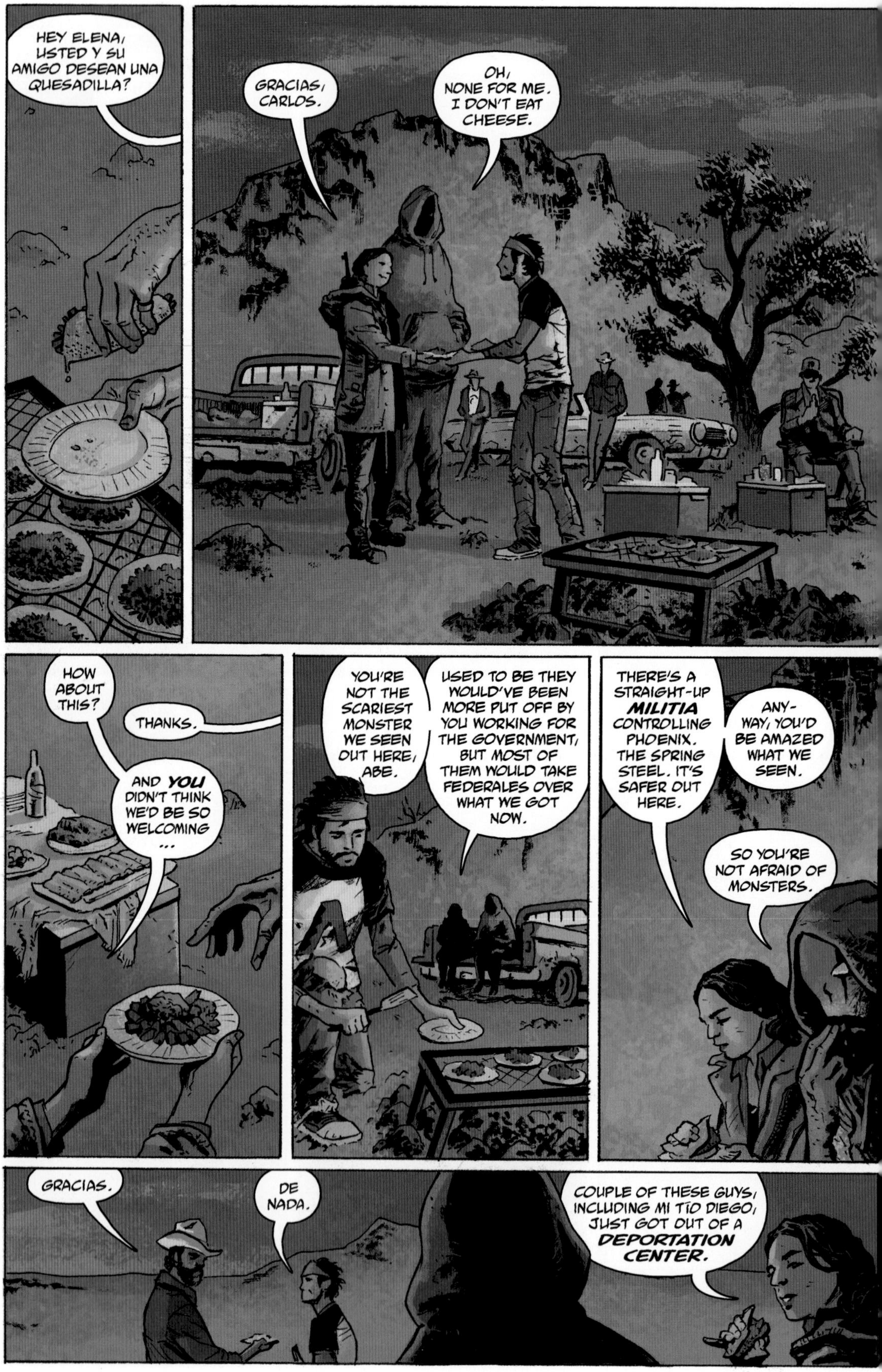
HEY ELENA, USTED Y SU AMIGO DESEAN UNA QUESADILLA?
GRACIAS, CARLOS.
OH, NONE FOR ME. I DON'T EAT CHEESE.
HOW ABOUT THIS?
THANKS.
AND YOU DIDN'T THINK WE'D BE SO WELCOMING...
YOU'RE NOT THE SCARIEST MONSTER WE SEEN OUT HERE, ABE.
USED TO BE THEY WOULD'VE BEEN MORE PUT OFF BY YOU WORKING FOR THE GOVERNMENT, BUT MOST OF THEM WOULD TAKE FEDERALES OVER WHAT WE GOT NOW.
THERE'S A STRAIGHT-UP MILITIA CONTROLLING PHOENIX. THE SPRING STEEL. IT'S SAFER OUT HERE.
ANYWAY, YOU'D BE AMAZED WHAT WE SEEN.
SO YOU'RE NOT AFRAID OF MONSTERS.
GRACIAS.
DE NADA.
COUPLE OF THESE GUYS, INCLUDING MI TÍO DIEGO, JUST GOT OUT OF A DEPORTATION CENTER.

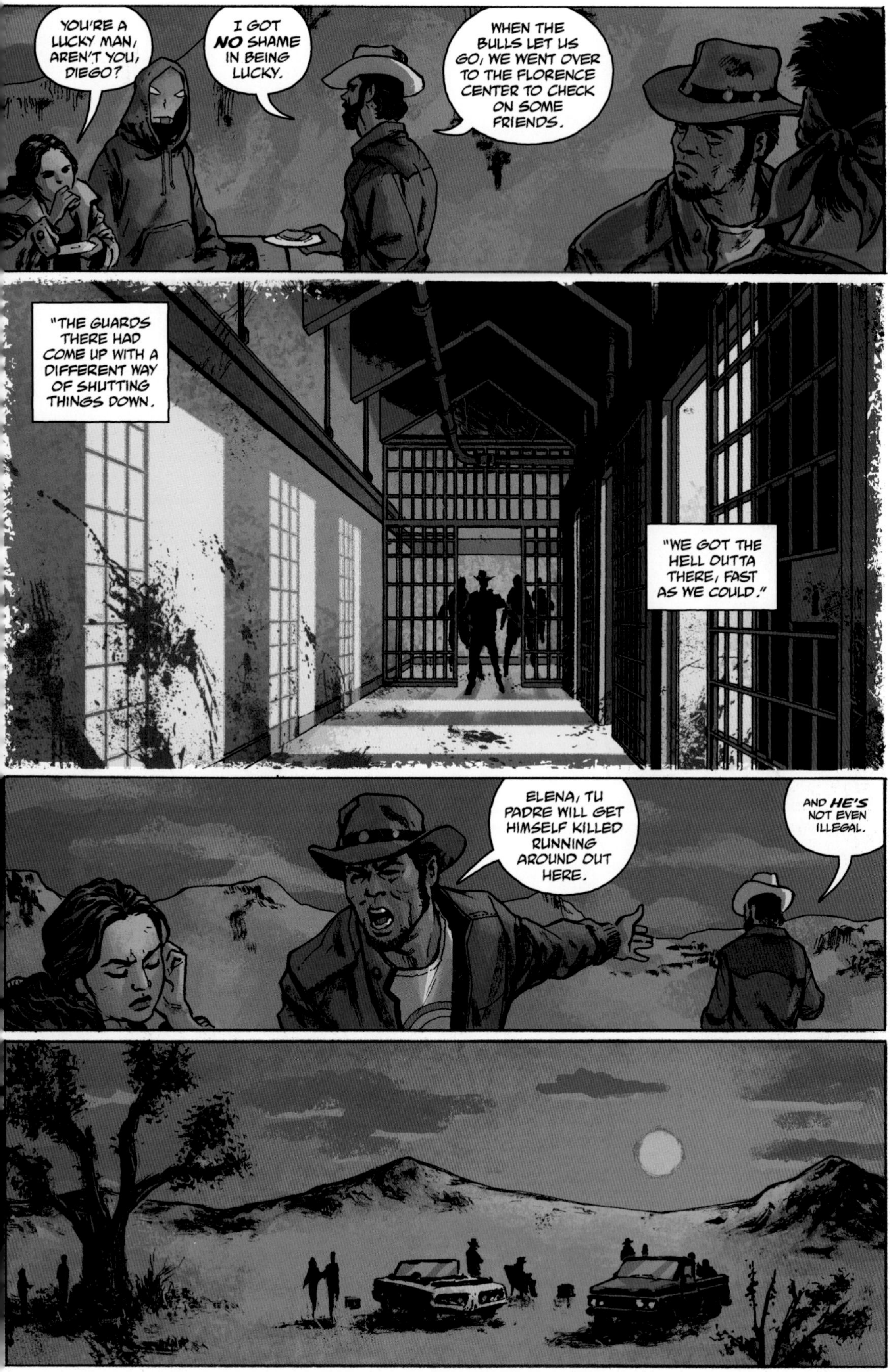
YOU'RE A LUCKY MAN, AREN'T YOU, DIEGO?
I GOT NO SHAME IN BEING LUCKY.
WHEN THE BULLS LET US GO, WE WENT OVER TO THE FLORENCE CENTER TO CHECK ON SOME FRIENDS.
"THE GUARDS THERE HAD COME UP WITH A DIFFERENT WAY OF SHUTTING THINGS DOWN.
"WE GOT THE HELL OUTTA THERE, FAST AS WE COULD."
ELENA, TU PADRE WILL GET HIMSELF KILLED RUNNING AROUND OUT HERE.
AND HE'S NOT EVEN ILLEGAL.

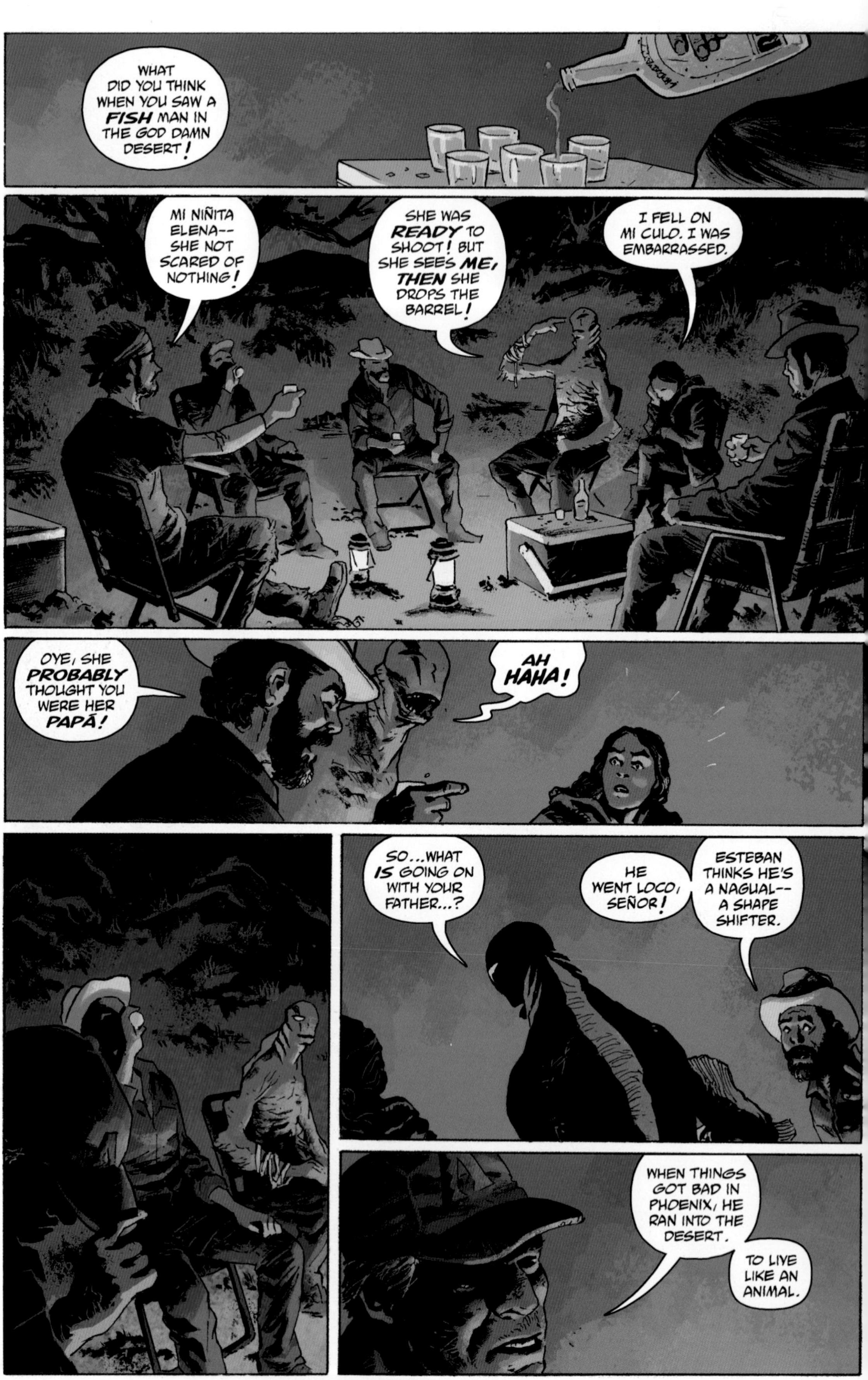
WHAT DID YOU THINK WHEN YOU SAW A FISH MAN IN THE GOD DAMN DESERT!
MI NIÑITA ELENA-- SHE NOT SCARED OF NOTHING!
SHE WAS READY TO SHOOT! BUT SHE SEES ME, THEN SHE DROPS THE BARREL!
I FELL ON MI CULO. I WAS EMBARRASSED.
OYE, SHE PROBABLY THOUGHT YOU WERE HER PAPÁ!
AH HAHA!
SO...WHAT IS GOING ON WITH YOUR FATHER...?
HE WENT LOCO, SEÑOR!
ESTEBAN THINKS HE'S A NAGUAL-- A SHAPE SHIFTER.
WHEN THINGS GOT BAD IN PHOENIX, HE RAN INTO THE DESERT.
TO LIVE LIKE AN ANIMAL.

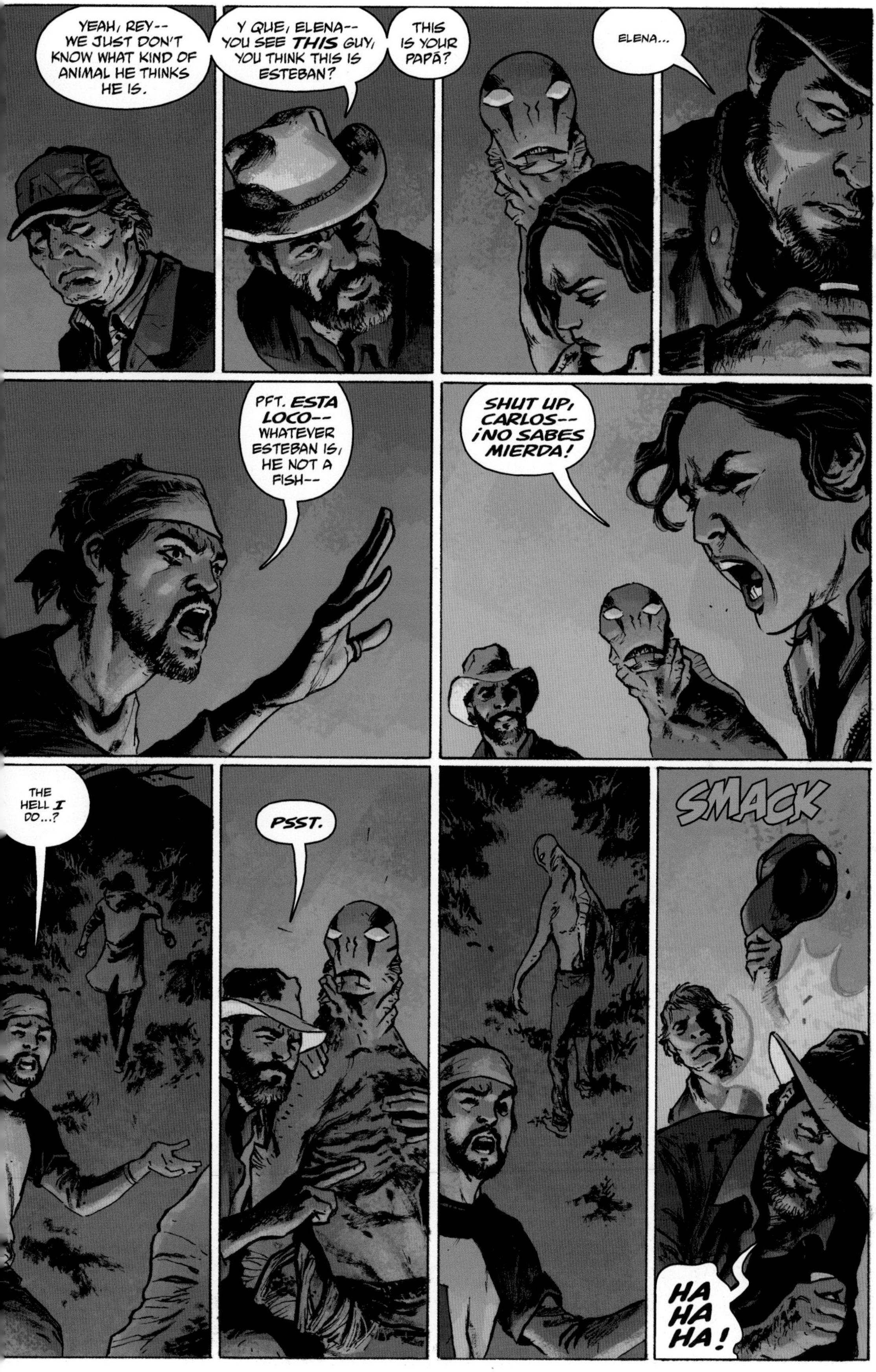
YEAH, REY--
WE JUST DON'T KNOW WHAT KIND OF ANIMAL HE THINKS HE IS.
Y QUE, ELENA--
YOU SEE THIS GUY, YOU THINK THIS IS ESTEBAN?
THIS IS YOUR PAPÁ?
ELENA...
PFT. ESTA LOCO--
WHATEVER ESTEBAN IS, HE NOT A FISH--
SHUT UP, CARLOS--
¡NO SABES MIERDA!
THE HELL I DO...?
PSST.
SMACK
HA HA HA!

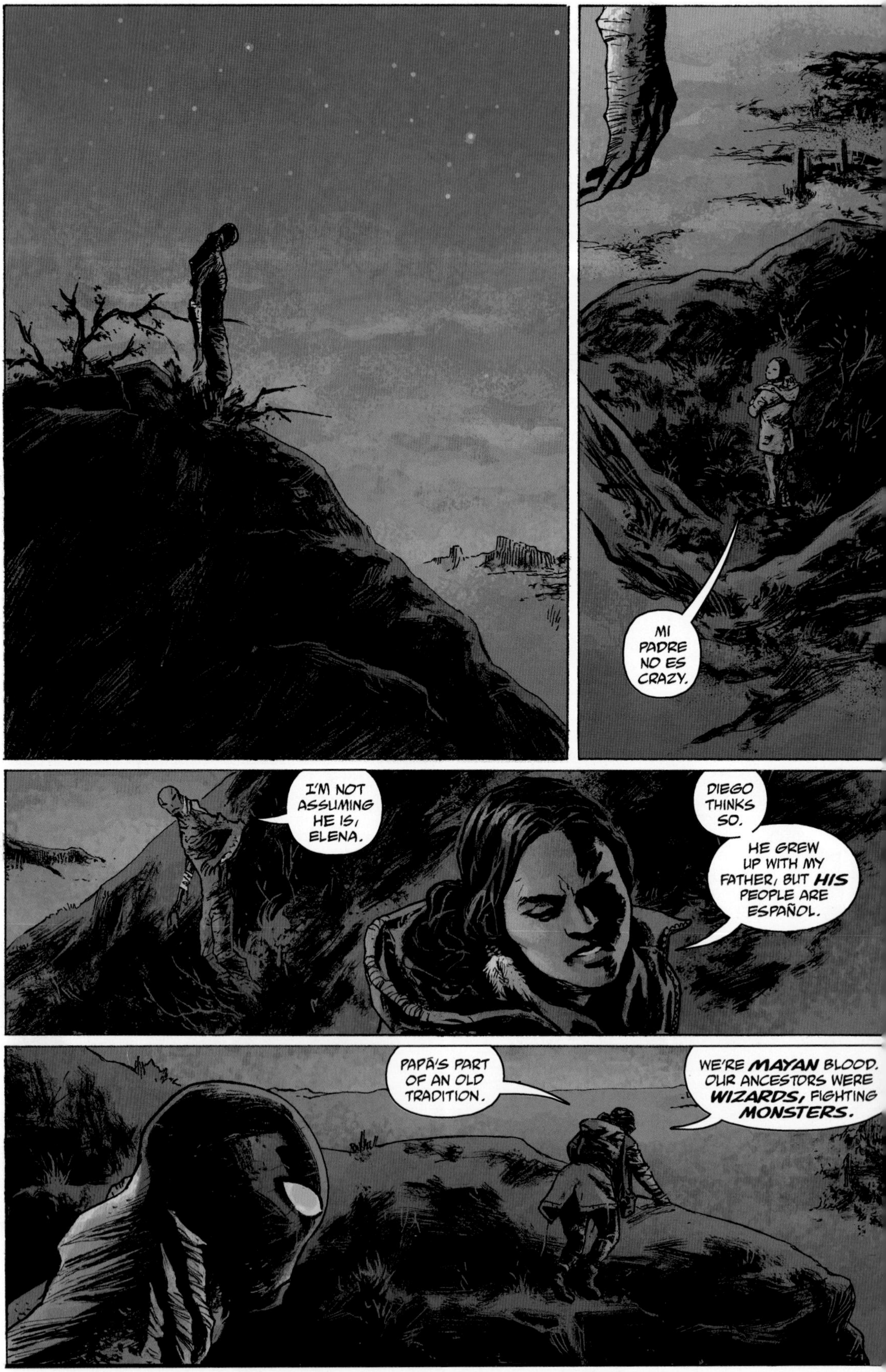
MI PADRE NO ES CRAZY.
I'M NOT ASSUMING HE IS, ELENA.
DIEGO THINKS SO.
HE GREW UP WITH MY FATHER, BUT **HIS** PEOPLE ARE ESPAÑOL.
PAPÁ'S PART OF AN OLD TRADITION.
WE'RE **MAYAN** BLOOD. OUR ANCESTORS WERE **WIZARDS,** FIGHTING **MONSTERS.**

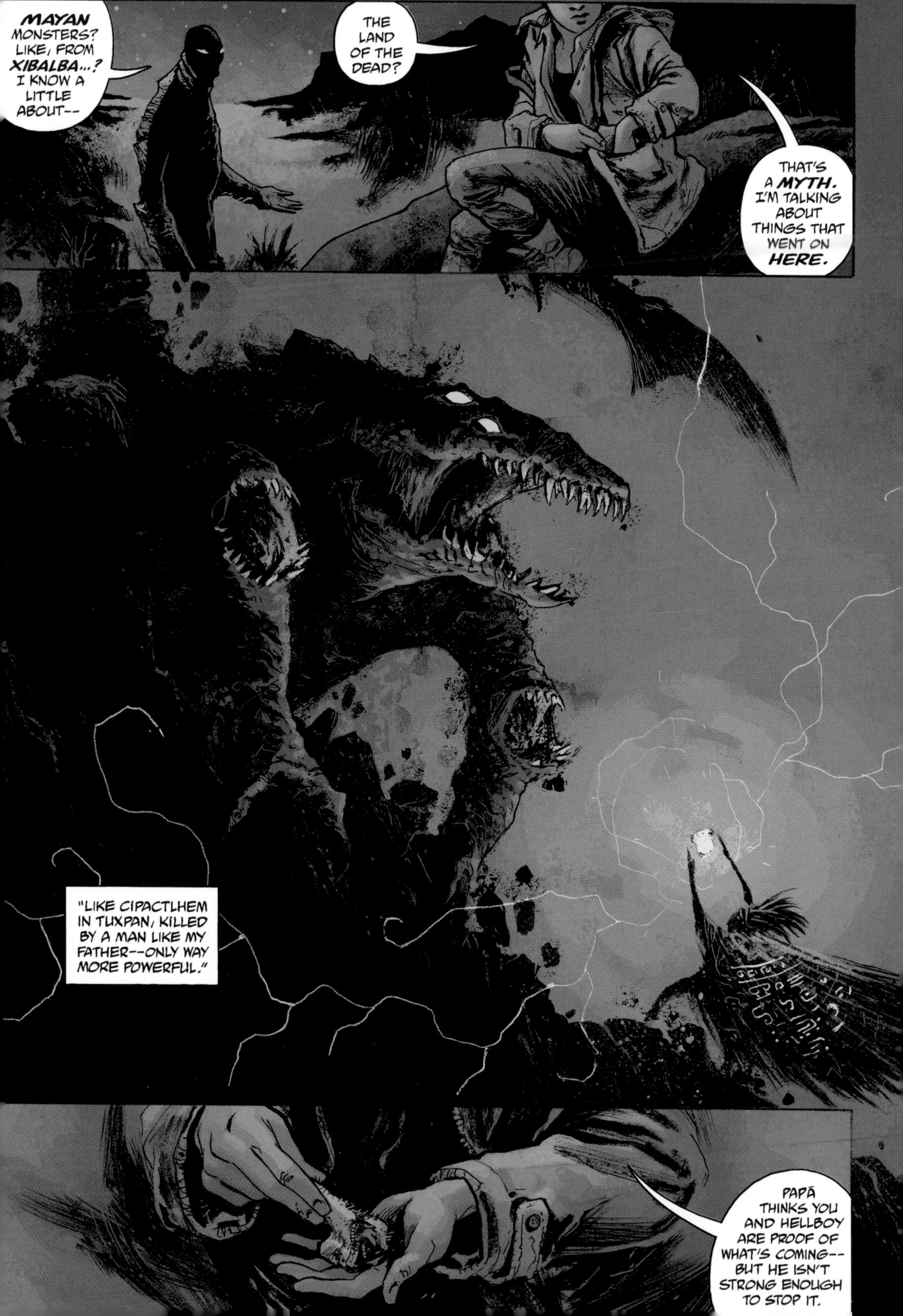
MAYAN MONSTERS? LIKE, FROM XIBALBA...? I KNOW A LITTLE ABOUT--
THE LAND OF THE DEAD?
THAT'S A MYTH. I'M TALKING ABOUT THINGS THAT WENT ON HERE.
"LIKE CIPACTLHEM IN TUXPAN, KILLED BY A MAN LIKE MY FATHER--ONLY WAY MORE POWERFUL."
PAPÁ THINKS YOU AND HELLBOY ARE PROOF OF WHAT'S COMING-- BUT HE ISN'T STRONG ENOUGH TO STOP IT.

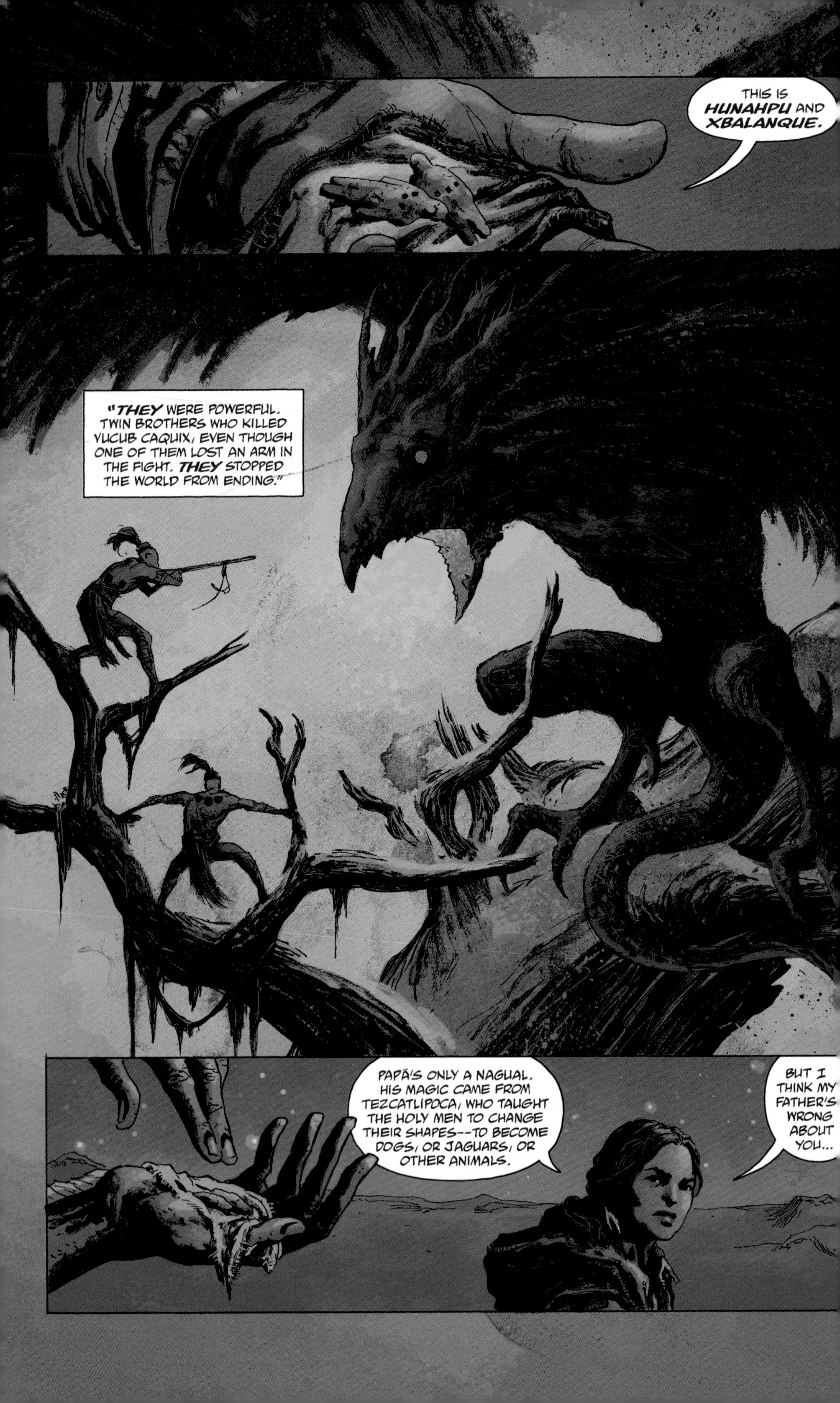
THIS IS HUNAHPU AND XBALANQUE.
"THEY WERE POWERFUL. TWIN BROTHERS WHO KILLED VUCUB CAQUIX, EVEN THOUGH ONE OF THEM LOST AN ARM IN THE FIGHT. THEY STOPPED THE WORLD FROM ENDING."
PAPÁ'S ONLY A NAGUAL. HIS MAGIC CAME FROM TEZCATLIPOCA, WHO TAUGHT THE HOLY MEN TO CHANGE THEIR SHAPES--TO BECOME DOGS, OR JAGUARS, OR OTHER ANIMALS.
BUT I THINK MY FATHER'S WRONG ABOUT YOU...

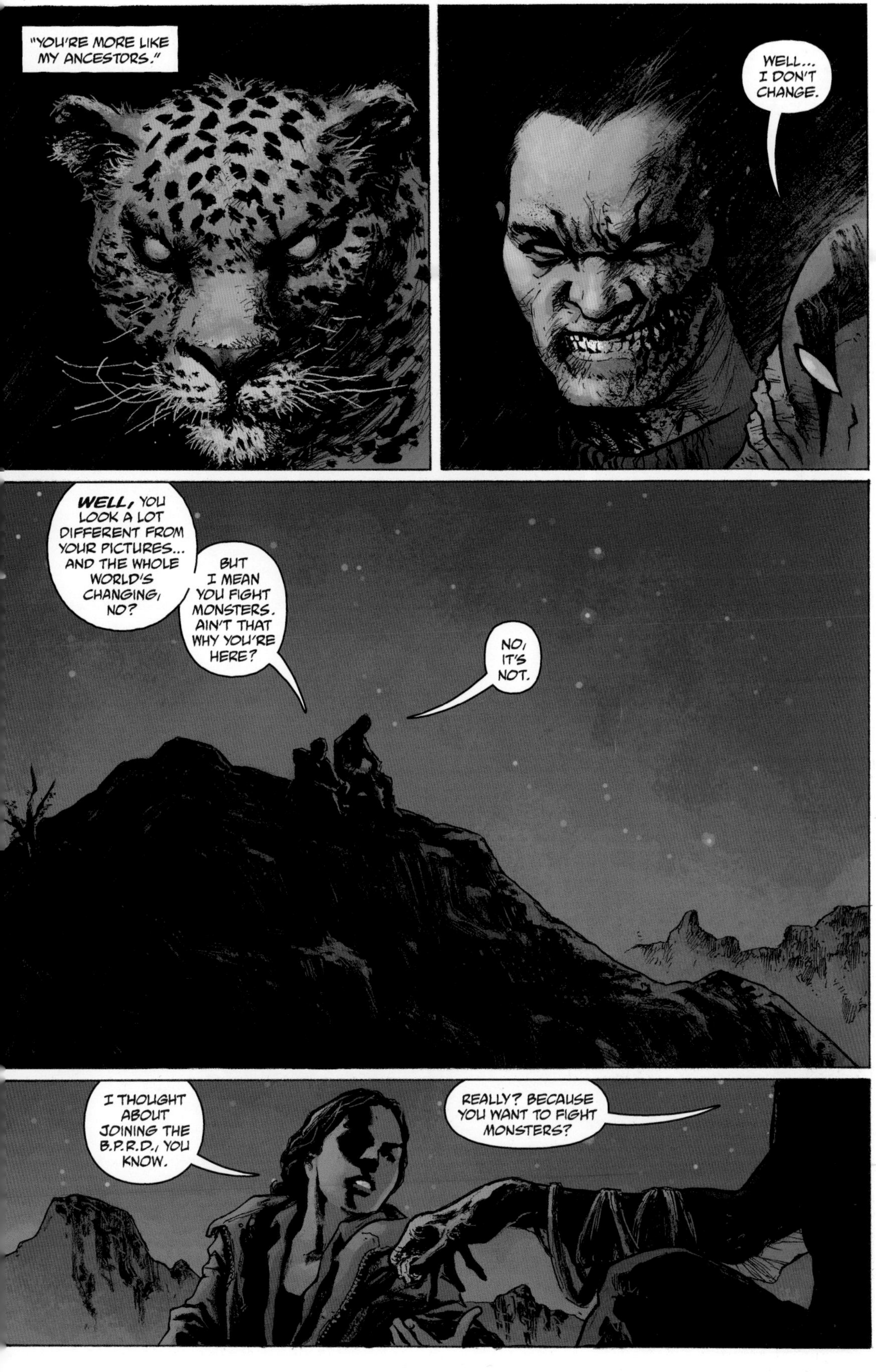
"YOU'RE MORE LIKE MY ANCESTORS."
WELL... I DON'T CHANGE.
WELL, YOU LOOK A LOT DIFFERENT FROM YOUR PICTURES... AND THE WHOLE WORLD'S CHANGING, NO?
BUT I MEAN YOU FIGHT MONSTERS. AIN'T THAT WHY YOU'RE HERE?
NO, IT'S NOT.
I THOUGHT ABOUT JOINING THE B.P.R.D., YOU KNOW.
REALLY? BECAUSE YOU WANT TO FIGHT MONSTERS?

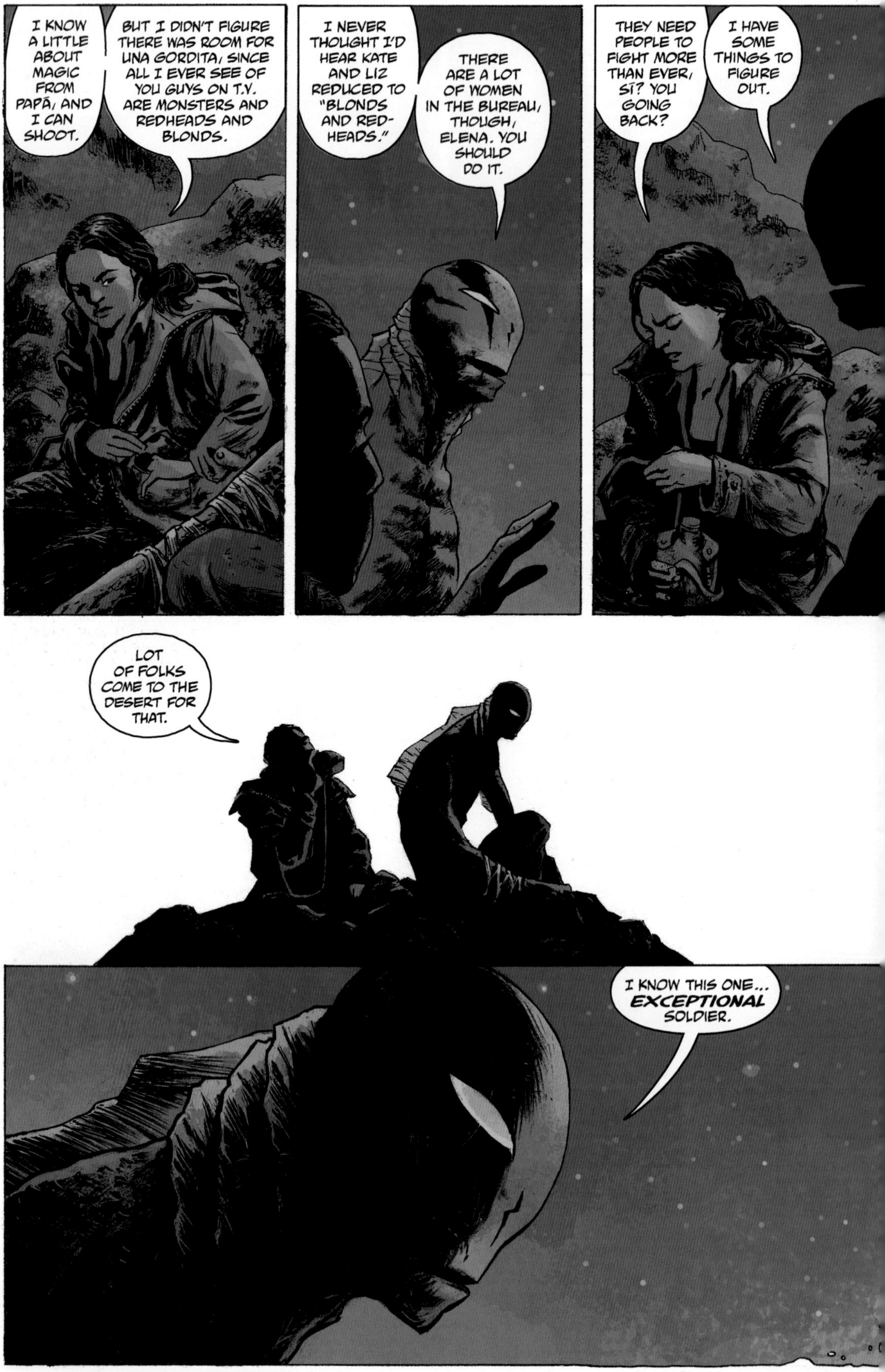
I KNOW A LITTLE ABOUT MAGIC FROM PAPÁ, AND I CAN SHOOT.
BUT I DIDN'T FIGURE THERE WAS ROOM FOR UNA GORDITA, SINCE ALL I EVER SEE OF YOU GUYS ON T.V. ARE MONSTERS AND REDHEADS AND BLONDS.
I NEVER THOUGHT I'D HEAR KATE AND LIZ REDUCED TO "BLONDS AND RED-HEADS."
THERE ARE A LOT OF WOMEN IN THE BUREAU, THOUGH, ELENA. YOU SHOULD DO IT.
THEY NEED PEOPLE TO FIGHT MORE THAN EVER, SÍ? YOU GOING BACK?
I HAVE SOME THINGS TO FIGURE OUT.
LOT OF FOLKS COME TO THE DESERT FOR THAT.
I KNOW THIS ONE... *EXCEPTIONAL* SOLDIER.

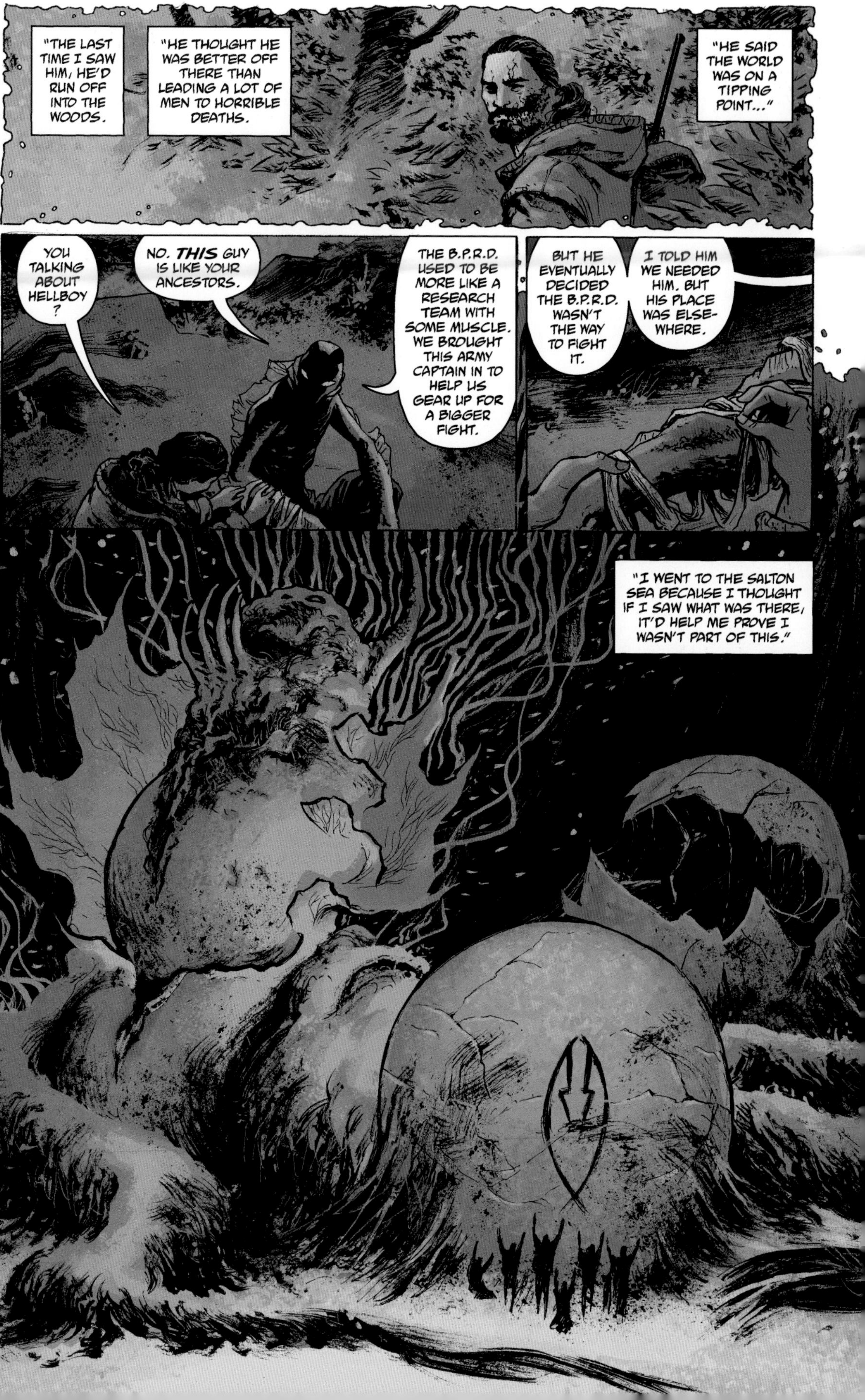
"THE LAST TIME I SAW HIM, HE'D RUN OFF INTO THE WOODS.
"HE THOUGHT HE WAS BETTER OFF THERE THAN LEADING A LOT OF MEN TO HORRIBLE DEATHS.
"HE SAID THE WORLD WAS ON A TIPPING POINT..."
YOU TALKING ABOUT HELLBOY?
NO. *THIS* GUY IS LIKE YOUR ANCESTORS.
THE B.P.R.D. USED TO BE MORE LIKE A RESEARCH TEAM WITH SOME MUSCLE. WE BROUGHT THIS ARMY CAPTAIN IN TO HELP US GEAR UP FOR A BIGGER FIGHT.
BUT HE EVENTUALLY DECIDED THE B.P.R.D. WASN'T THE WAY TO FIGHT IT.
I TOLD HIM WE NEEDED HIM. BUT HIS PLACE WAS ELSE-WHERE.
"I WENT TO THE SALTON SEA BECAUSE I THOUGHT IF I SAW WHAT WAS THERE, IT'D HELP ME PROVE I WASN'T PART OF THIS."

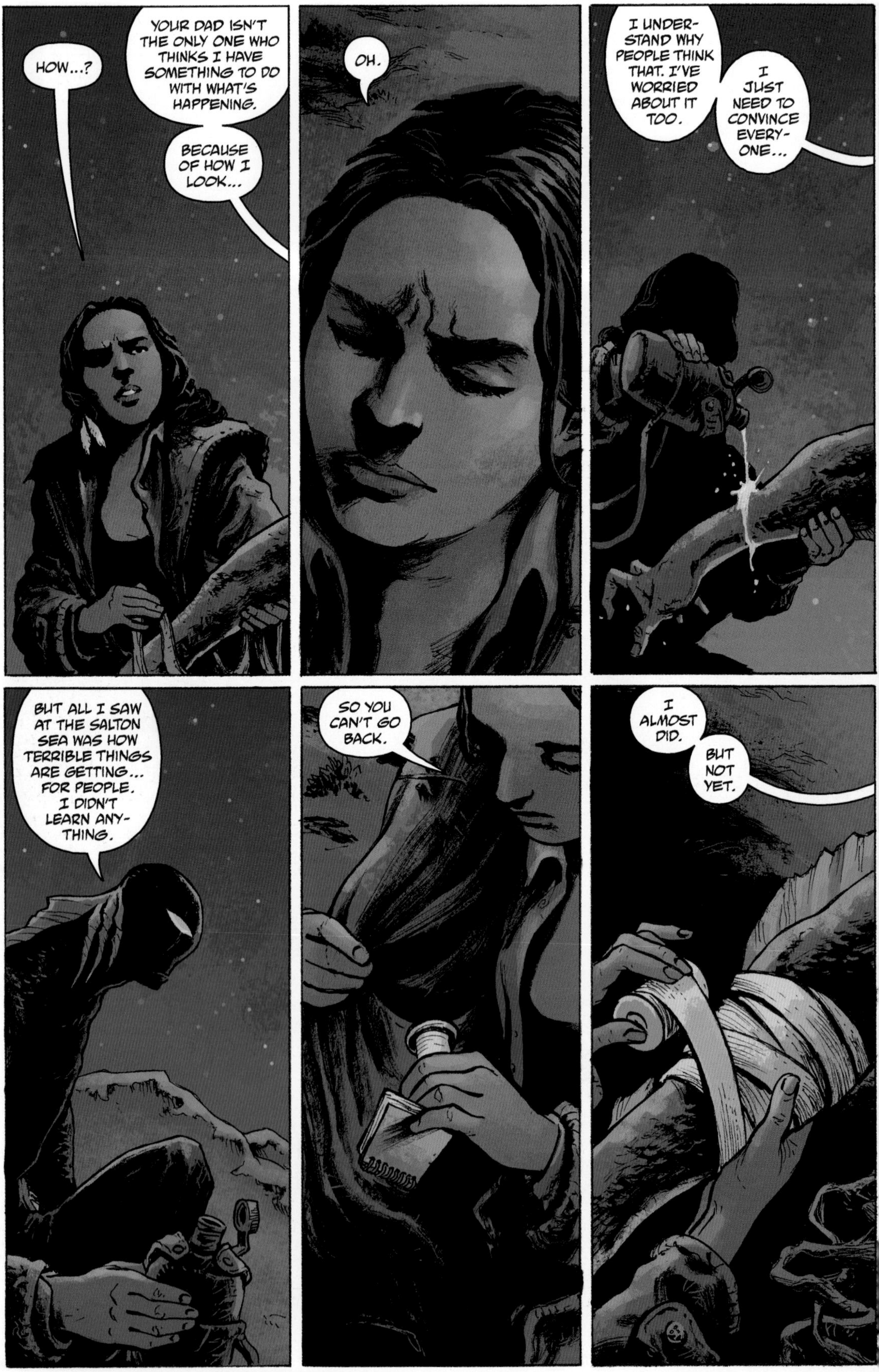
HOW...?
YOUR DAD ISN'T THE ONLY ONE WHO THINKS I HAVE SOMETHING TO DO WITH WHAT'S HAPPENING.
BECAUSE OF HOW I LOOK...
OH.
I UNDERSTAND WHY PEOPLE THINK THAT. I'VE WORRIED ABOUT IT TOO.
I JUST NEED TO CONVINCE EVERYONE...
BUT ALL I SAW AT THE SALTON SEA WAS HOW TERRIBLE THINGS ARE GETTING... FOR PEOPLE. I DIDN'T LEARN ANYTHING.
SO YOU CAN'T GO BACK.
I ALMOST DID.
BUT NOT YET.

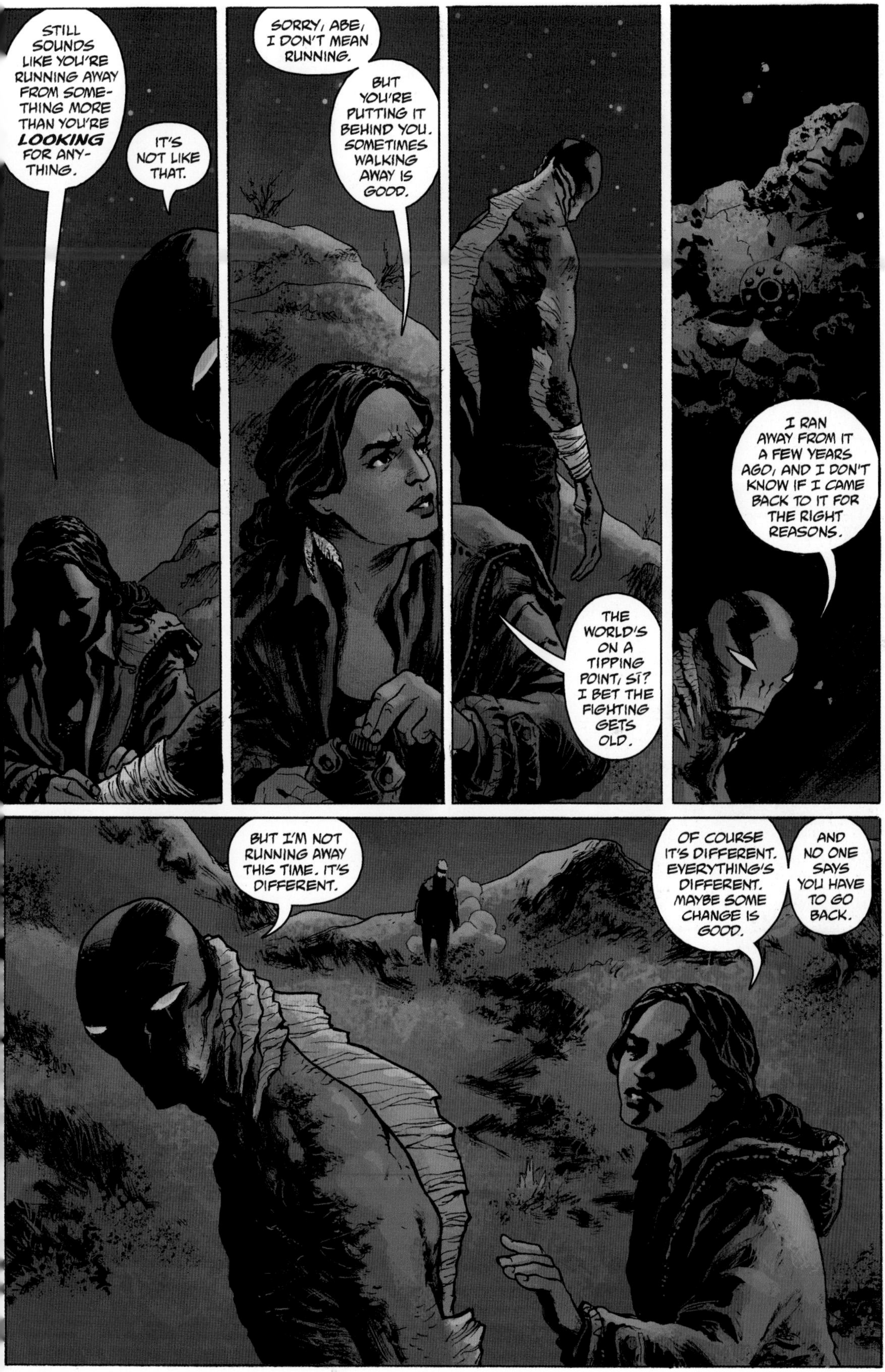
STILL SOUNDS LIKE YOU'RE RUNNING AWAY FROM SOME-THING MORE THAN YOU'RE **LOOKING** FOR ANY-THING.
IT'S NOT LIKE THAT.
SORRY, ABE, I DON'T MEAN RUNNING.
BUT YOU'RE PUTTING IT BEHIND YOU. SOMETIMES WALKING AWAY IS GOOD.
THE WORLD'S ON A TIPPING POINT, SÍ? I BET THE FIGHTING GETS OLD.
I RAN AWAY FROM IT A FEW YEARS AGO, AND I DON'T KNOW IF I CAME BACK TO IT FOR THE RIGHT REASONS.
BUT I'M NOT RUNNING AWAY THIS TIME. IT'S DIFFERENT.
OF COURSE IT'S DIFFERENT. EVERYTHING'S DIFFERENT. MAYBE SOME CHANGE IS GOOD.
AND NO ONE SAYS YOU HAVE TO GO BACK.

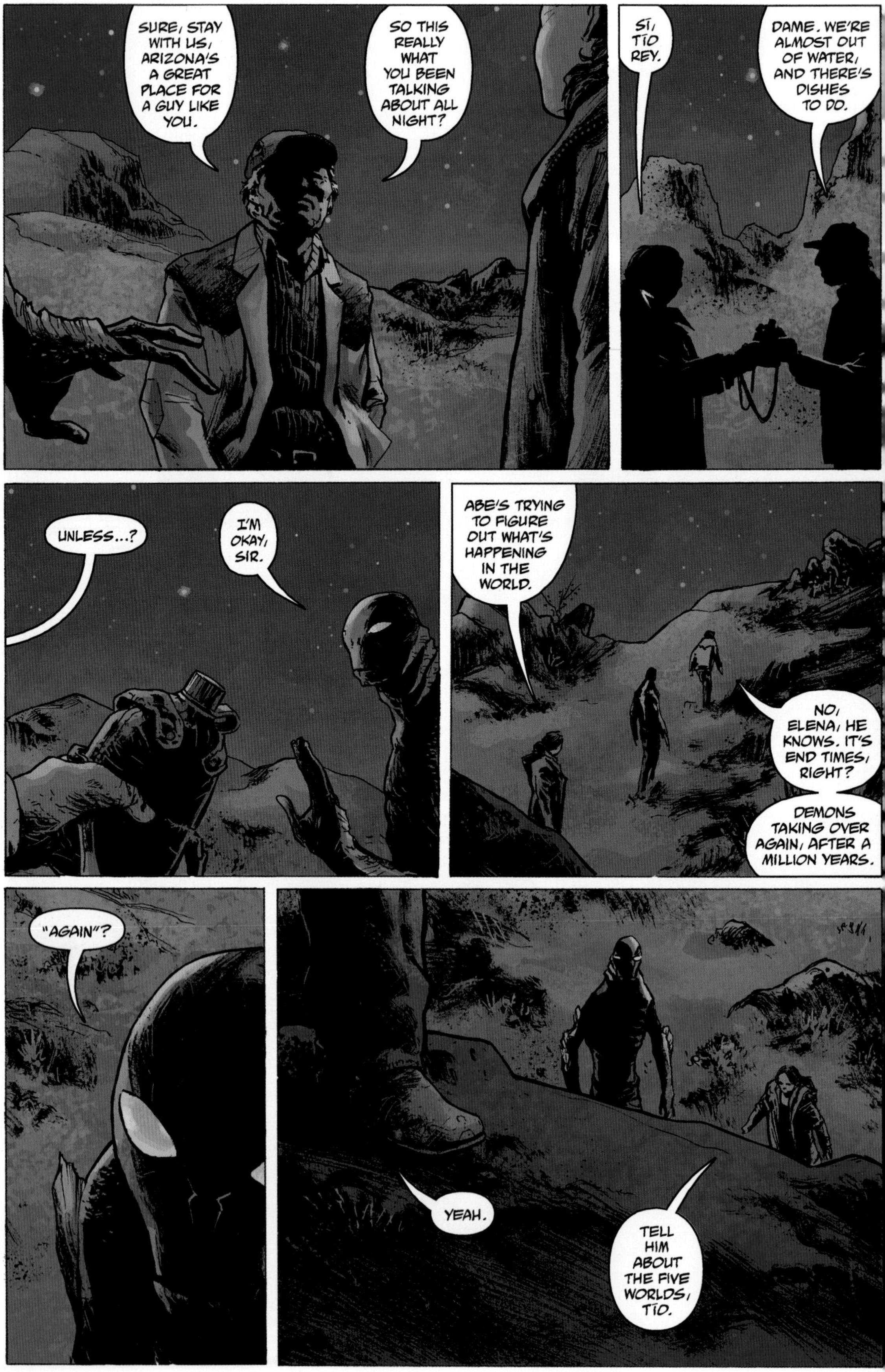

SURE, STAY WITH US, ARIZONA'S A GREAT PLACE FOR A GUY LIKE YOU.
SO THIS REALLY WHAT YOU BEEN TALKING ABOUT ALL NIGHT?
SÍ, TÍO REY.
DAME. WE'RE ALMOST OUT OF WATER, AND THERE'S DISHES TO DO.
UNLESS...?
I'M OKAY, SIR.
ABE'S TRYING TO FIGURE OUT WHAT'S HAPPENING IN THE WORLD.
NO, ELENA, HE KNOWS. IT'S END TIMES, RIGHT?
DEMONS TAKING OVER AGAIN, AFTER A MILLION YEARS.
"AGAIN"?
YEAH.
TELL HIM ABOUT THE FIVE WORLDS, TÍO.

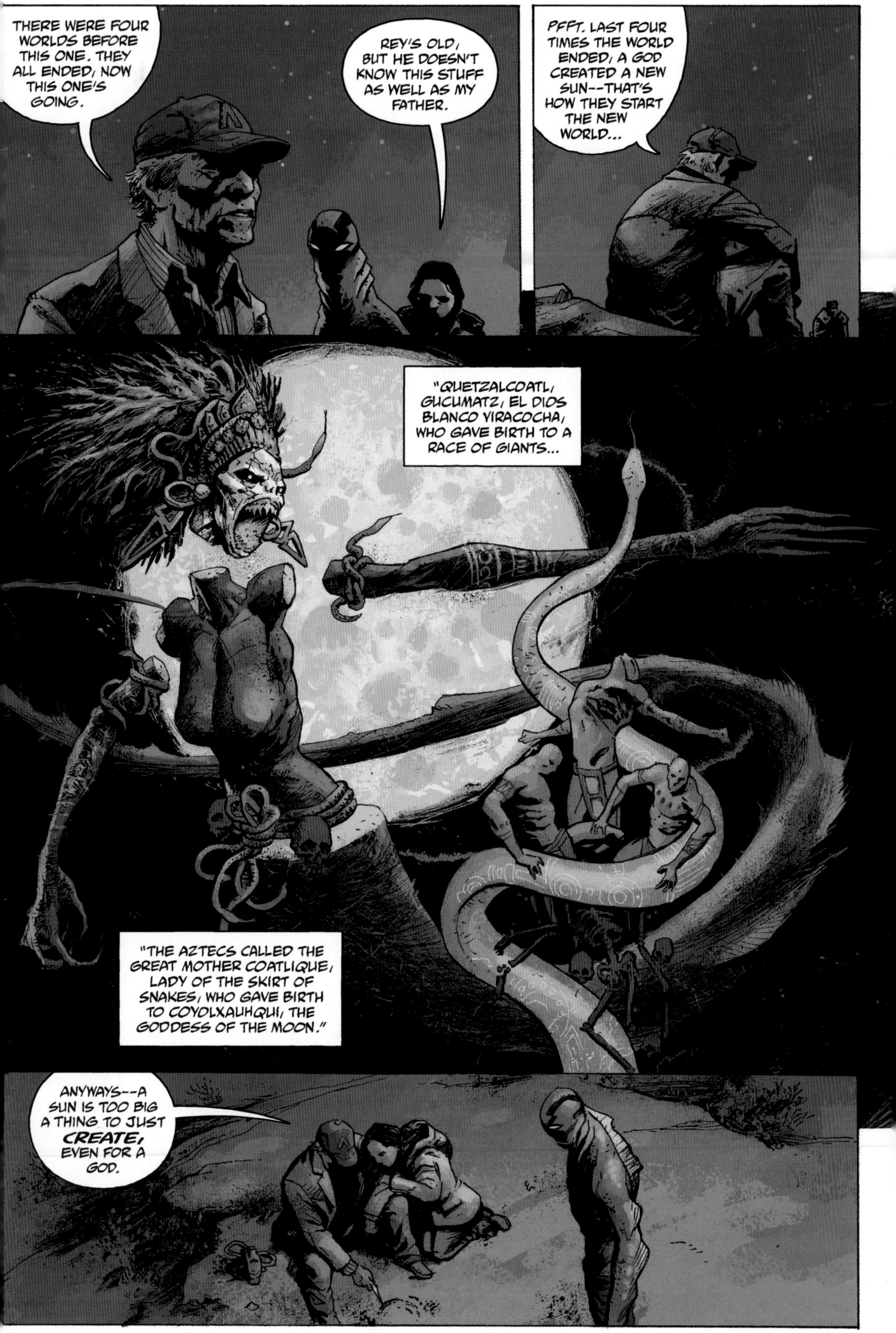
THERE WERE FOUR WORLDS BEFORE THIS ONE. THEY ALL ENDED; NOW THIS ONE'S GOING.
REY'S OLD, BUT HE DOESN'T KNOW THIS STUFF AS WELL AS MY FATHER.
PFFT. LAST FOUR TIMES THE WORLD ENDED, A GOD CREATED A NEW SUN--THAT'S HOW THEY START THE NEW WORLD...
"QUETZALCOATL, GUCUMATZ, EL DIOS BLANCO VIRACOCHA, WHO GAVE BIRTH TO A RACE OF GIANTS...
"THE AZTECS CALLED THE GREAT MOTHER COATLIQUE, LADY OF THE SKIRT OF SNAKES, WHO GAVE BIRTH TO COYOLXAUHQUI, THE GODDESS OF THE MOON."
ANYWAYS--A SUN IS TOO BIG A THING TO JUST **CREATE,** EVEN FOR A GOD.

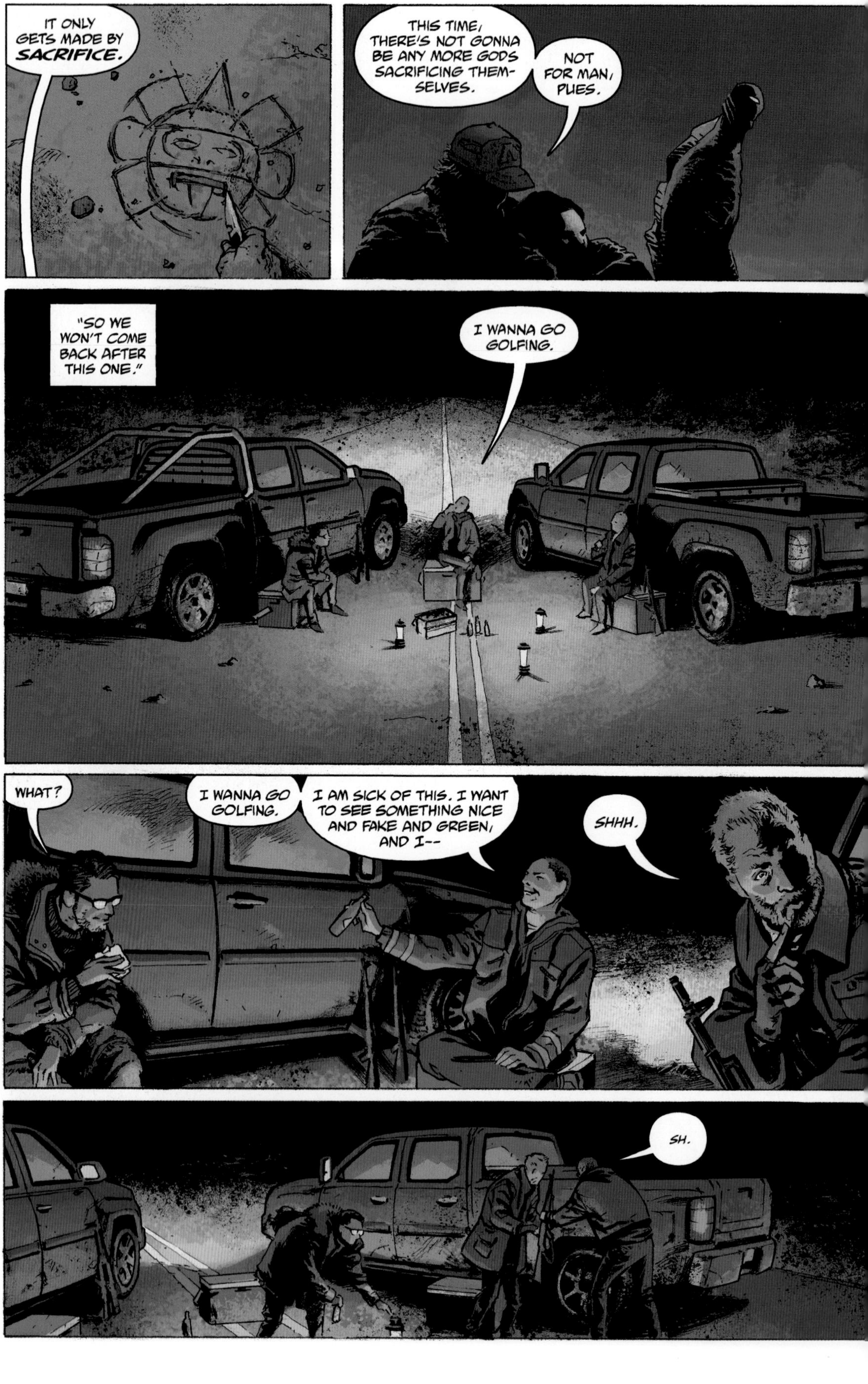
IT ONLY GETS MADE BY SACRIFICE.
THIS TIME, THERE'S NOT GONNA BE ANY MORE GODS SACRIFICING THEM-SELVES.
NOT FOR MAN, PUES.
"SO WE WON'T COME BACK AFTER THIS ONE."
I WANNA GO GOLFING.
WHAT?
I WANNA GO GOLFING.
I AM SICK OF THIS. I WANT TO SEE SOMETHING NICE AND FAKE AND GREEN, AND I--
SHHH.
SH.

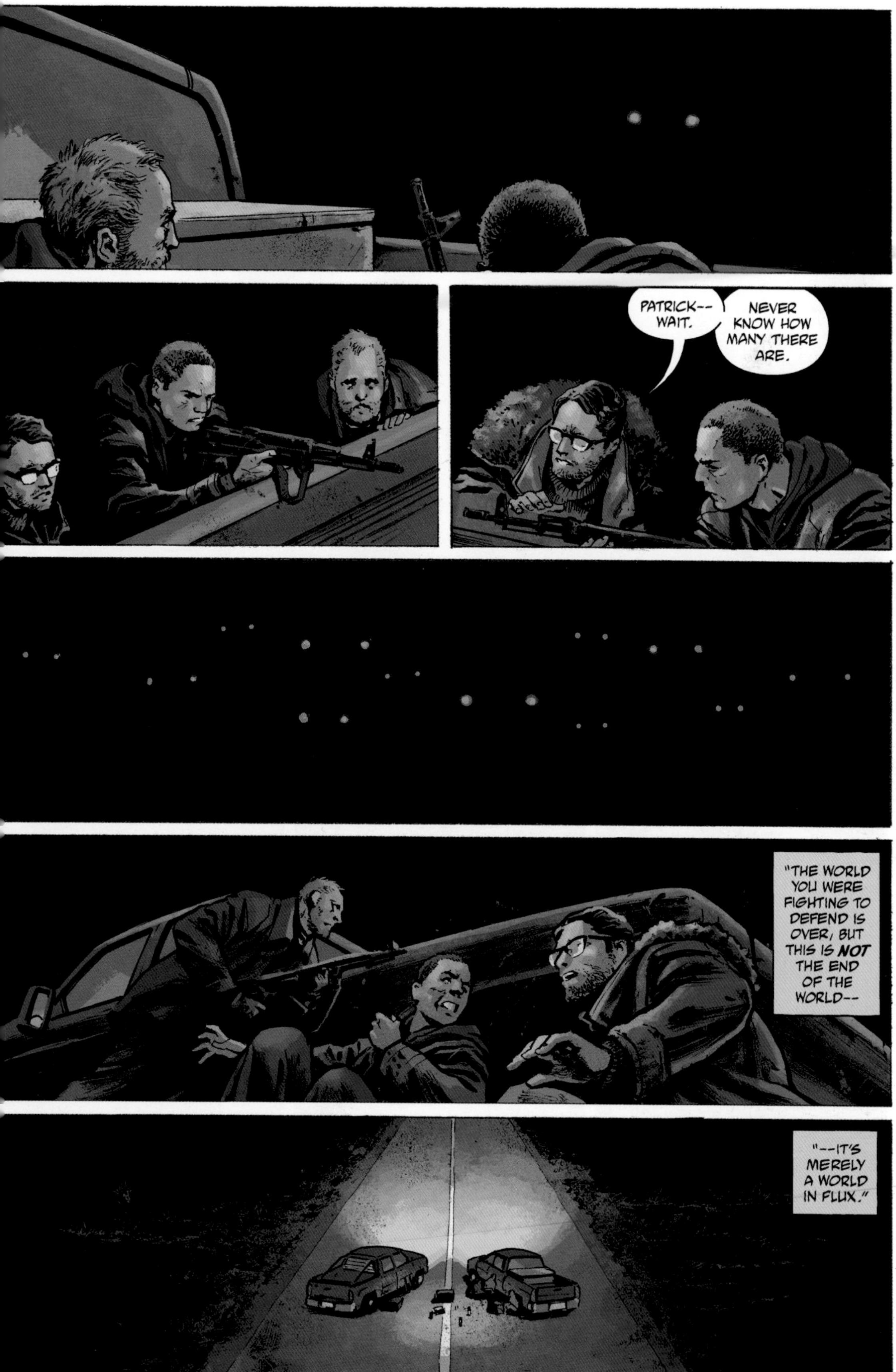
PATRICK--
WAIT.
NEVER KNOW HOW MANY THERE ARE.
"THE WORLD YOU WERE FIGHTING TO DEFEND IS OVER, BUT THIS IS NOT THE END OF THE WORLD--
"--IT'S MERELY A WORLD IN FLUX."

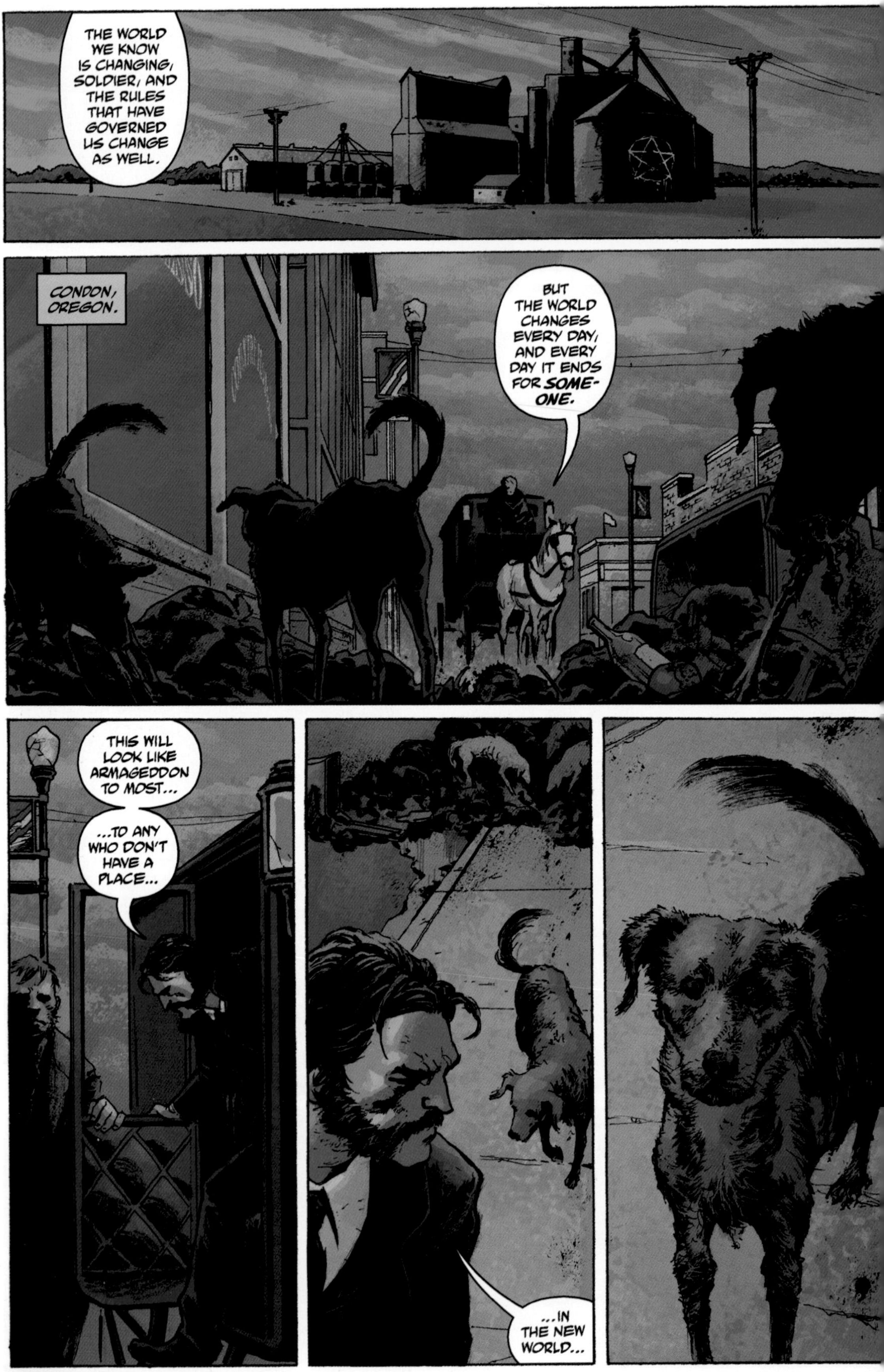
THE WORLD WE KNOW IS CHANGING, SOLDIER, AND THE RULES THAT HAVE GOVERNED US CHANGE AS WELL.
CONDON, OREGON.
BUT THE WORLD CHANGES EVERY DAY, AND EVERY DAY IT ENDS FOR SOME-ONE.
THIS WILL LOOK LIKE ARMAGEDDON TO MOST...
...TO ANY WHO DON'T HAVE A PLACE...
...IN THE NEW WORLD...

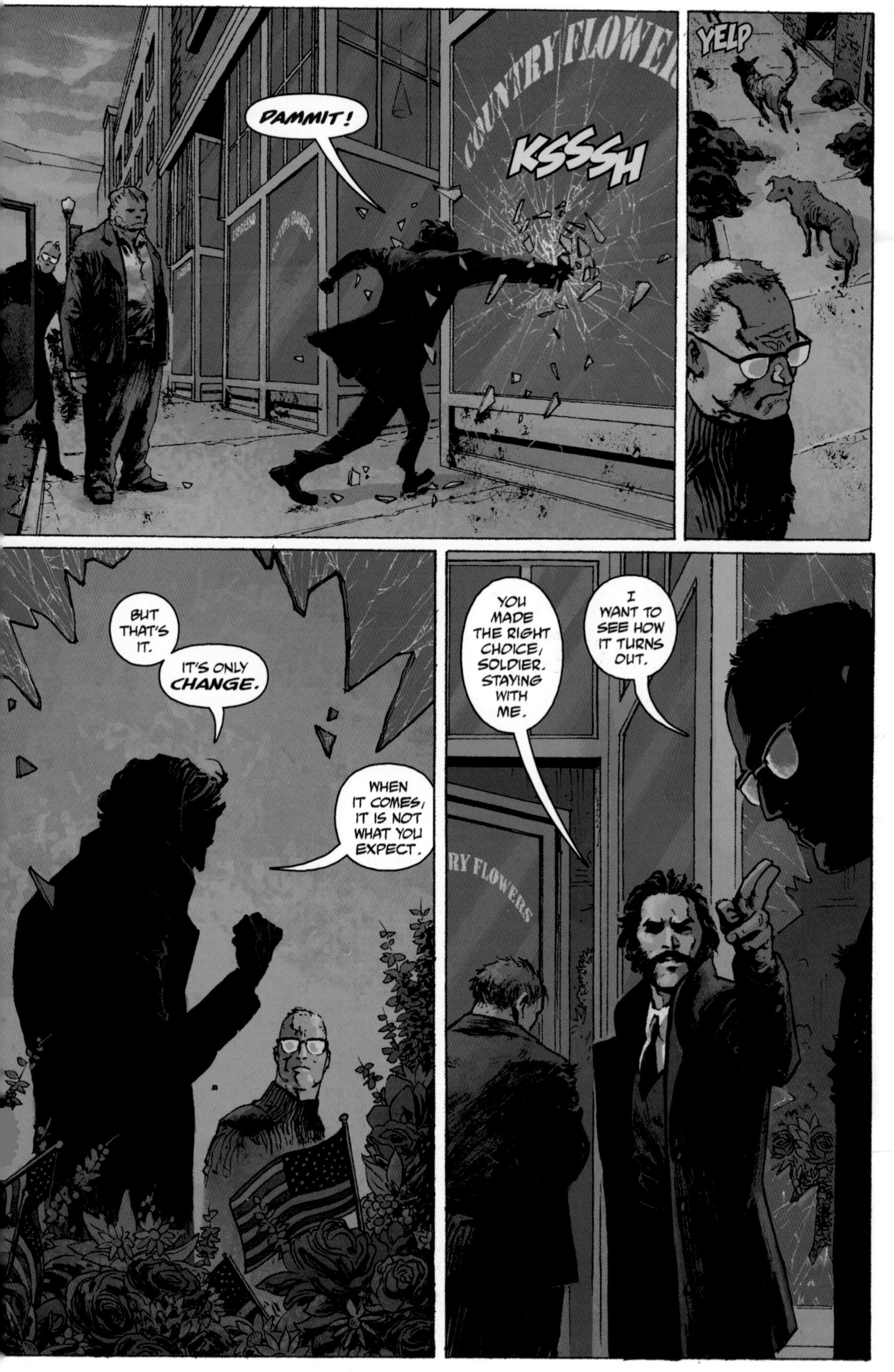
DAMMIT!
KSSSH
COUNTRY FLOWERS
YELP
BUT THAT'S IT.
IT'S ONLY CHANGE.
WHEN IT COMES, IT IS NOT WHAT YOU EXPECT.
YOU MADE THE RIGHT CHOICE, SOLDIER. STAYING WITH ME.
I WANT TO SEE HOW IT TURNS OUT.

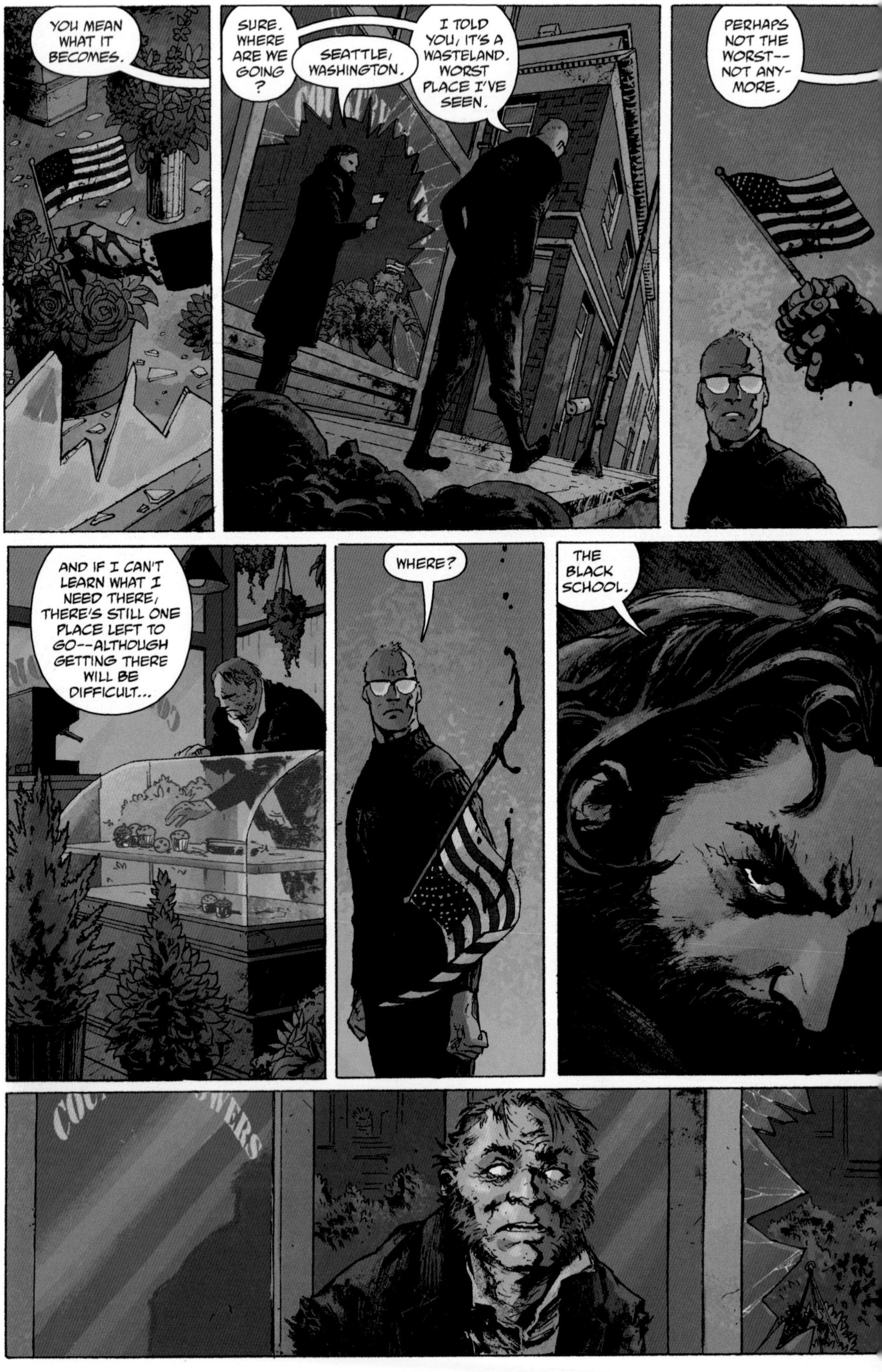
YOU MEAN WHAT IT BECOMES.
SURE. WHERE ARE WE GOING?
SEATTLE, WASHINGTON.
I TOLD YOU, IT'S A WASTELAND. WORST PLACE I'VE SEEN.
PERHAPS NOT THE WORST--NOT ANY-MORE.
AND IF I CAN'T LEARN WHAT I NEED THERE, THERE'S STILL ONE PLACE LEFT TO GO--ALTHOUGH GETTING THERE WILL BE DIFFICULT...
WHERE?
THE BLACK SCHOOL.

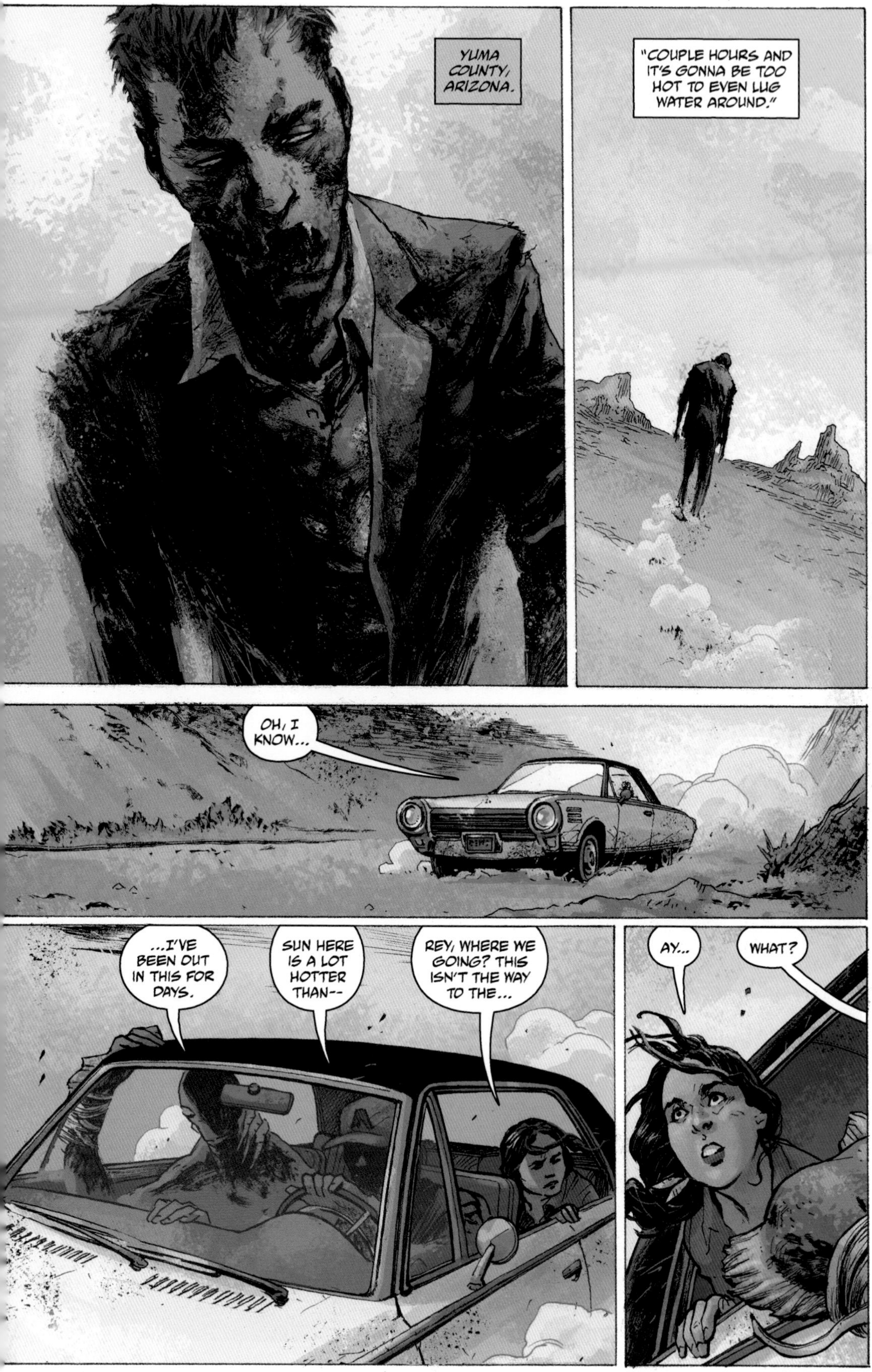
YUMA COUNTY, ARIZONA.
"COUPLE HOURS AND IT'S GONNA BE TOO HOT TO EVEN LUG WATER AROUND."
OH, I KNOW...
...I'VE BEEN OUT IN THIS FOR DAYS.
SUN HERE IS A LOT HOTTER THAN--
REY, WHERE WE GOING? THIS ISN'T THE WAY TO THE...
AY...
WHAT?

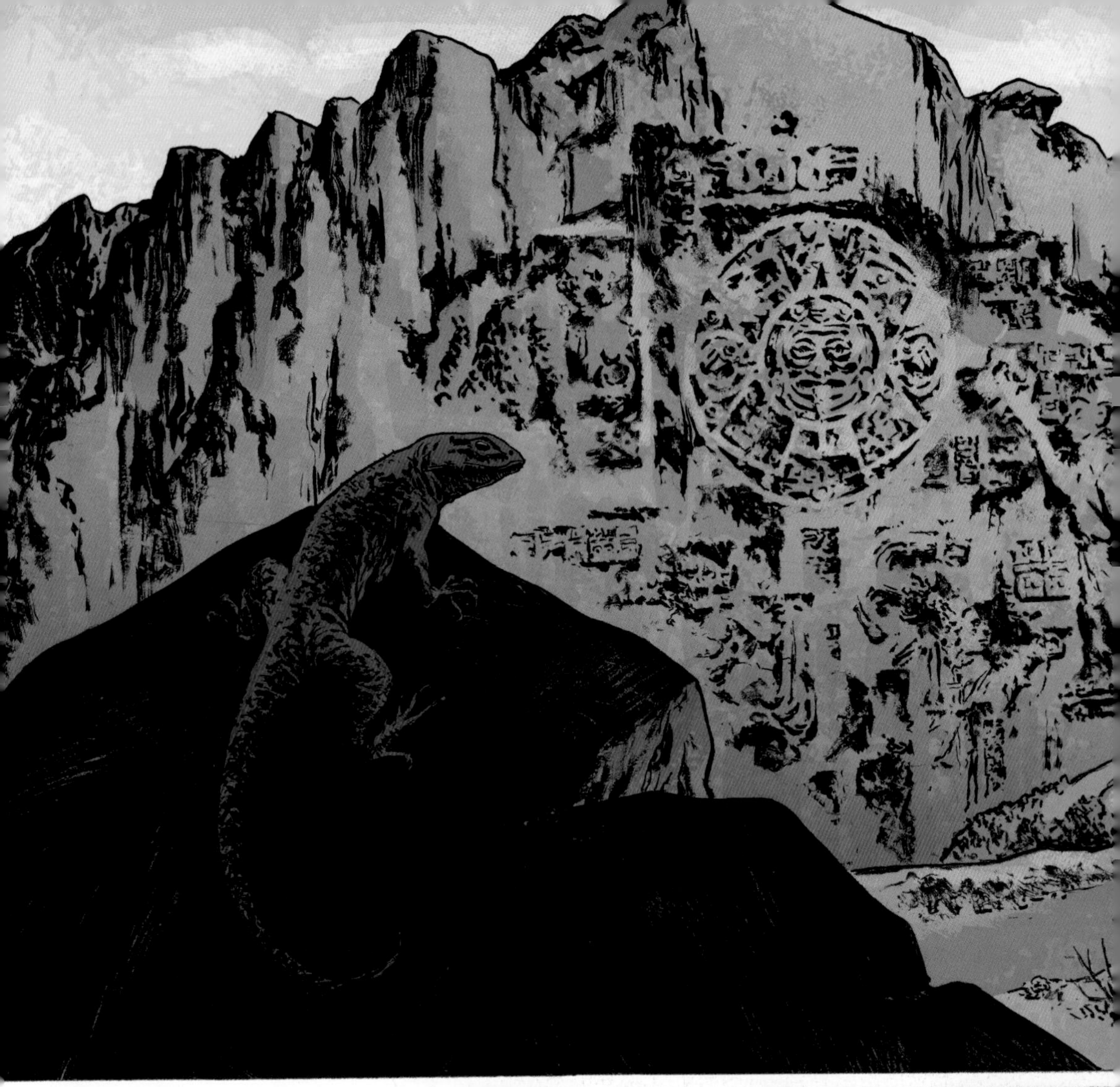
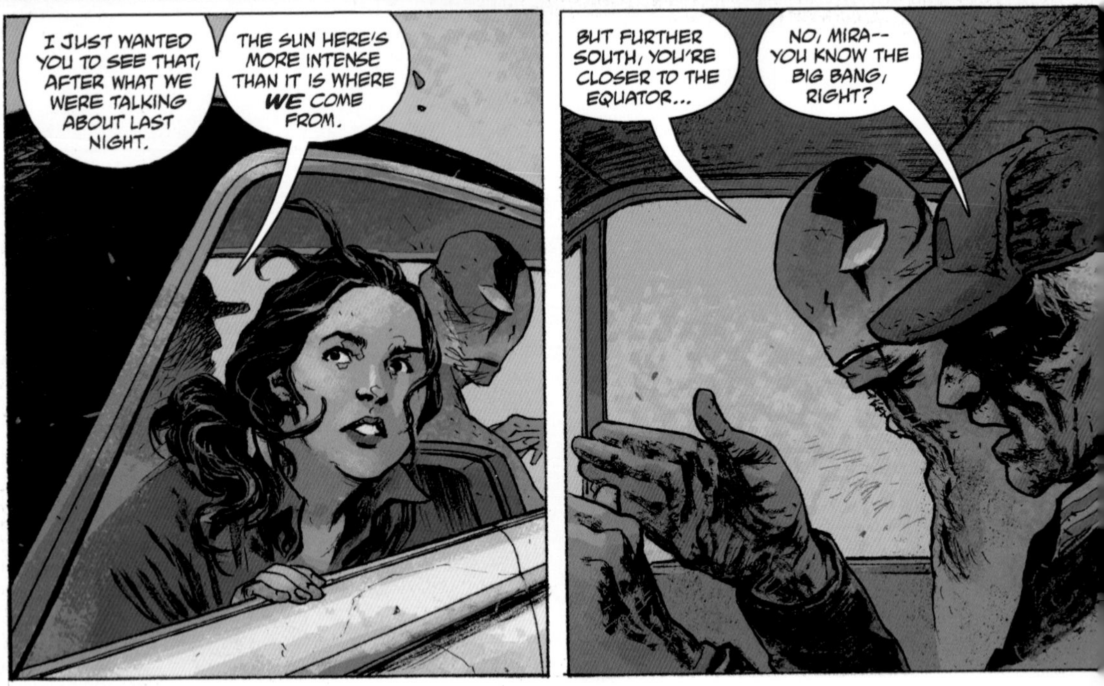
I JUST WANTED YOU TO SEE THAT, AFTER WHAT WE WERE TALKING ABOUT LAST NIGHT.
THE SUN HERE'S MORE INTENSE THAN IT IS WHERE **WE** COME FROM.
BUT FURTHER SOUTH, YOU'RE CLOSER TO THE EQUATOR...
NO, MIRA-- YOU KNOW THE BIG BANG, RIGHT?

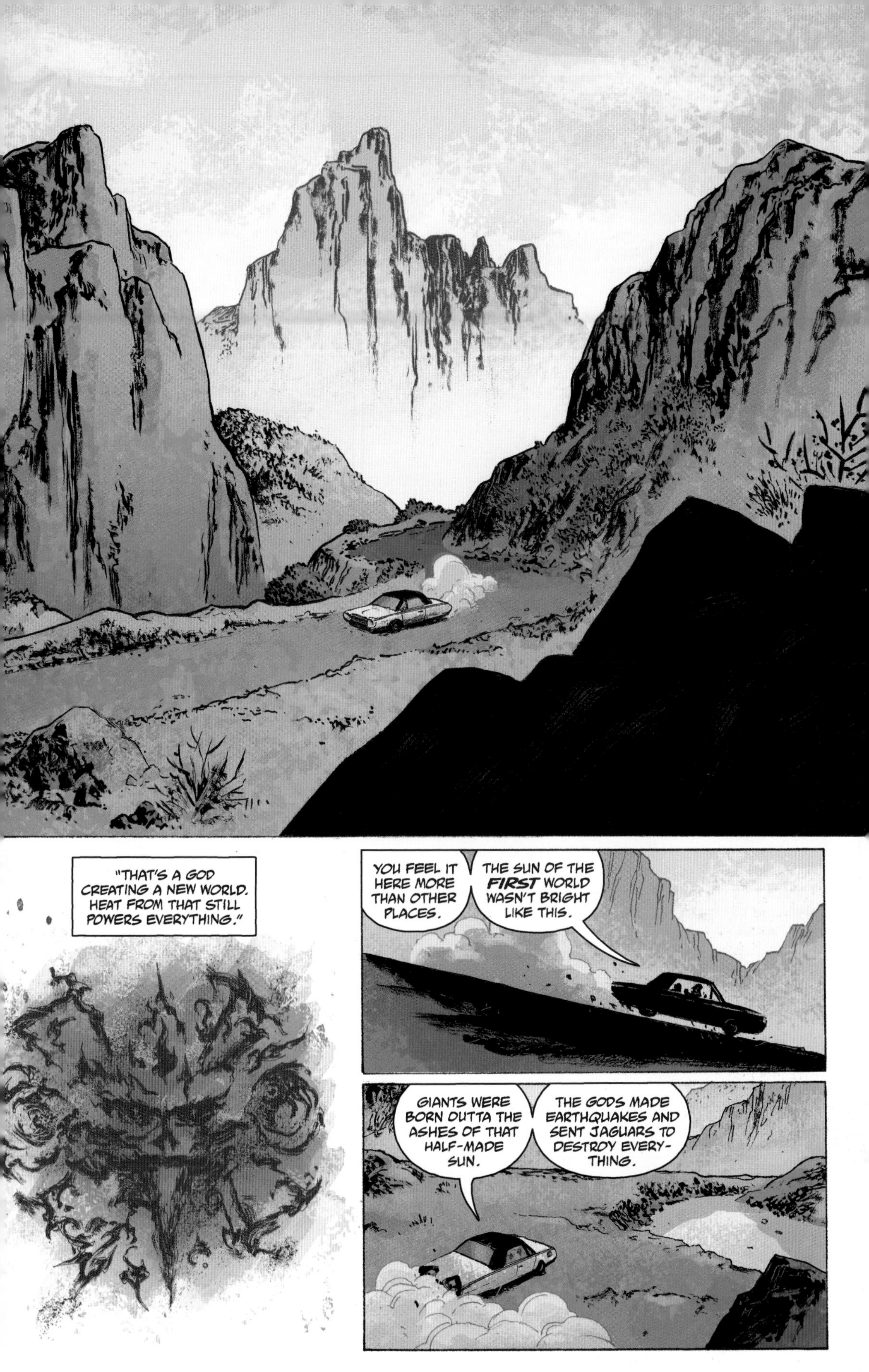
"THAT'S A GOD CREATING A NEW WORLD. HEAT FROM THAT STILL POWERS EVERYTHING."
YOU FEEL IT HERE MORE THAN OTHER PLACES.
THE SUN OF THE **FIRST** WORLD WASN'T BRIGHT LIKE THIS.
GIANTS WERE BORN OUTTA THE ASHES OF THAT HALF-MADE SUN.
THE GODS MADE EARTHQUAKES AND SENT JAGUARS TO DESTROY EVERY-THING.

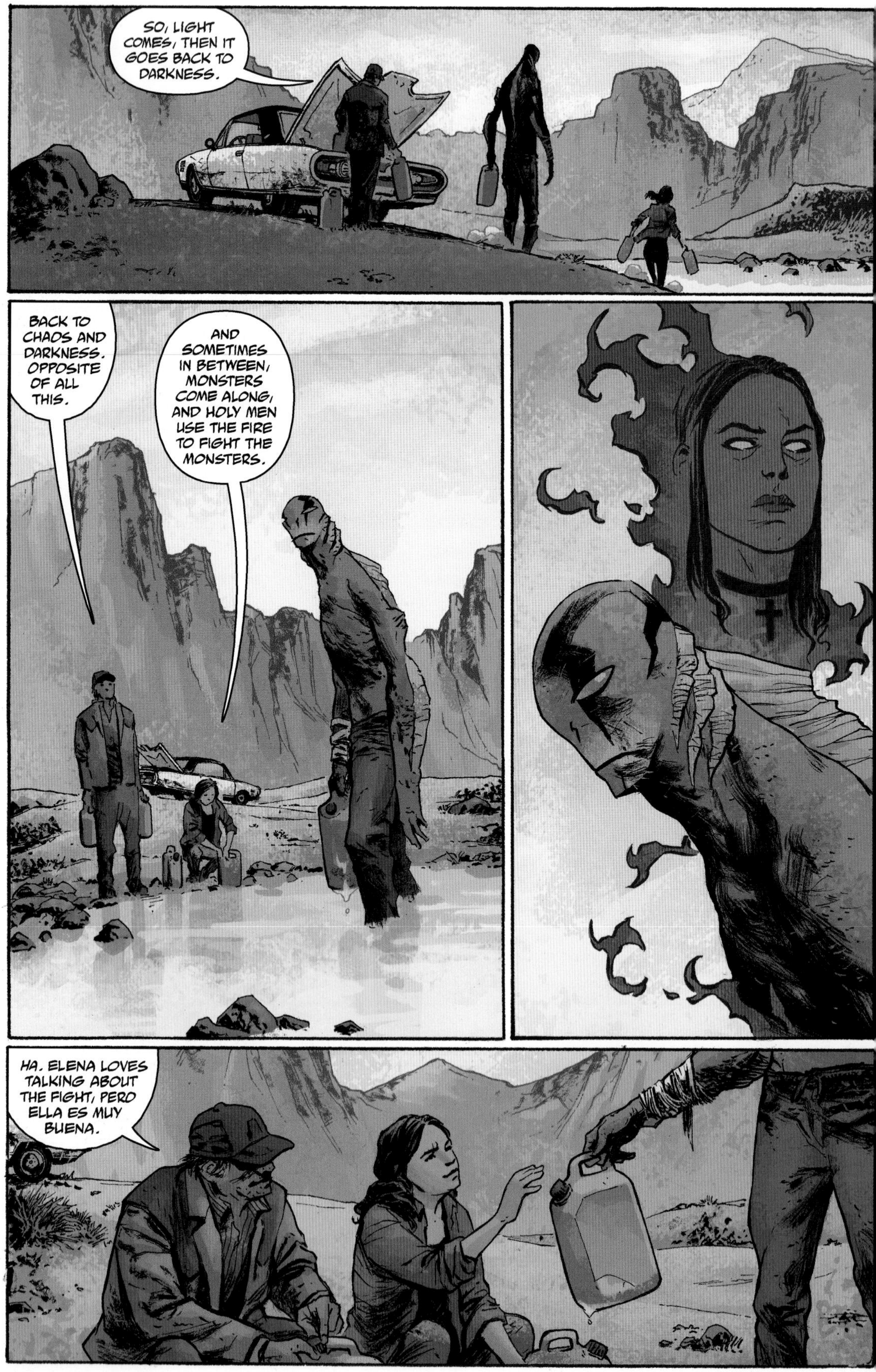
SO, LIGHT COMES, THEN IT GOES BACK TO DARKNESS.
BACK TO CHAOS AND DARKNESS. OPPOSITE OF ALL THIS.
AND SOMETIMES IN BETWEEN, MONSTERS COME ALONG, AND HOLY MEN USE THE FIRE TO FIGHT THE MONSTERS.
HA. ELENA LOVES TALKING ABOUT THE FIGHT, PERO ELLA ES MUY BUENA.

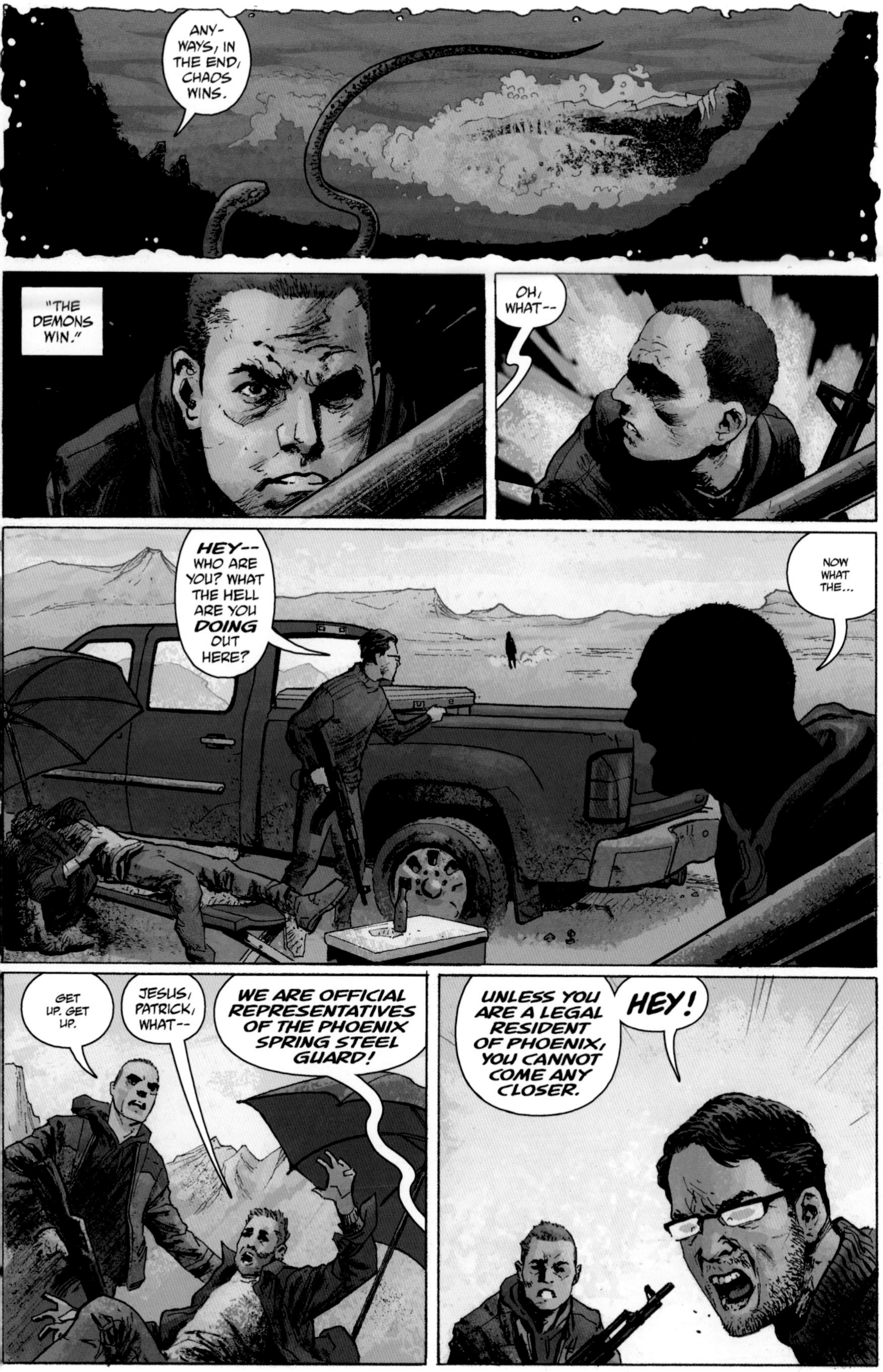
ANY-WAYS, IN THE END, CHAOS WINS.
"THE DEMONS WIN."
OH, WHAT--
HEY-- WHO ARE YOU? WHAT THE HELL ARE YOU DOING OUT HERE?
NOW WHAT THE...
GET UP. GET UP.
JESUS, PATRICK, WHAT--
WE ARE OFFICIAL REPRESENTATIVES OF THE PHOENIX SPRING STEEL GUARD!
UNLESS YOU ARE A LEGAL RESIDENT OF PHOENIX, YOU CANNOT COME ANY CLOSER.
HEY!

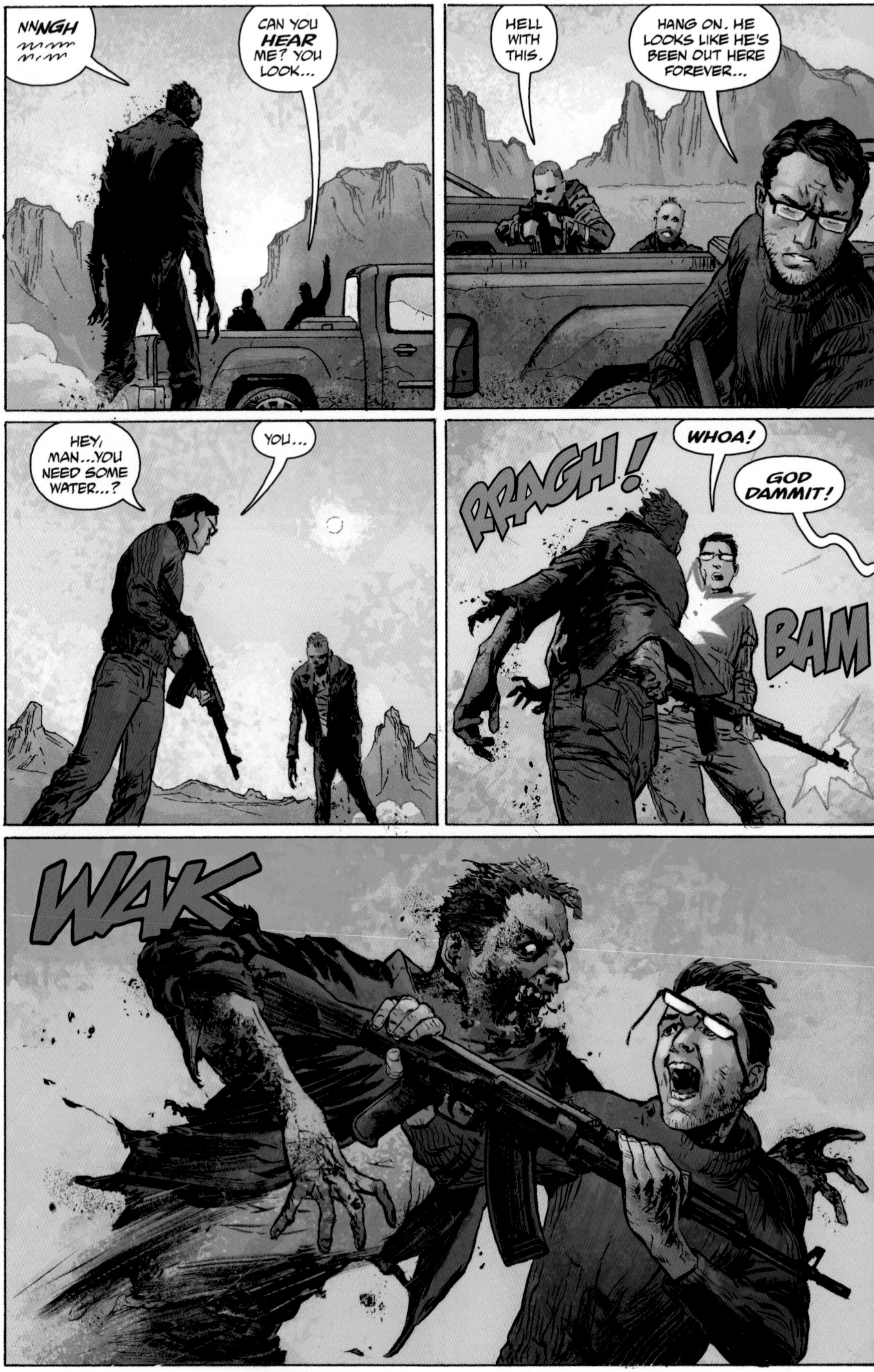
NNNGH
CAN YOU HEAR ME? YOU LOOK...
HELL WITH THIS.
HANG ON. HE LOOKS LIKE HE'S BEEN OUT HERE FOREVER...
HEY, MAN...YOU NEED SOME WATER...?
YOU...
RRAGH!
WHOA!
GOD DAMMIT!
BAM
WAK

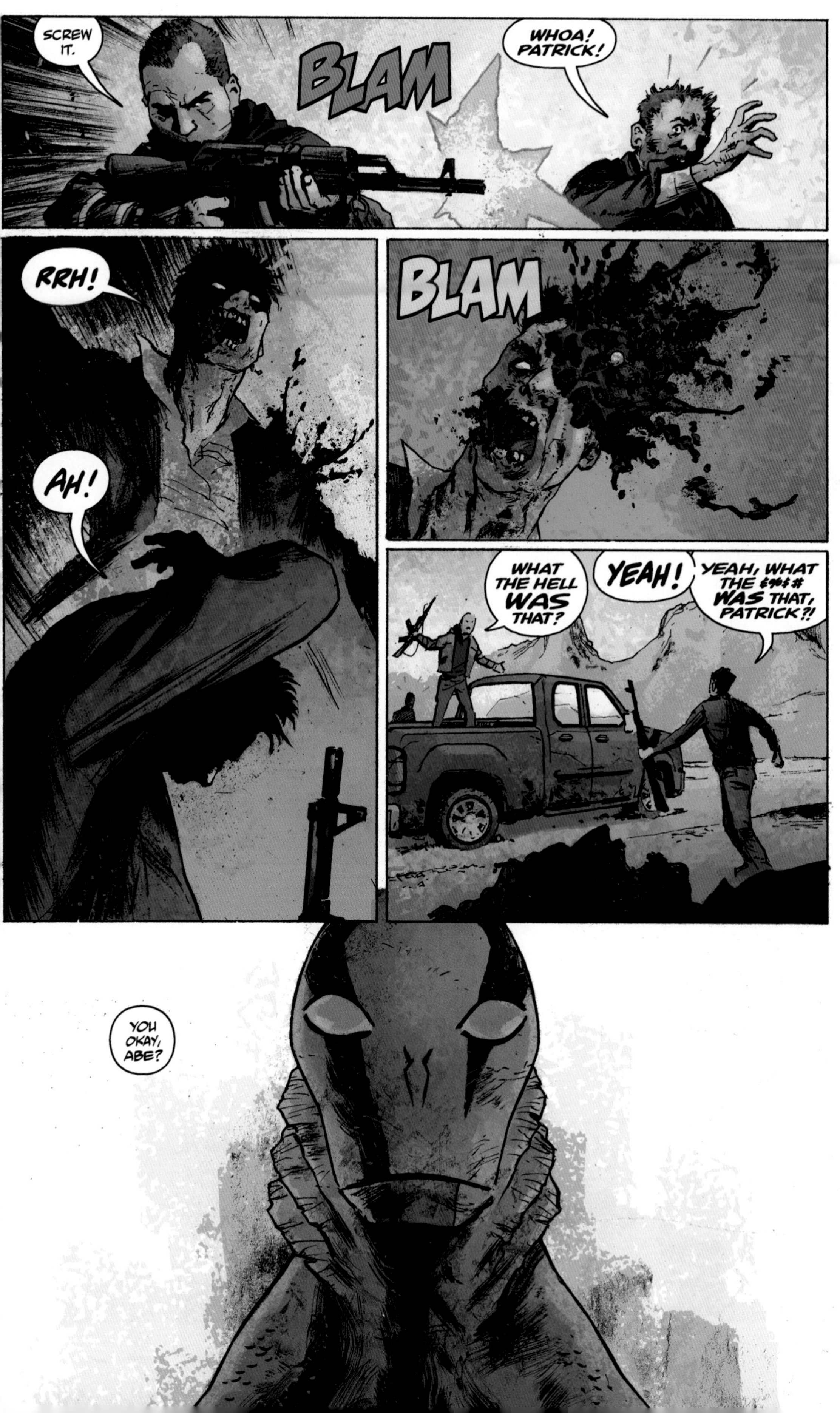
SCREW IT.
BLAM
WHOA! PATRICK!
RRH!
AH!
BLAM
WHAT THE HELL WAS THAT?
YEAH!
YEAH, WHAT THE $%$# WAS THAT, PATRICK?!
YOU OKAY, ABE?

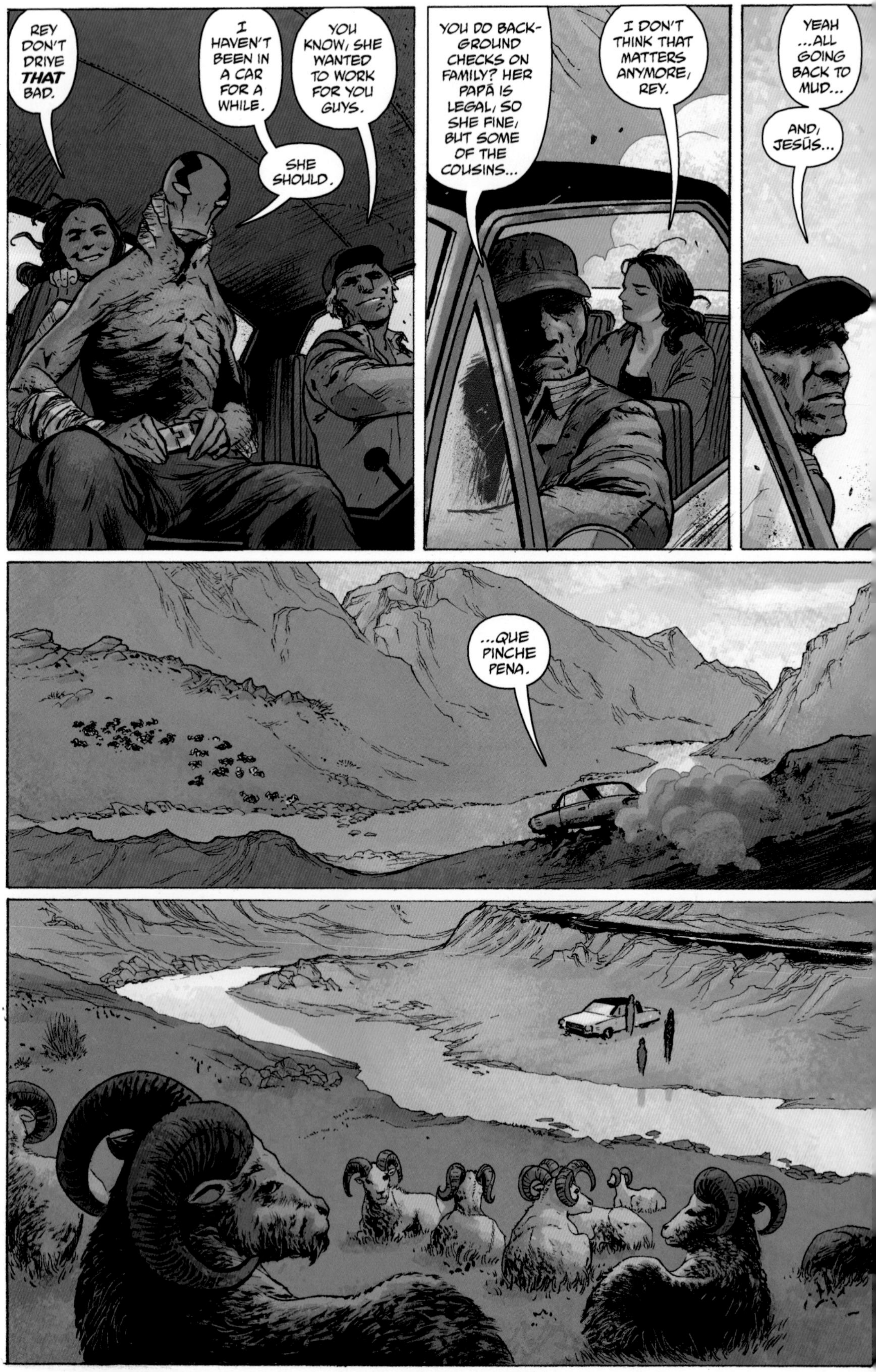
REY DON'T DRIVE *THAT* BAD.
I HAVEN'T BEEN IN A CAR FOR A WHILE.
YOU KNOW, SHE WANTED TO WORK FOR YOU GUYS.
SHE SHOULD.
YOU DO BACK-GROUND CHECKS ON FAMILY? HER PAPÁ IS LEGAL, SO SHE FINE, BUT SOME OF THE COUSINS...
I DON'T THINK THAT MATTERS ANYMORE, REY.
YEAH ...ALL GOING BACK TO MUD...
AND, JESÚS...
...QUE PINCHE PENA.

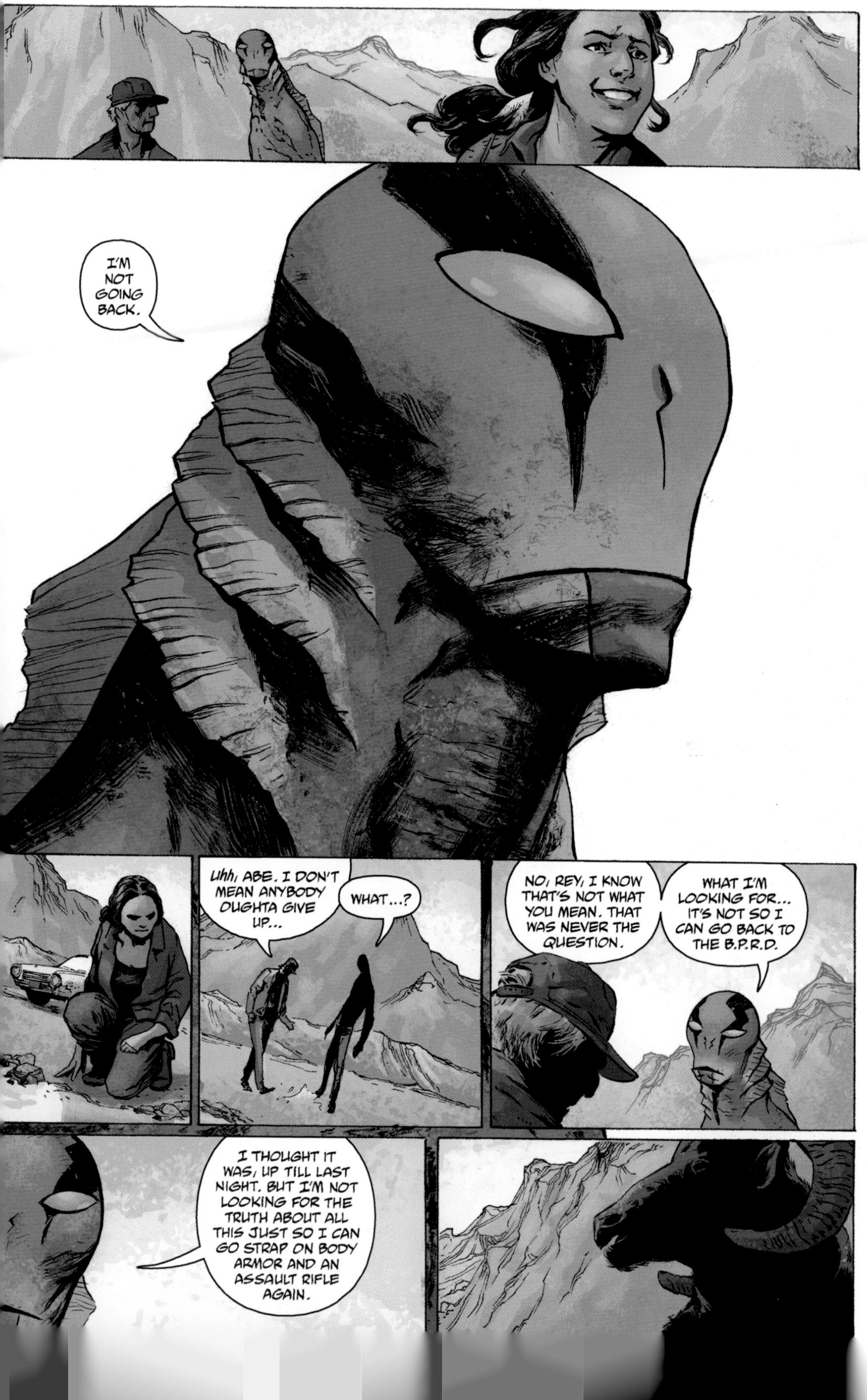
I'M NOT GOING BACK.
Uhh, ABE. I DON'T MEAN ANYBODY OUGHTA GIVE UP...
WHAT...?
NO, REY, I KNOW THAT'S NOT WHAT YOU MEAN. THAT WAS NEVER THE QUESTION.
WHAT I'M LOOKING FOR... IT'S NOT SO I CAN GO BACK TO THE B.P.R.D.
I THOUGHT IT WAS, UP TILL LAST NIGHT. BUT I'M NOT LOOKING FOR THE TRUTH ABOUT ALL THIS JUST SO I CAN GO STRAP ON BODY ARMOR AND AN ASSAULT RIFLE AGAIN.

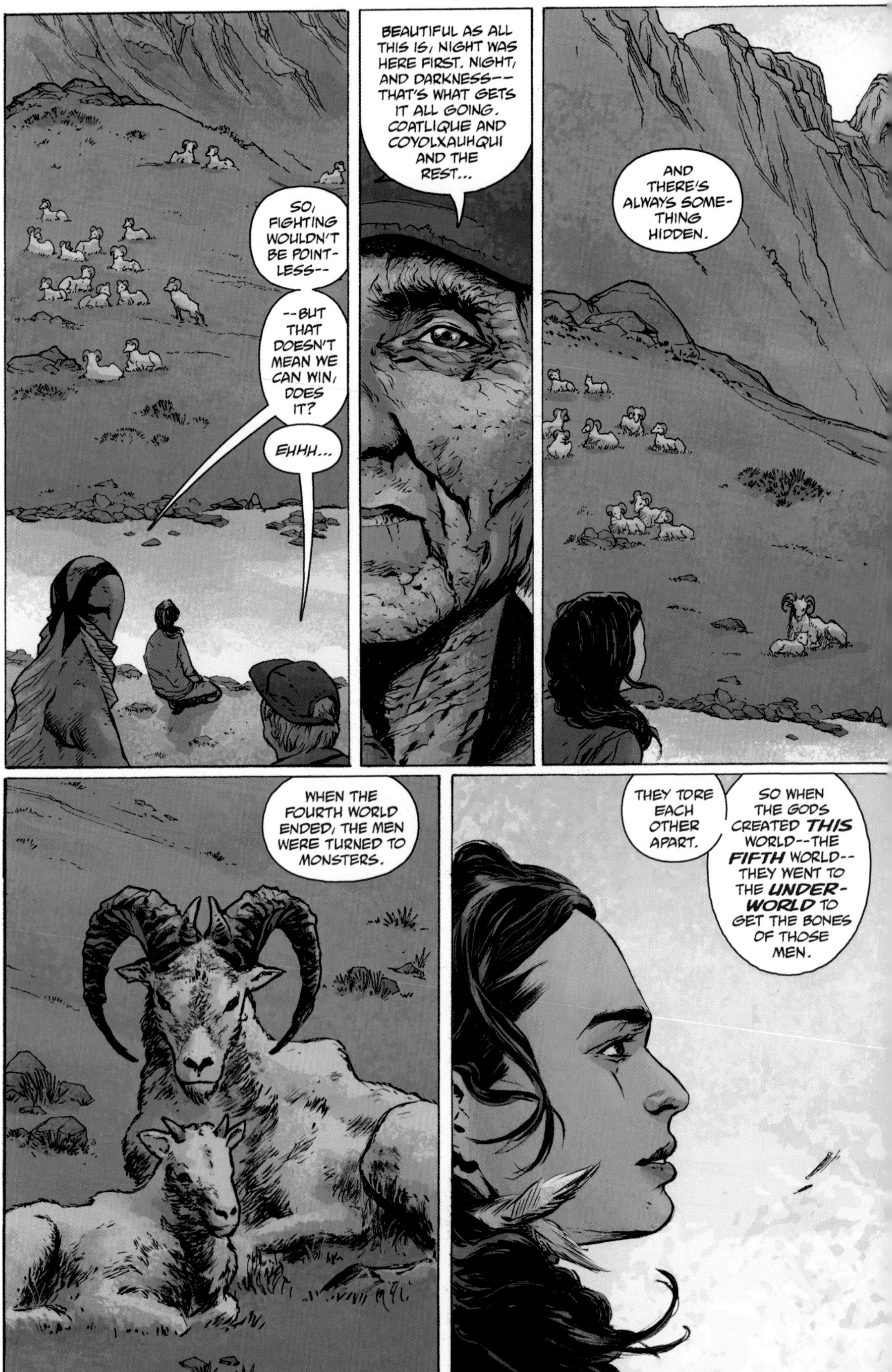
SO, FIGHTING WOULDN'T BE POINT-LESS--
--BUT THAT DOESN'T MEAN WE CAN WIN, DOES IT?
EHHH...
BEAUTIFUL AS ALL THIS IS, NIGHT WAS HERE FIRST. NIGHT, AND DARKNESS-- THAT'S WHAT GETS IT ALL GOING. COATLIQUE AND COYOLXAUHQUI AND THE REST...
AND THERE'S ALWAYS SOME-THING HIDDEN.
WHEN THE FOURTH WORLD ENDED, THE MEN WERE TURNED TO MONSTERS.
THEY TORE EACH OTHER APART.
SO WHEN THE GODS CREATED **THIS** WORLD--THE **FIFTH** WORLD-- THEY WENT TO THE **UNDER-WORLD** TO GET THE BONES OF THOSE MEN.

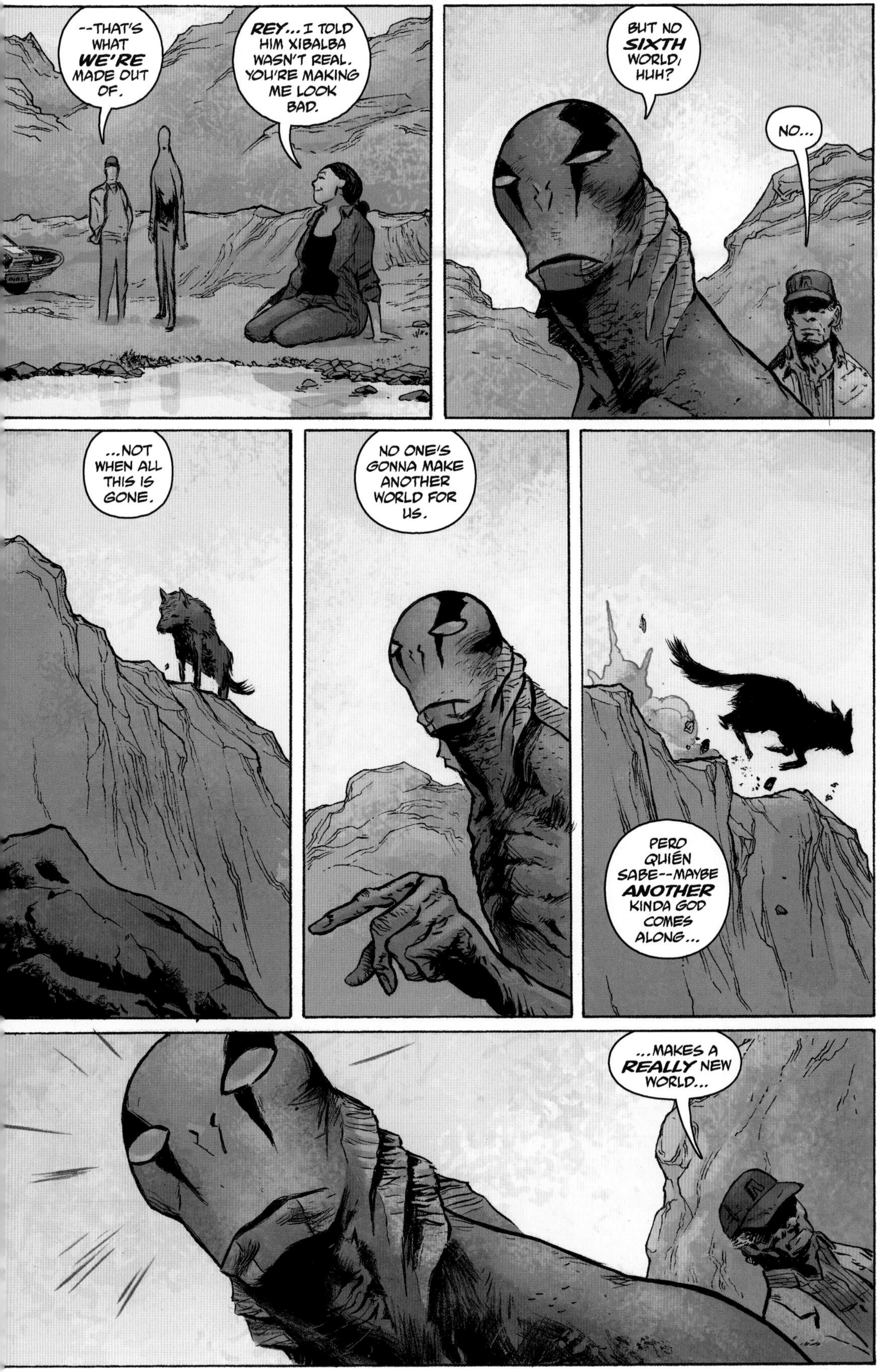
--THAT'S WHAT WE'RE MADE OUT OF.
REY... I TOLD HIM XIBALBA WASN'T REAL. YOU'RE MAKING ME LOOK BAD.
BUT NO SIXTH WORLD, HUH?
NO...
...NOT WHEN ALL THIS IS GONE.
NO ONE'S GONNA MAKE ANOTHER WORLD FOR US.
PERO QUIÉN SABE--MAYBE ANOTHER KINDA GOD COMES ALONG...
...MAKES A REALLY NEW WORLD...

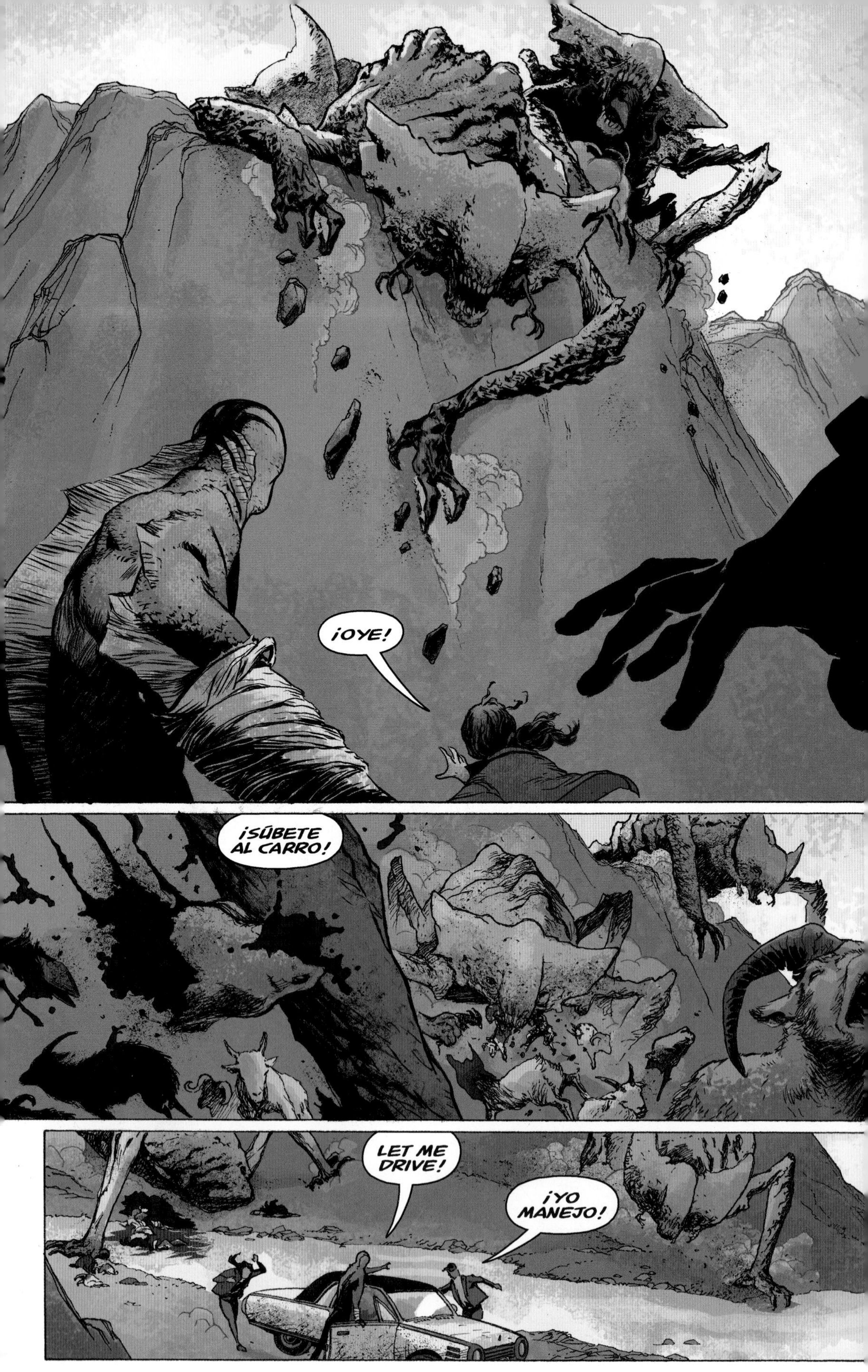
¡OYE!
¡SÚBETE AL CARRO!
LET ME DRIVE!
¡YO MANEJO!

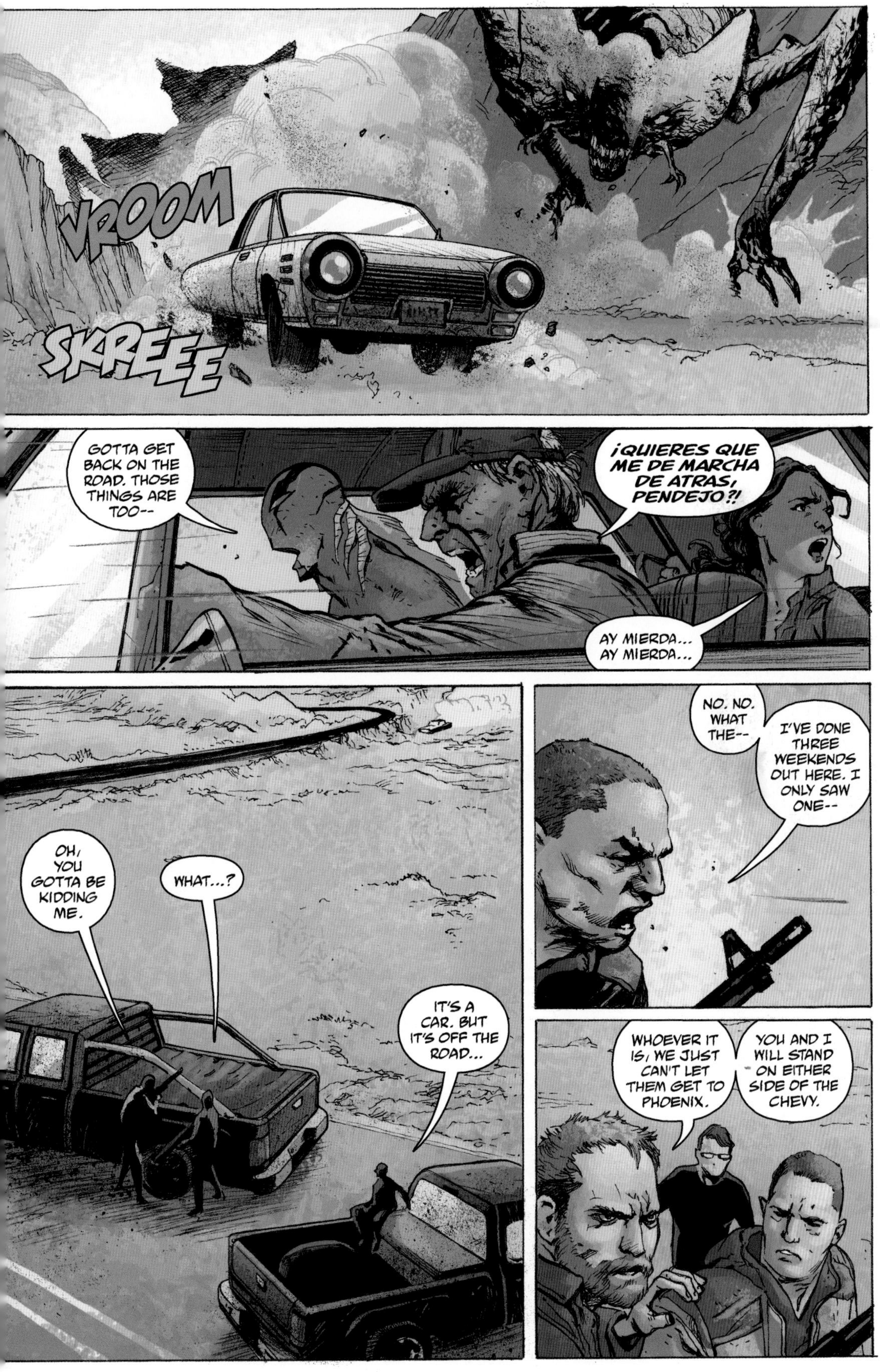
VROOM
SKREEEE
GOTTA GET BACK ON THE ROAD. THOSE THINGS ARE TOO--
¡QUIERES QUE ME DE MARCHA DE ATRAS, PENDEJO?!
AY MIERDA... AY MIERDA...
OH, YOU GOTTA BE KIDDING ME.
WHAT...?
IT'S A CAR. BUT IT'S OFF THE ROAD...
NO. NO. WHAT THE--
I'VE DONE THREE WEEKENDS OUT HERE. I ONLY SAW ONE--
WHOEVER IT IS, WE JUST CAN'T LET THEM GET TO PHOENIX.
YOU AND I WILL STAND ON EITHER SIDE OF THE CHEVY.

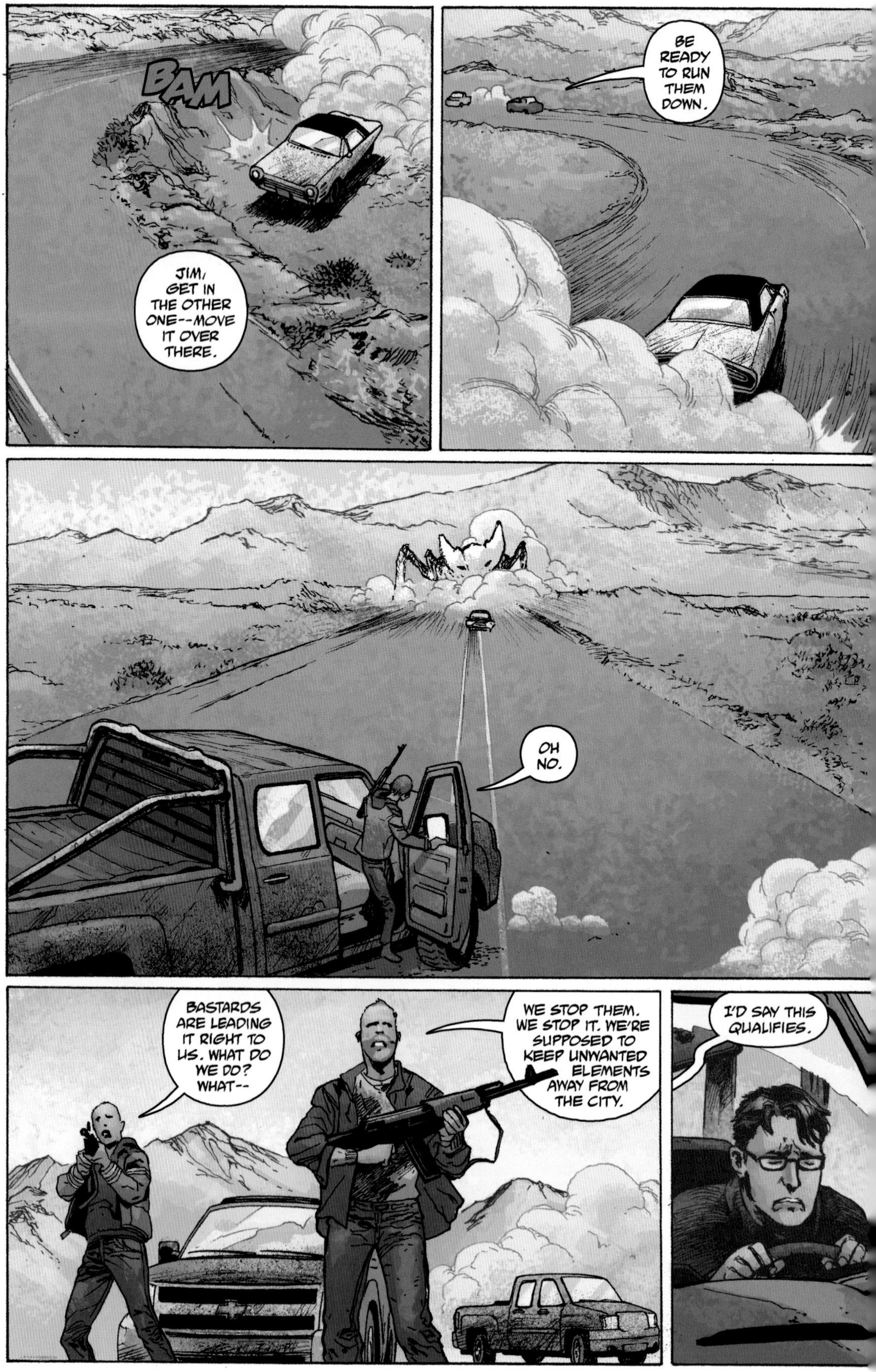
BAM
JIM, GET IN THE OTHER ONE--MOVE IT OVER THERE.
BE READY TO RUN THEM DOWN.
OH NO.
BASTARDS ARE LEADING IT RIGHT TO US. WHAT DO WE DO? WHAT--
WE STOP THEM. WE STOP IT. WE'RE SUPPOSED TO KEEP UNWANTED ELEMENTS AWAY FROM THE CITY.
I'D SAY THIS QUALIFIES.

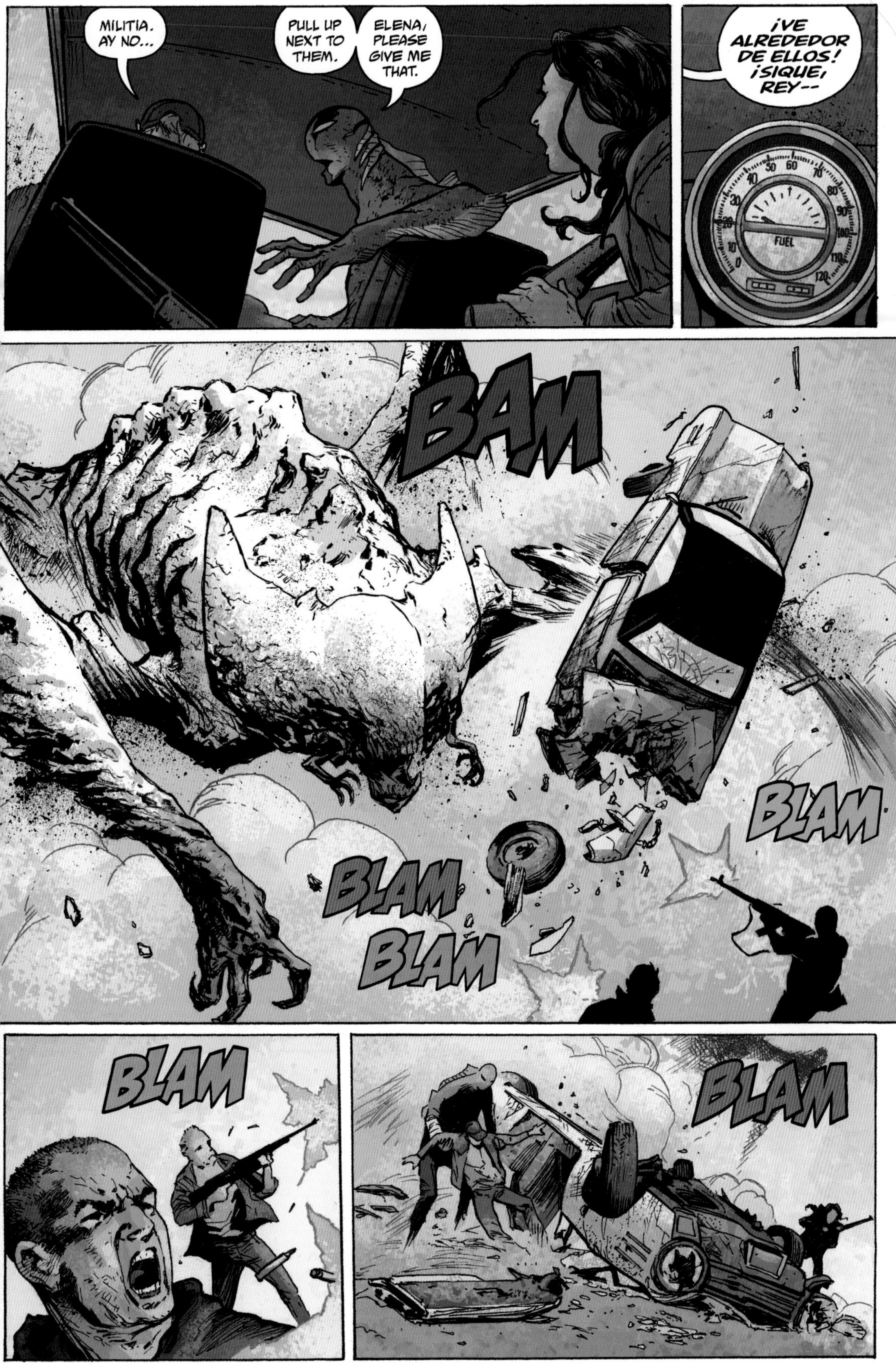

MILITIA. AY NO...
PULL UP NEXT TO THEM.
ELENA, PLEASE GIVE ME THAT.
¡VE ALREDEDOR DE ELLOS! ¡SIQUE, REY--
FUEL
BAM
BLAM
BLAM
BLAM
BLAM
BLAM

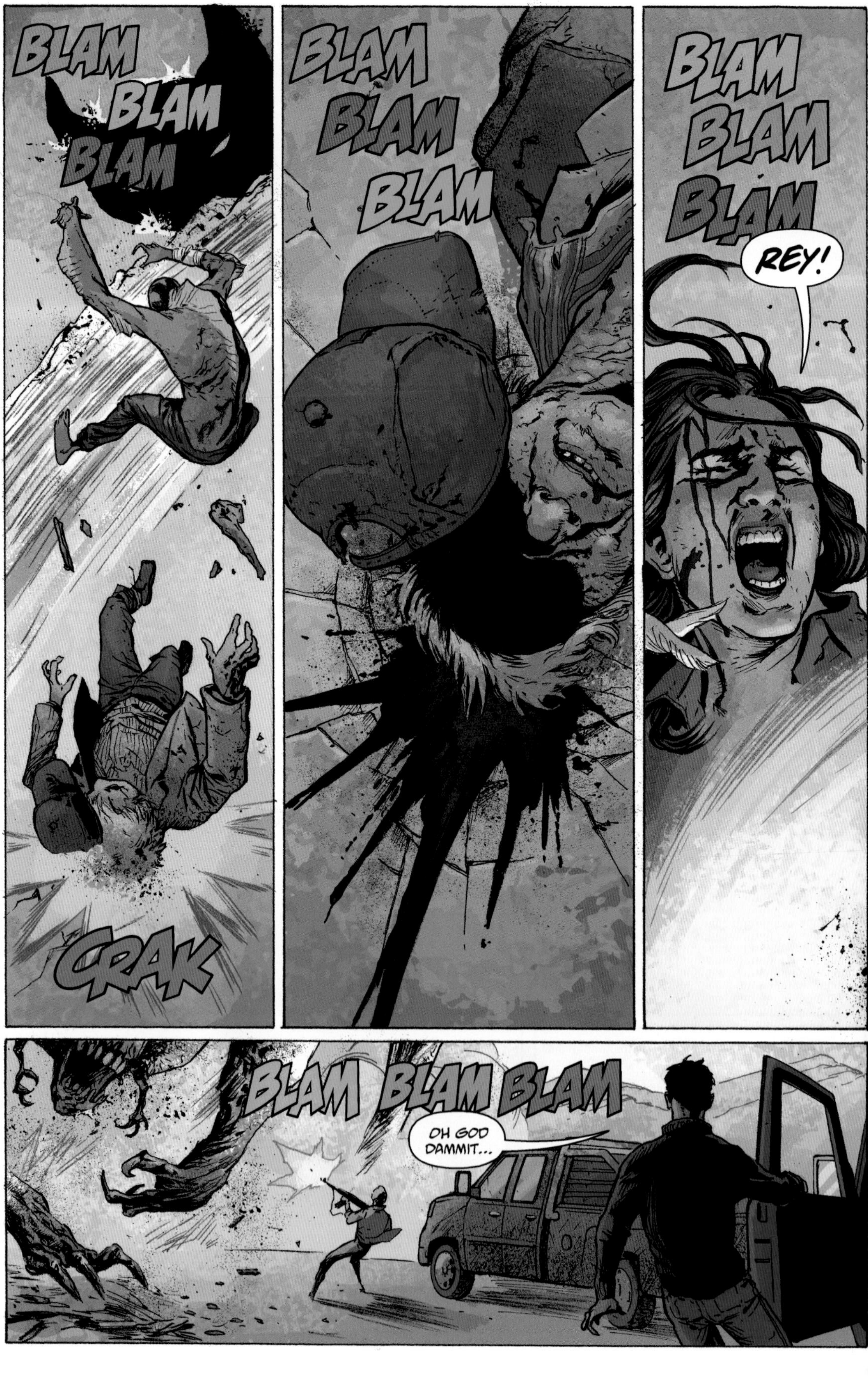
BLAM
BLAM
BLAM
CRAK
BLAM
BLAM
BLAM
BLAM
BLAM
BLAM
REY!
BLAM BLAM BLAM
OH GOD DAMMIT...

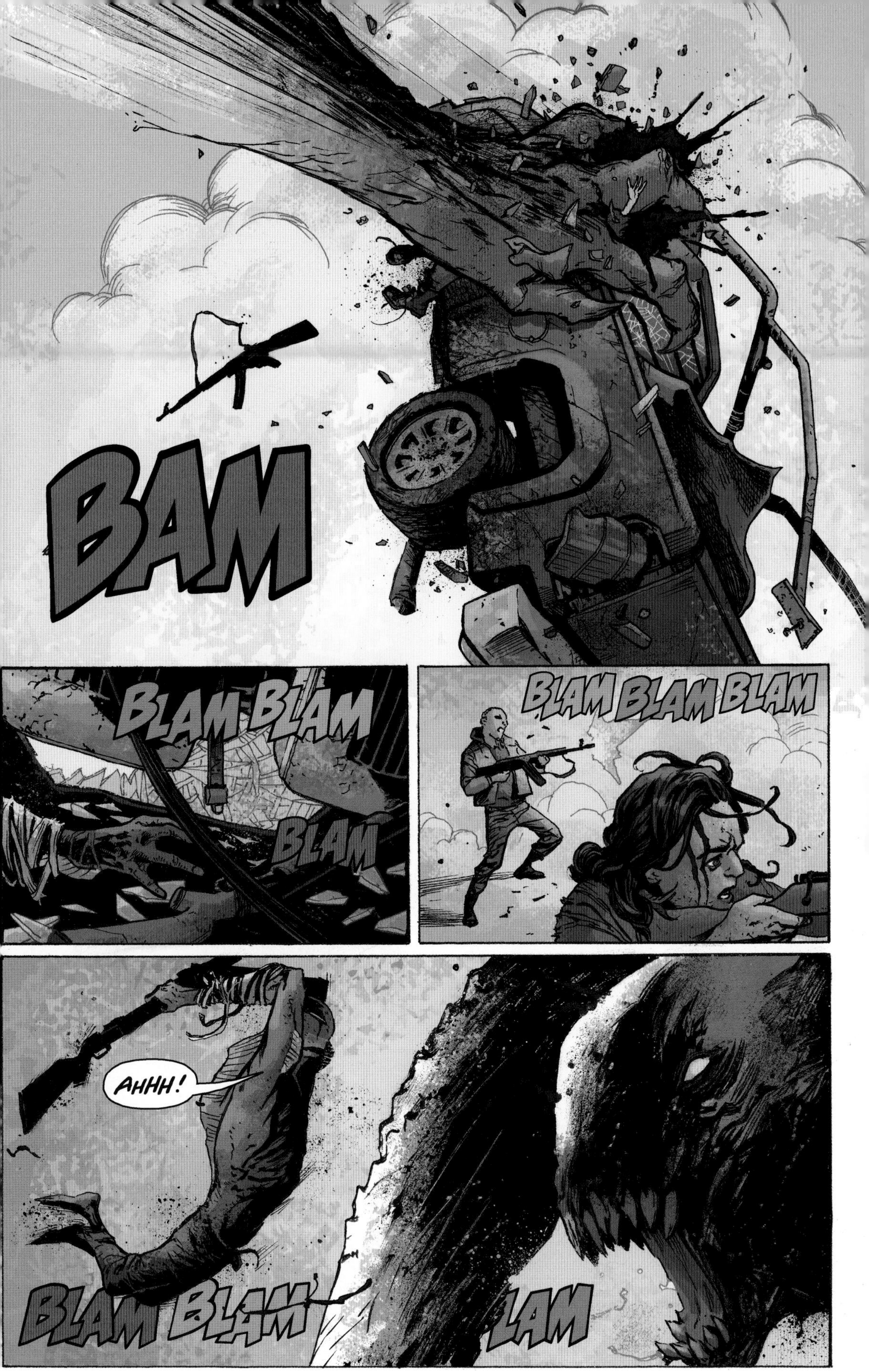

BAM
BLAM BLAM
BLAM
BLAM BLAM BLAM
AHHH!
BLAM BLAM
LAM

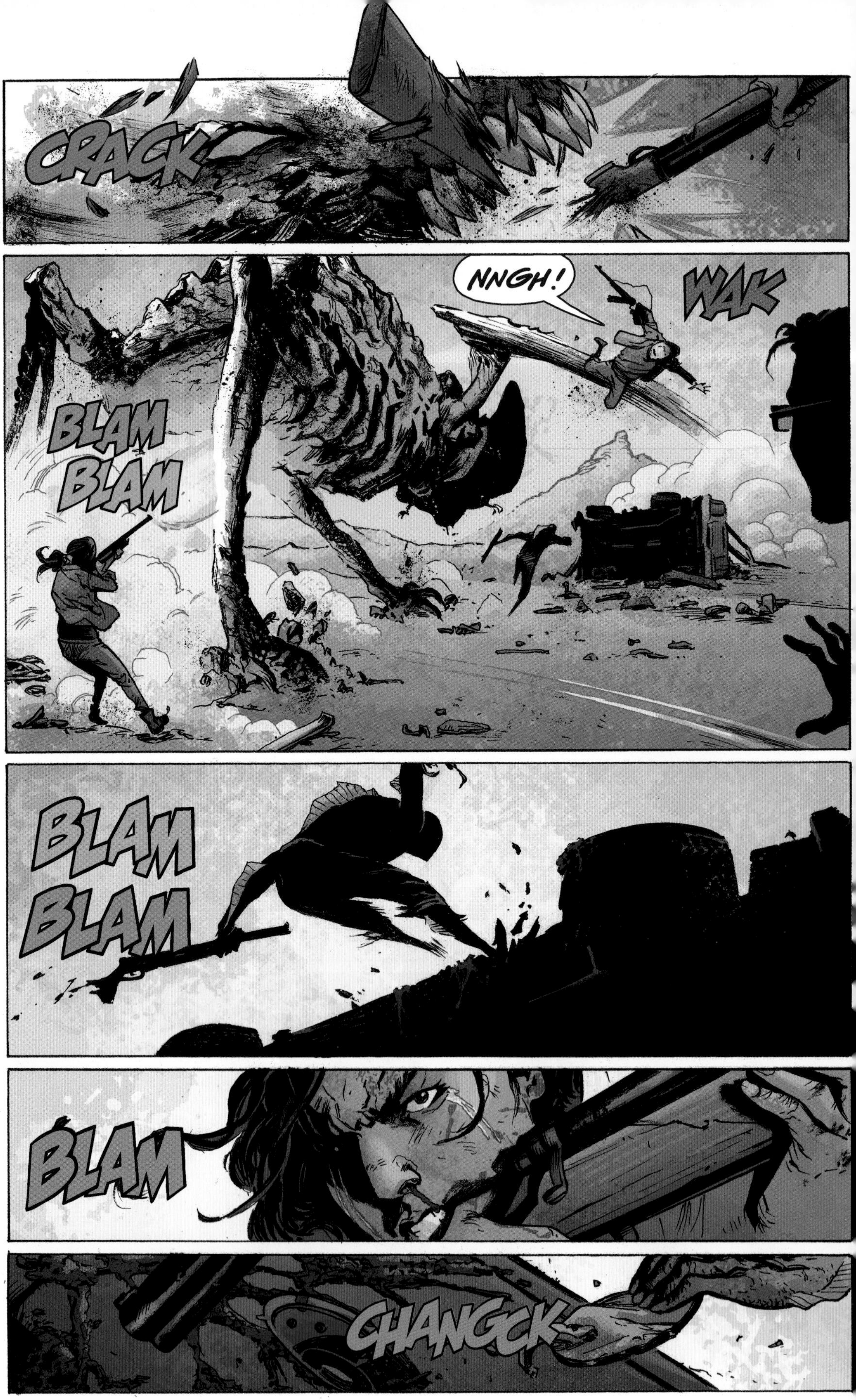
CRACK
NNGH!
WAK
BLAM
BLAM
BLAM
BLAM
BLAM
CHANGCK

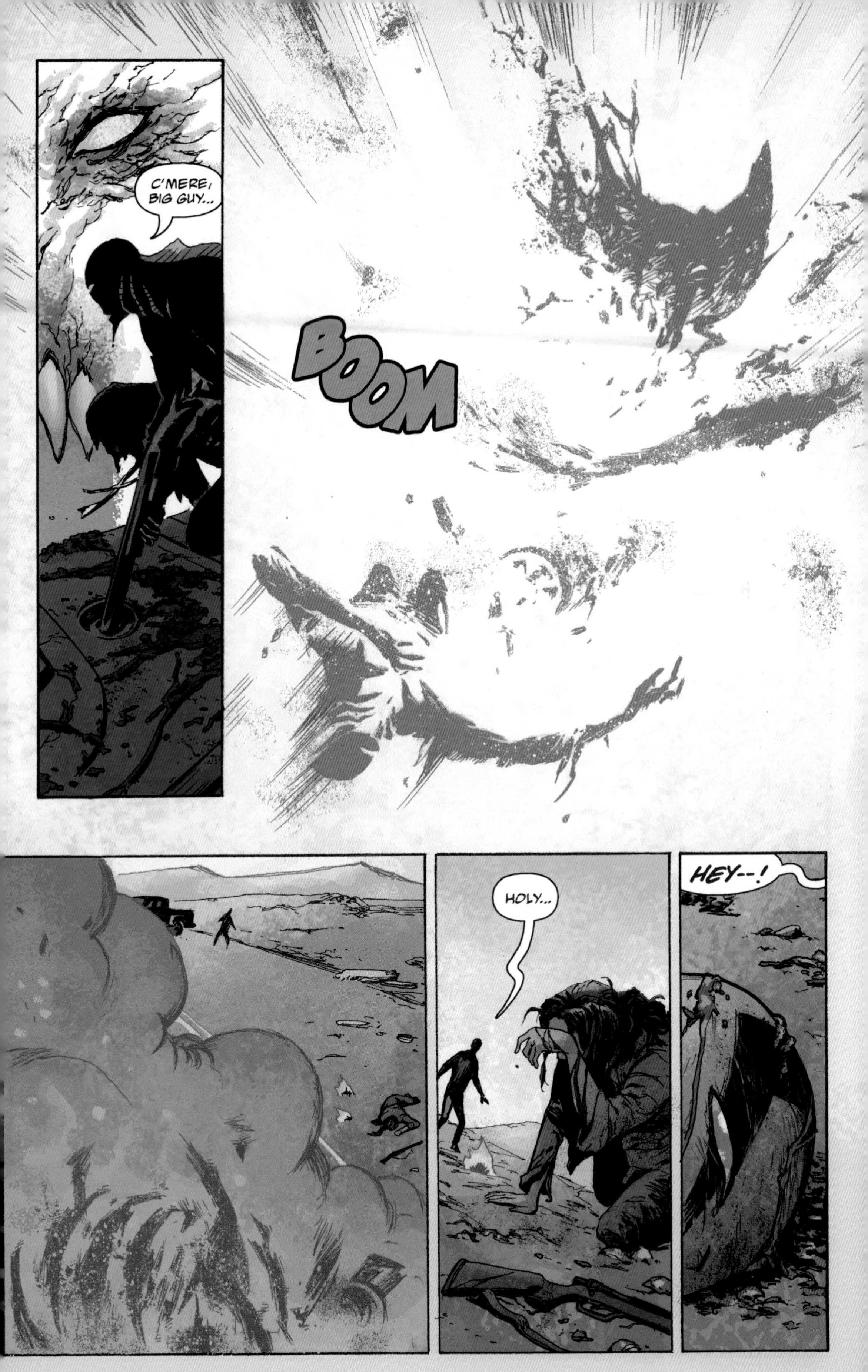
C'MERE, BIG GUY...
BOOM
HOLY...
HEY--!

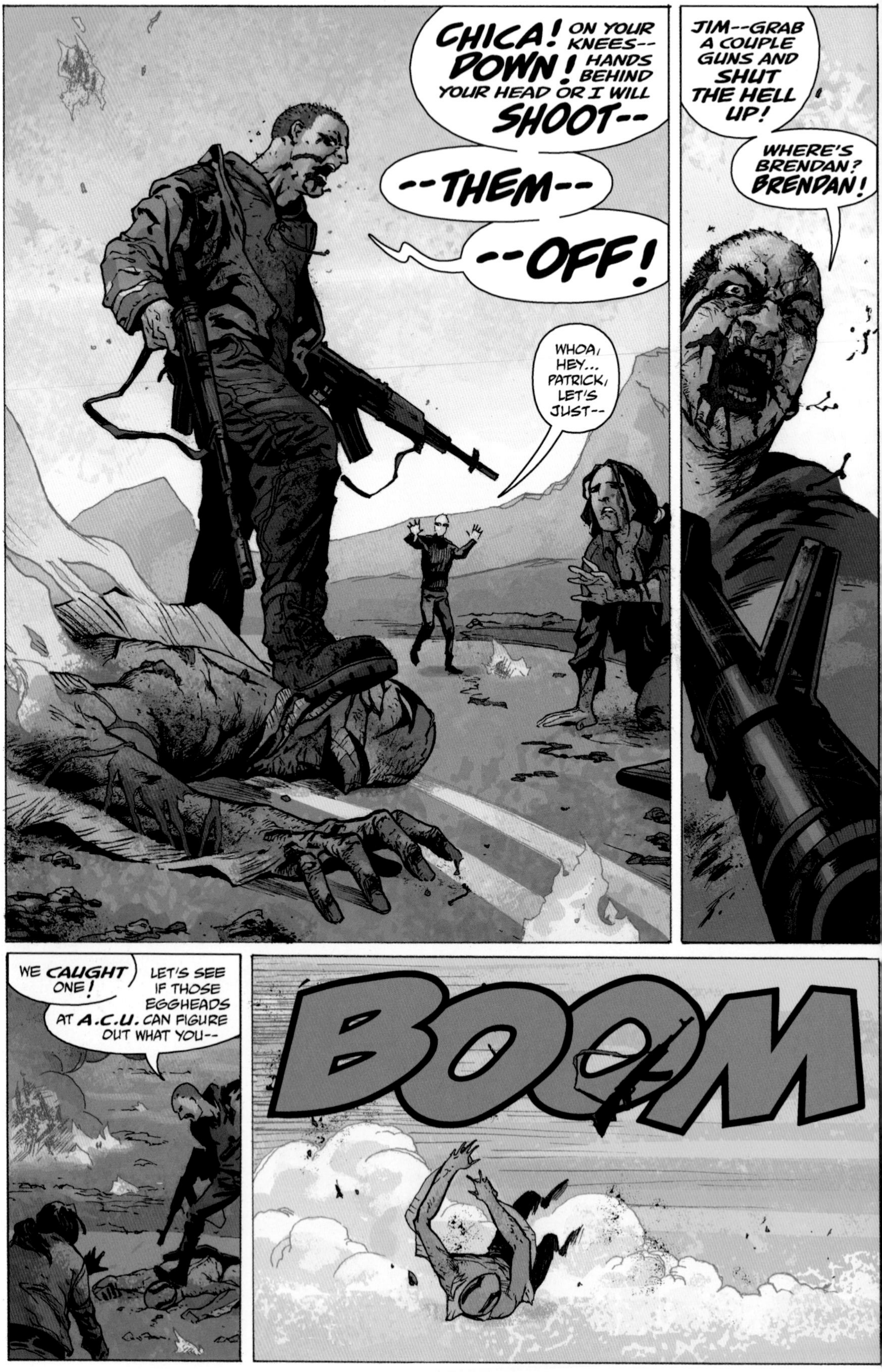
CHICA! ON YOUR KNEES-- DOWN! HANDS BEHIND YOUR HEAD OR I WILL SHOOT--
--THEM--
--OFF!
WHOA, HEY... PATRICK, LET'S JUST--
JIM--GRAB A COUPLE GUNS AND SHUT THE HELL UP!
WHERE'S BRENDAN? BRENDAN!
WE CAUGHT ONE!
LET'S SEE IF THOSE EGGHEADS AT A.C.U. CAN FIGURE OUT WHAT YOU--
BOOM

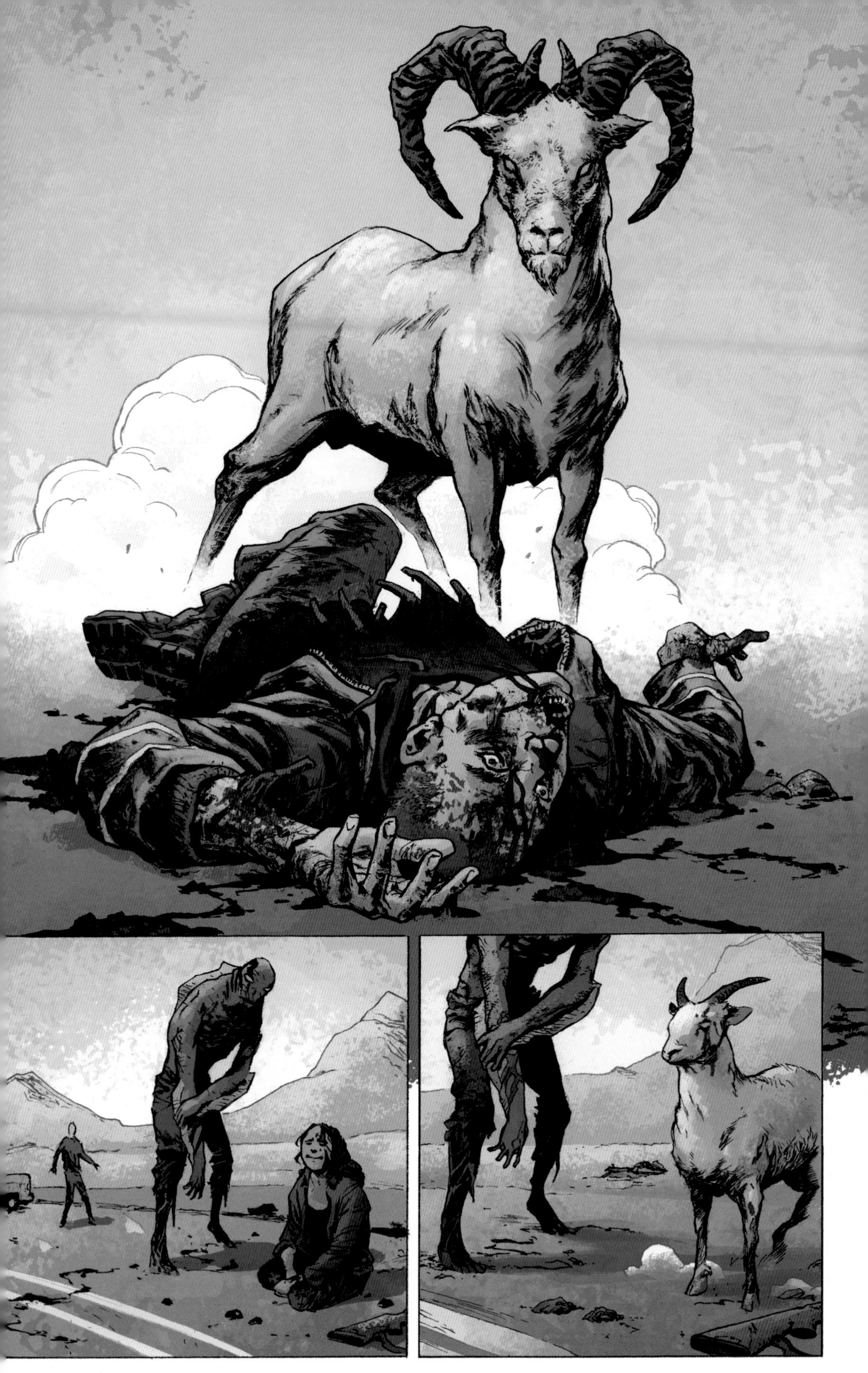

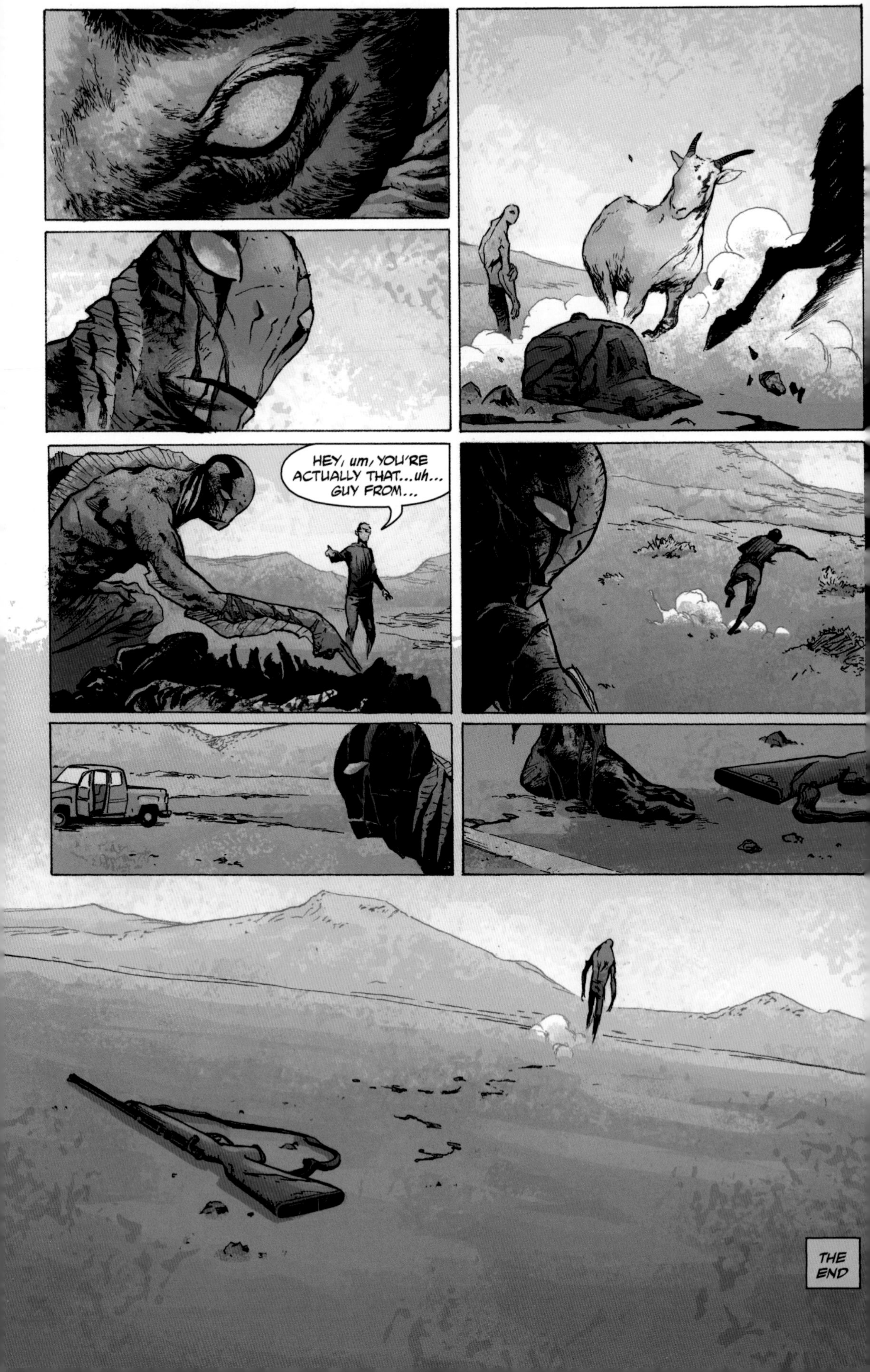

HEY, um, YOU'RE ACTUALLY THAT...uh... GUY FROM...
THE END

TO THE LAST MAN

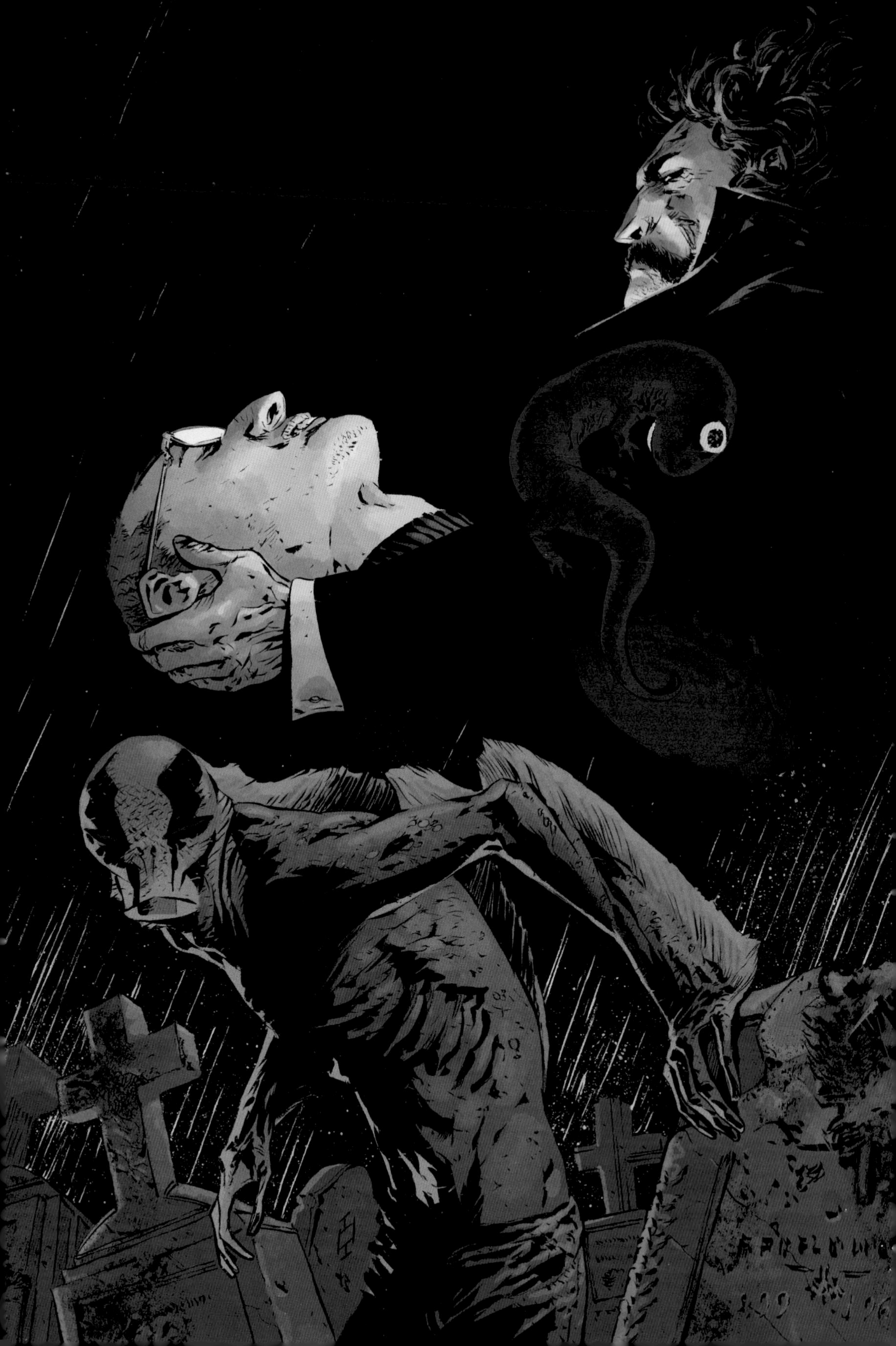

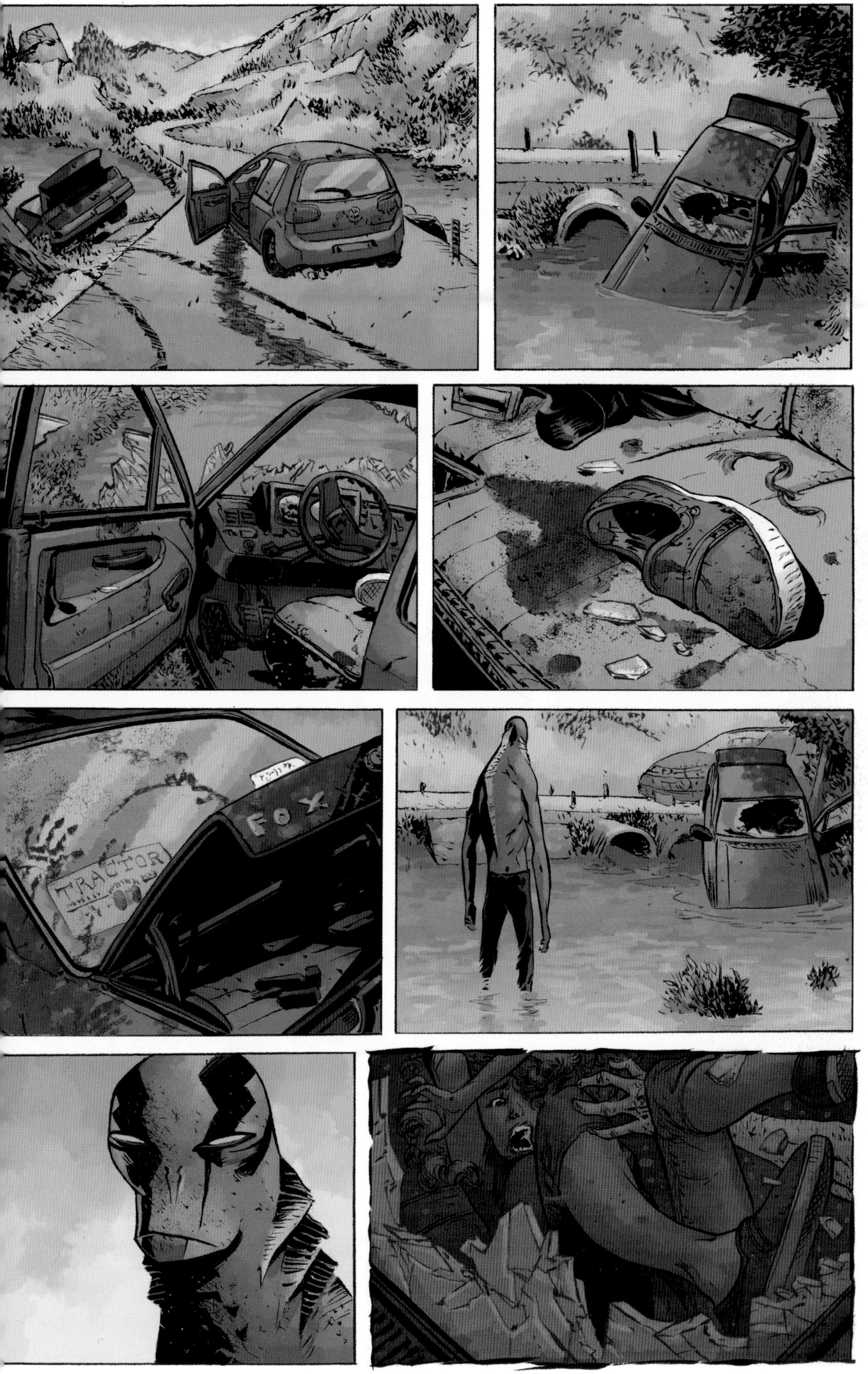
FOX
TRACTOR

"IF THOSE DEMONS DON'T ANSWER WHEN YOU CALL..."

...HOW'D YOU BRING ME BACK...?

THERE ARE MANY SOURCES OF POWER IN THE WORLD, SOLDIER...

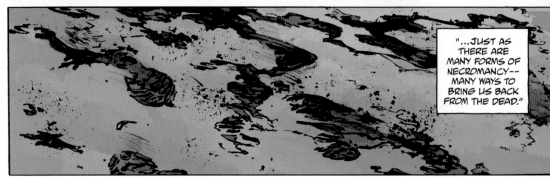

"...JUST AS THERE ARE MANY FORMS OF NECROMANCY-- MANY WAYS TO BRING US BACK FROM THE DEAD."

THE OREGON-WASHINGTON BORDER.

WHATEVER THE TROUBLE IN HELL MAY BE, IT SEEMS TO HAVE CUT OFF THE GREATEST OF MY POWERS--

--BUT NOT *ALL* OF THEM.

YOU SEE, MY... *FAUSTIAN* GAMBLE HAS NOT PAID OUT. IF HELL HAS LOST INTEREST IN THIS WORLD, IT HAS NO INTEREST IN ME!

"IF THAT IS THE CASE, ONE MUST ASK WHERE *IS* THE NEW POWER? FROM WHERE DOES THIS CHANGE *COME?*"

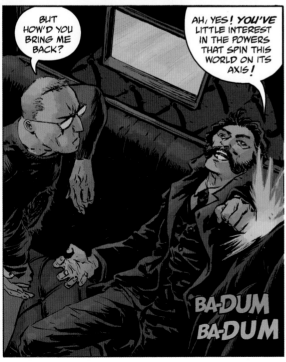

BUT HOW'D YOU BRING ME BACK?

AH, YES! *YOU'VE* LITTLE INTEREST IN THE POWERS THAT SPIN THIS WORLD ON ITS AXIS!

BA-DUM BA-DUM

IN ALL THE COSMOS THE ONLY SOUND *YOU* HEAR IS THE FAINT POUNDING OF YOUR OWN DEAD HEART!

THE POWER I USED TO REVIVE YOU AND WILLIS IS SOMETHING I CAPTURED LONG AGO.

BA-DUM BA-DUM

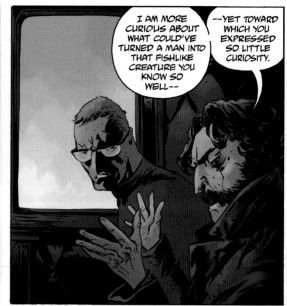

"A SIMPLE POWER, ROOTED IN THE EARTH ITSELF, IN THAT MAGIC-RICH ISLE OF BRITAIN. *IT* CAUSES YOUR THICK LIMBS TO PLOD ON."

I AM MORE CURIOUS ABOUT WHAT COULD'VE TURNED A MAN INTO THAT FISHLIKE CREATURE YOU KNOW SO WELL--

--YET TOWARD WHICH YOU EXPRESSED SO LITTLE CURIOSITY.

"*IMAGINE!* MAN'S UNDOING MAY HAVE DWELT BENEATH YOUR ROOF FOR DECADES--

"YET YOUR '*BUREAU* OF *RESEARCH*'--

"YOU NEVER THOUGHT TO...*CUT IT OPEN*...

"...TO *LOOK INSIDE*..."

IN LOVING MEMORY
MARIANNE POIRIER
AUGUST 7 2008
March 19 2012

PAYSON, ARIZONA.

"YOU MEN OF SCIENCE. YOU SICKEN ME.

"BUT I FORGET! *YOU* ARE A SOLDIER!"

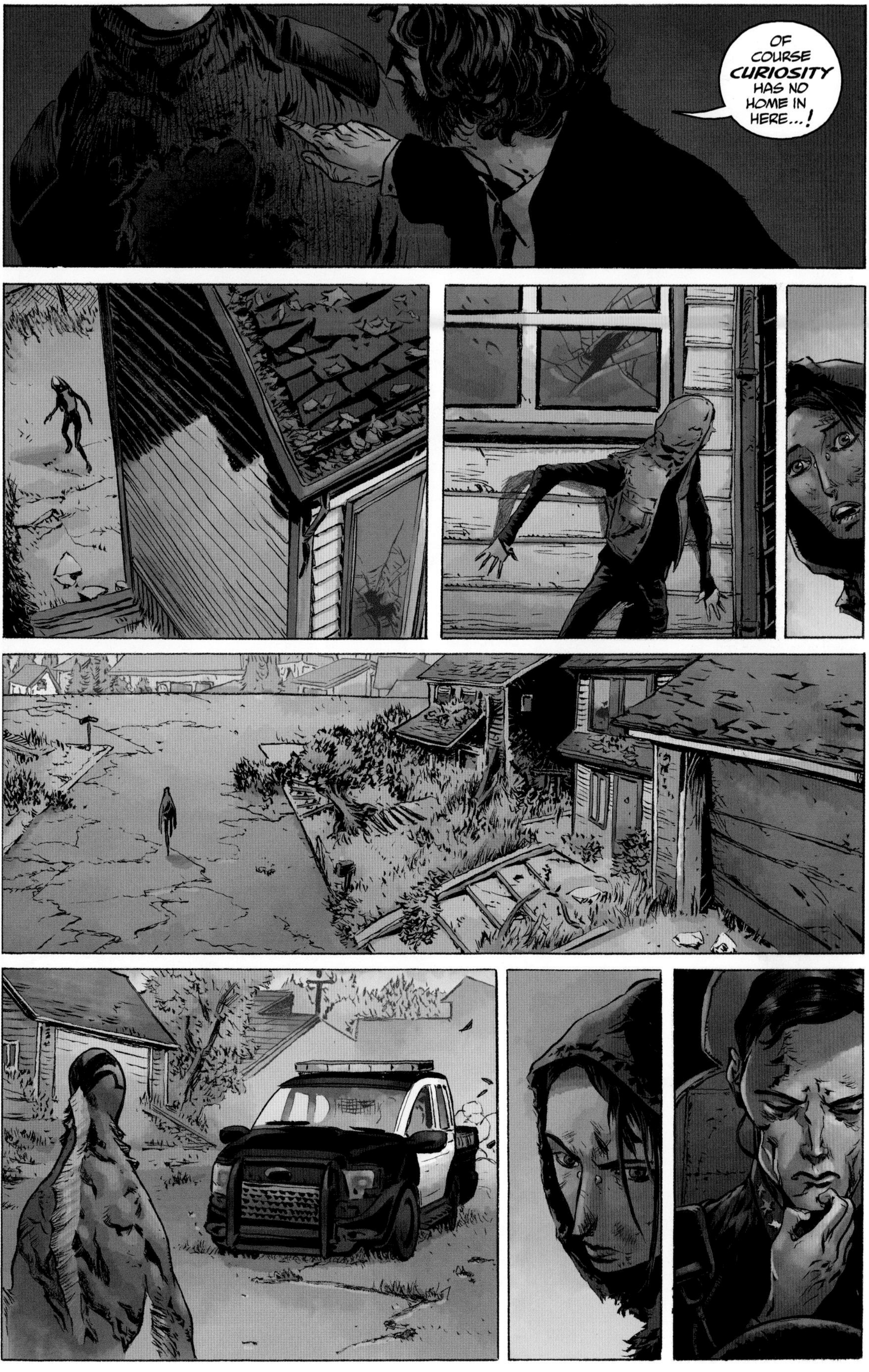
OF COURSE CURIOSITY HAS NO HOME IN HERE...!

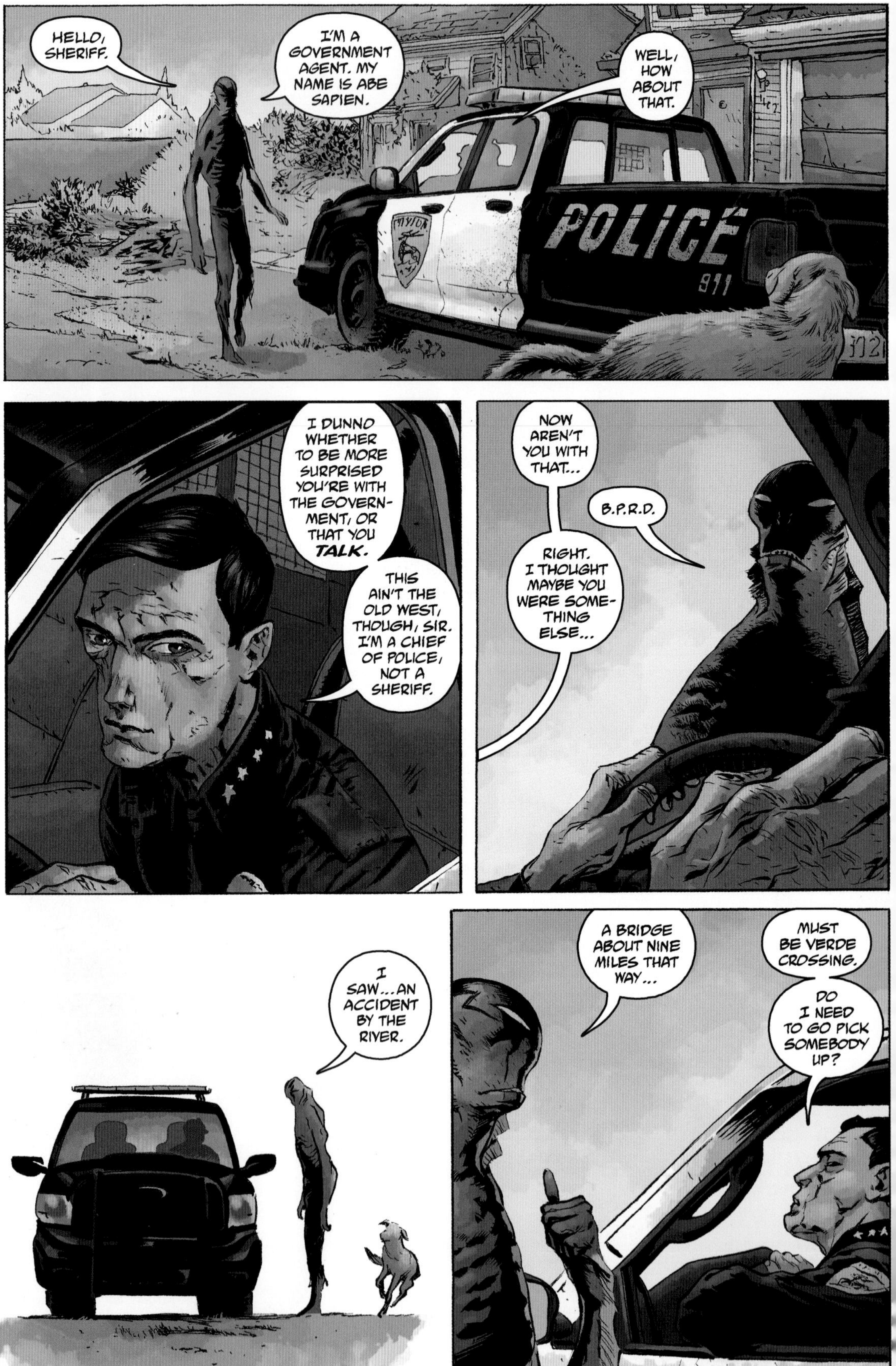
HELLO, SHERIFF.
I'M A GOVERNMENT AGENT. MY NAME IS ABE SAPIEN.
WELL, HOW ABOUT THAT.
POLICE
911
I DUNNO WHETHER TO BE MORE SURPRISED YOU'RE WITH THE GOVERNMENT, OR THAT YOU TALK.
THIS AIN'T THE OLD WEST, THOUGH, SIR. I'M A CHIEF OF POLICE, NOT A SHERIFF.
NOW AREN'T YOU WITH THAT...
B.P.R.D.
RIGHT. I THOUGHT MAYBE YOU WERE SOMETHING ELSE...
I SAW...AN ACCIDENT BY THE RIVER.
A BRIDGE ABOUT NINE MILES THAT WAY...
MUST BE VERDE CROSSING.
DO I NEED TO GO PICK SOMEBODY UP?

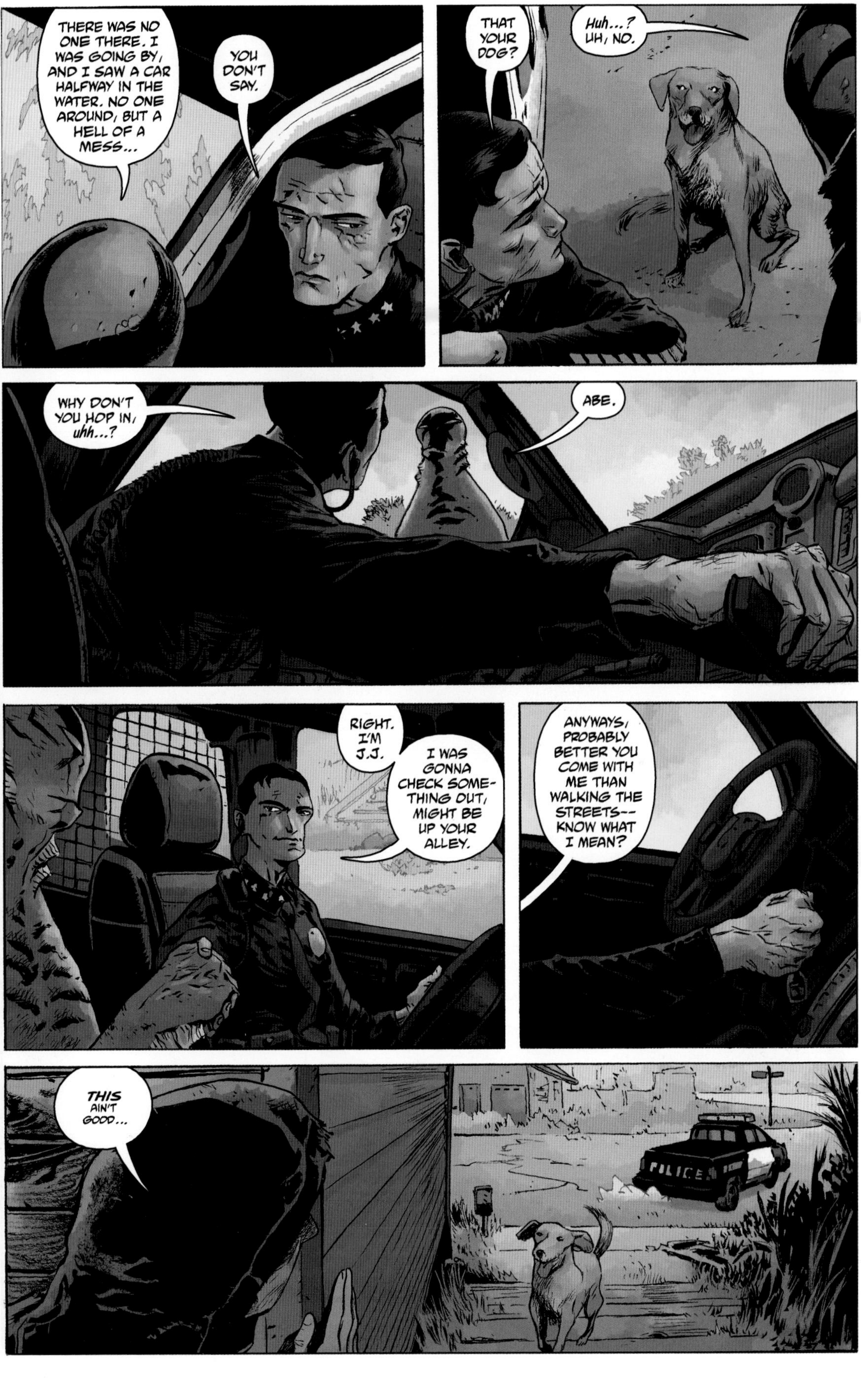

THERE WAS NO ONE THERE. I WAS GOING BY, AND I SAW A CAR HALFWAY IN THE WATER. NO ONE AROUND, BUT A HELL OF A MESS...
YOU DON'T SAY.
THAT YOUR DOG?
Huh...? UH, NO.
WHY DON'T YOU HOP IN, uhh...?
ABE.
RIGHT. I'M J.J.
I WAS GONNA CHECK SOME-THING OUT, MIGHT BE UP YOUR ALLEY.
ANYWAYS, PROBABLY BETTER YOU COME WITH ME THAN WALKING THE STREETS-- KNOW WHAT I MEAN?
THIS AIN'T GOOD...
POLICE

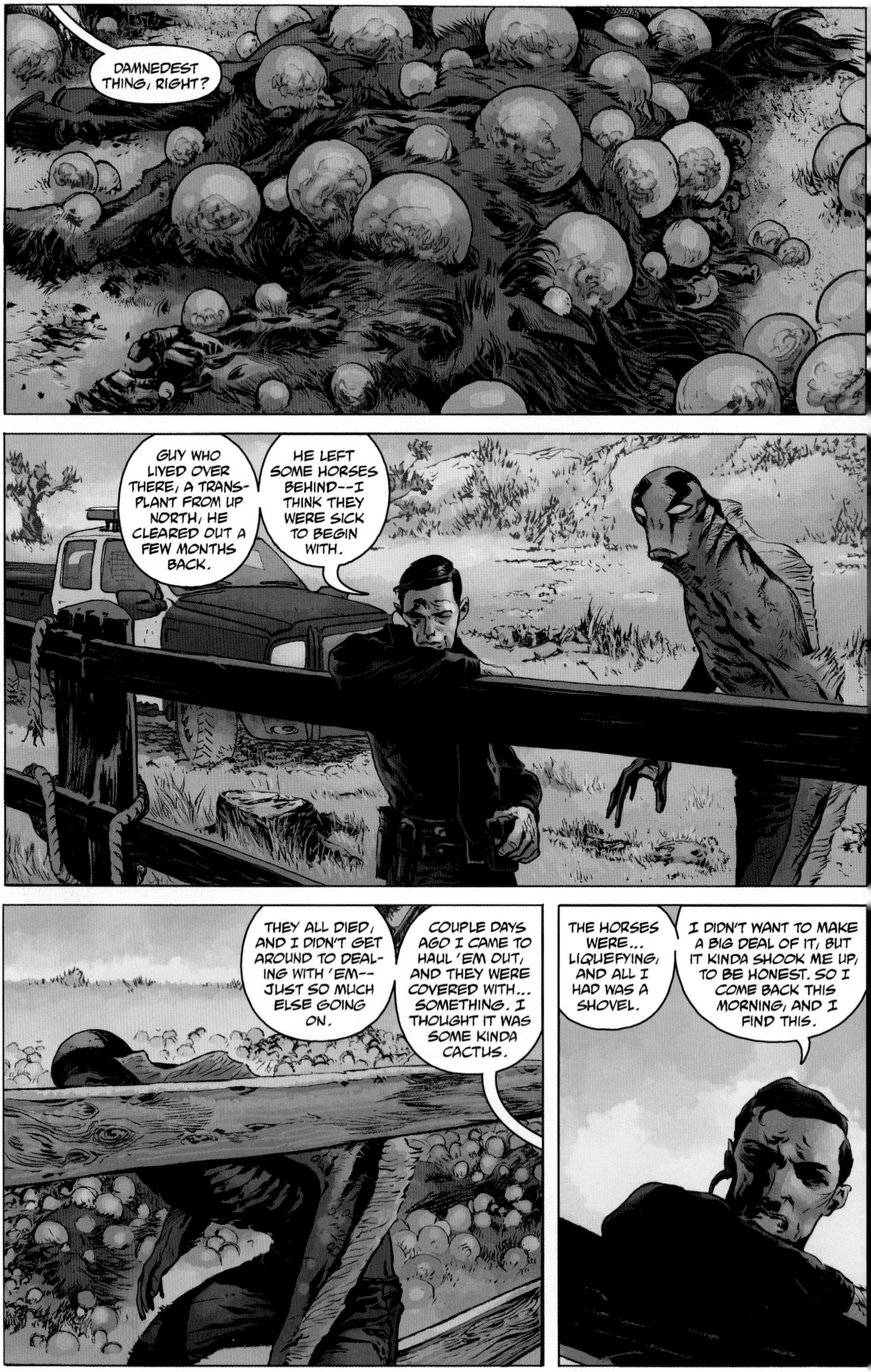
DAMNEDEST THING, RIGHT?
GUY WHO LIVED OVER THERE, A TRANS-PLANT FROM UP NORTH, HE CLEARED OUT A FEW MONTHS BACK.
HE LEFT SOME HORSES BEHIND--I THINK THEY WERE SICK TO BEGIN WITH.
THEY ALL DIED, AND I DIDN'T GET AROUND TO DEAL-ING WITH 'EM--JUST SO MUCH ELSE GOING ON.
COUPLE DAYS AGO I CAME TO HAUL 'EM OUT, AND THEY WERE COVERED WITH... SOMETHING. I THOUGHT IT WAS SOME KINDA CACTUS.
THE HORSES WERE... LIQUEFYING, AND ALL I HAD WAS A SHOVEL.
I DIDN'T WANT TO MAKE A BIG DEAL OF IT, BUT IT KINDA SHOOK ME UP, TO BE HONEST. SO I COME BACK THIS MORNING, AND I FIND THIS.

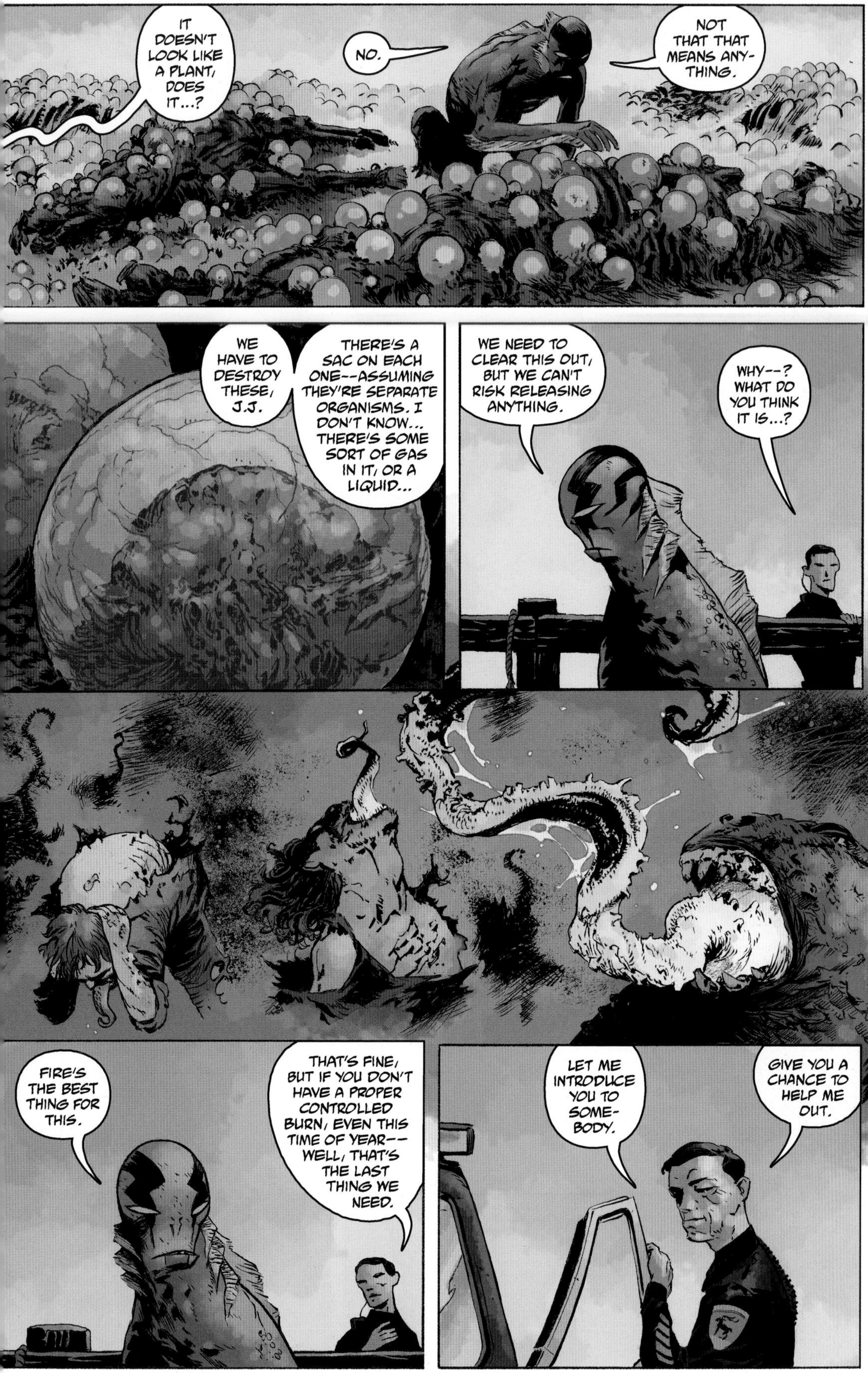
IT DOESN'T LOOK LIKE A PLANT, DOES IT...?
NO.
NOT THAT THAT MEANS ANYTHING.
WE HAVE TO DESTROY THESE, J.J.
THERE'S A SAC ON EACH ONE--ASSUMING THEY'RE SEPARATE ORGANISMS. I DON'T KNOW... THERE'S SOME SORT OF GAS IN IT, OR A LIQUID...
WE NEED TO CLEAR THIS OUT, BUT WE CAN'T RISK RELEASING ANYTHING.
WHY--? WHAT DO YOU THINK IT IS...?
FIRE'S THE BEST THING FOR THIS.
THAT'S FINE, BUT IF YOU DON'T HAVE A PROPER CONTROLLED BURN, EVEN THIS TIME OF YEAR--WELL, THAT'S THE LAST THING WE NEED.
LET ME INTRODUCE YOU TO SOMEBODY.
GIVE YOU A CHANCE TO HELP ME OUT.

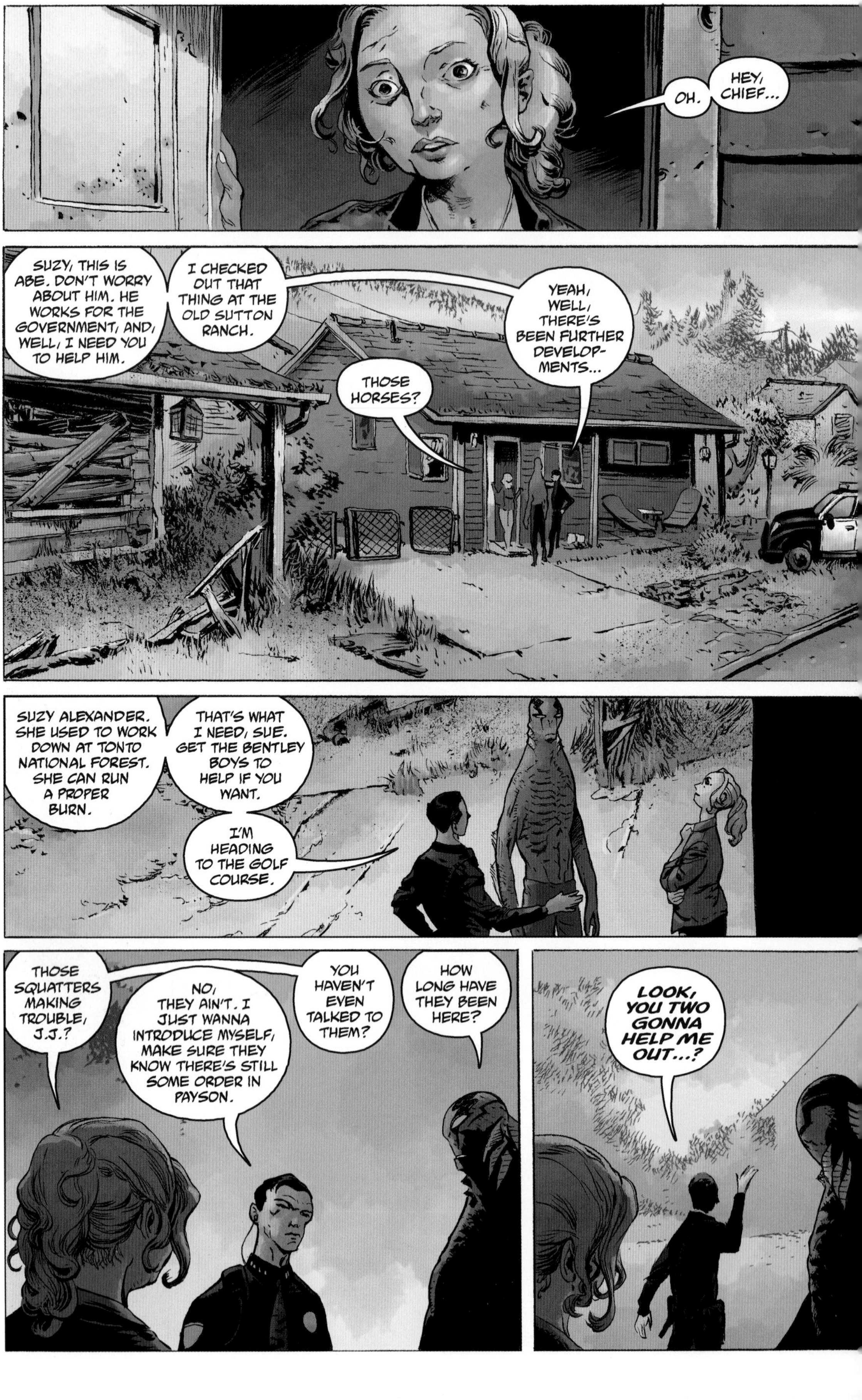

OH.
HEY, CHIEF...
SUZY, THIS IS ABE. DON'T WORRY ABOUT HIM. HE WORKS FOR THE GOVERNMENT, AND, WELL, I NEED YOU TO HELP HIM.
I CHECKED OUT THAT THING AT THE OLD SUTTON RANCH.
YEAH, WELL, THERE'S BEEN FURTHER DEVELOP-MENTS...
THOSE HORSES?
SUZY ALEXANDER. SHE USED TO WORK DOWN AT TONTO NATIONAL FOREST. SHE CAN RUN A PROPER BURN.
THAT'S WHAT I NEED, SUE. GET THE BENTLEY BOYS TO HELP IF YOU WANT.
I'M HEADING TO THE GOLF COURSE.
THOSE SQUATTERS MAKING TROUBLE, J.J.?
NO, THEY AIN'T. I JUST WANNA INTRODUCE MYSELF, MAKE SURE THEY KNOW THERE'S STILL SOME ORDER IN PAYSON.
YOU HAVEN'T EVEN TALKED TO THEM?
HOW LONG HAVE THEY BEEN HERE?
LOOK, YOU TWO GONNA HELP ME OUT...?

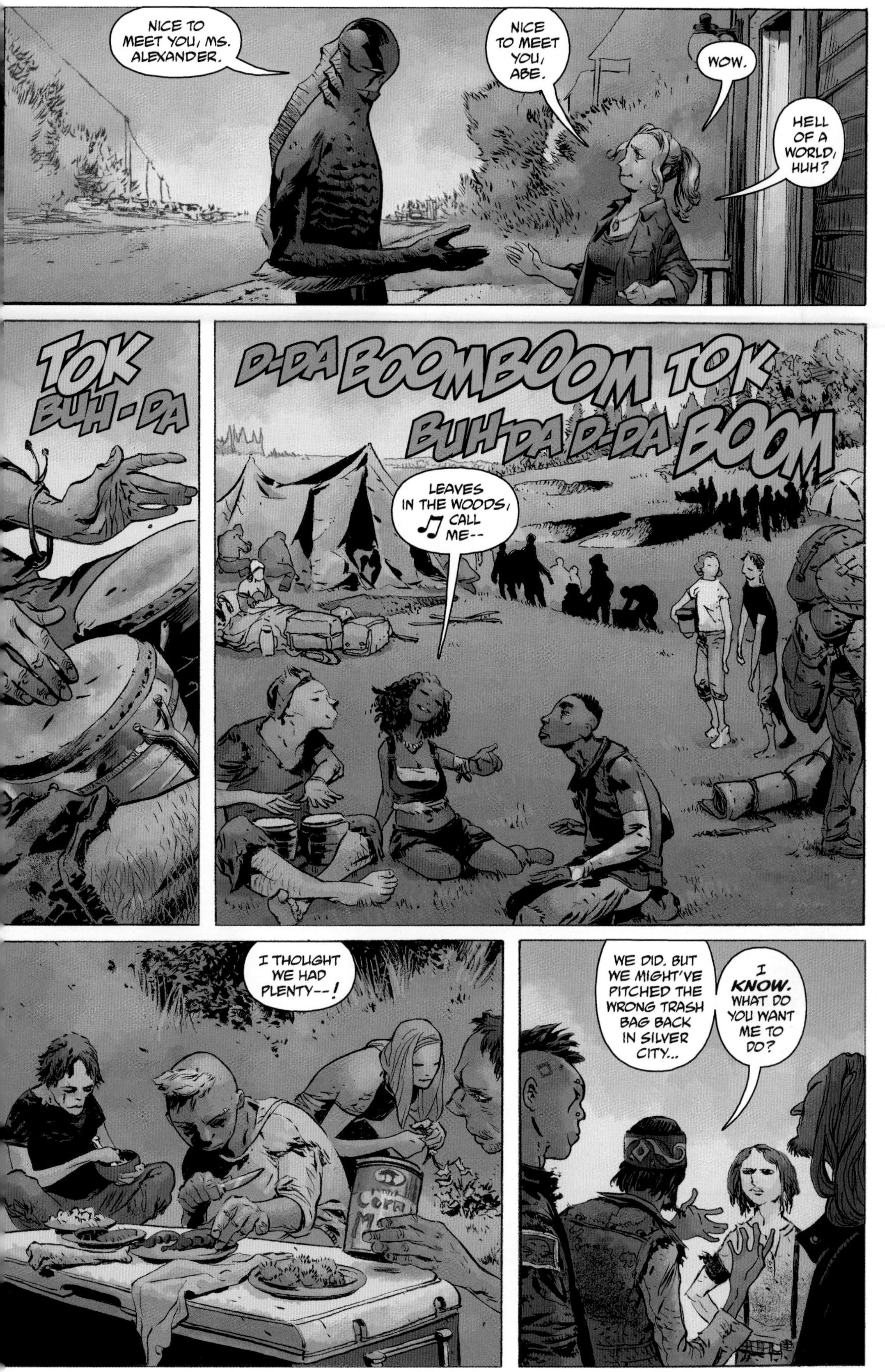

NICE TO MEET YOU, MS. ALEXANDER.
NICE TO MEET YOU, ABE.
WOW.
HELL OF A WORLD, HUH?
TOK BUH-DA
D-DA BOOMBOOM TOK BUH-DA D-DA BOOM
LEAVES IN THE WOODS, ♫ CALL ME--
I THOUGHT WE HAD PLENTY--!
WE DID. BUT WE MIGHT'VE PITCHED THE WRONG TRASH BAG BACK IN SILVER CITY...
I KNOW. WHAT DO YOU WANT ME TO DO?

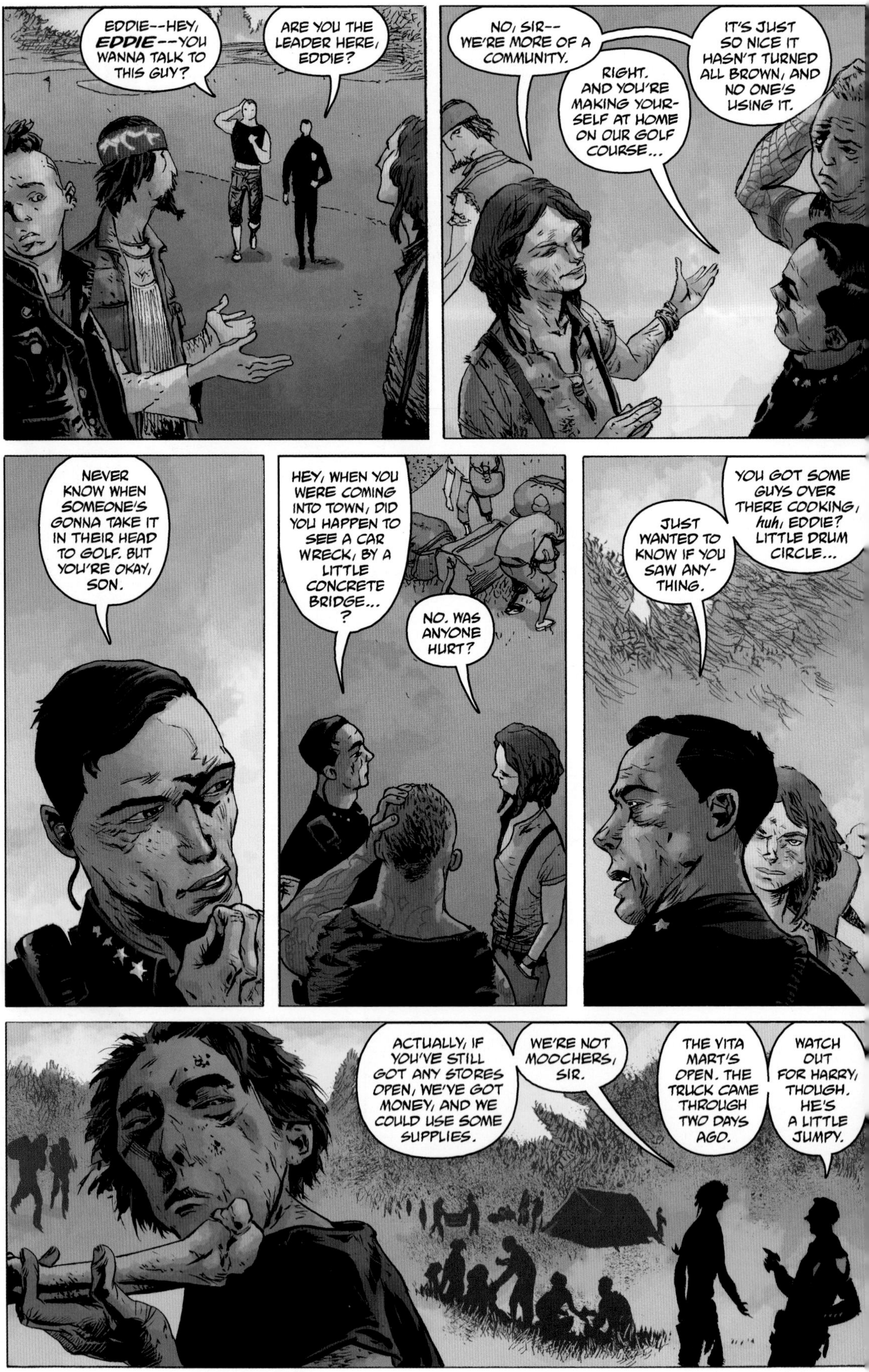
EDDIE--HEY, EDDIE--YOU WANNA TALK TO THIS GUY?
ARE YOU THE LEADER HERE, EDDIE?
NO, SIR-- WE'RE MORE OF A COMMUNITY.
RIGHT. AND YOU'RE MAKING YOUR-SELF AT HOME ON OUR GOLF COURSE...
IT'S JUST SO NICE IT HASN'T TURNED ALL BROWN, AND NO ONE'S USING IT.
NEVER KNOW WHEN SOMEONE'S GONNA TAKE IT IN THEIR HEAD TO GOLF. BUT YOU'RE OKAY, SON.
HEY, WHEN YOU WERE COMING INTO TOWN, DID YOU HAPPEN TO SEE A CAR WRECK, BY A LITTLE CONCRETE BRIDGE... ?
NO. WAS ANYONE HURT?
JUST WANTED TO KNOW IF YOU SAW ANY-THING.
YOU GOT SOME GUYS OVER THERE COOKING, huh, EDDIE? LITTLE DRUM CIRCLE...
ACTUALLY, IF YOU'VE STILL GOT ANY STORES OPEN, WE'VE GOT MONEY, AND WE COULD USE SOME SUPPLIES.
WE'RE NOT MOOCHERS, SIR.
THE VITA MART'S OPEN. THE TRUCK CAME THROUGH TWO DAYS AGO.
WATCH OUT FOR HARRY, THOUGH. HE'S A LITTLE JUMPY.

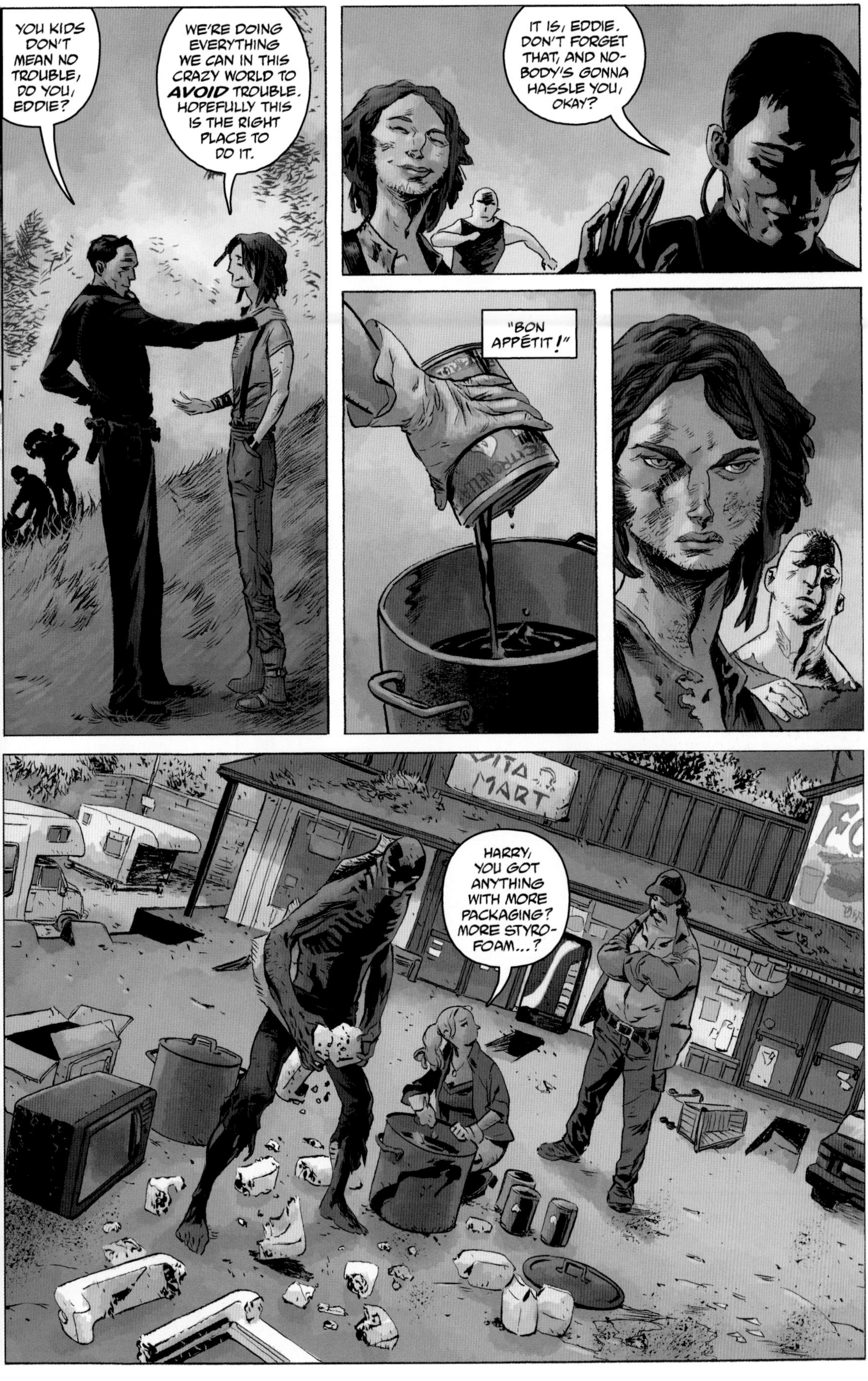

YOU KIDS DON'T MEAN NO TROUBLE, DO YOU, EDDIE?
WE'RE DOING EVERYTHING WE CAN IN THIS CRAZY WORLD TO **AVOID** TROUBLE. HOPEFULLY THIS IS THE RIGHT PLACE TO DO IT.
IT IS, EDDIE. DON'T FORGET THAT, AND NO-BODY'S GONNA HASSLE YOU, OKAY?
"BON APPÉTIT!"
HARRY, YOU GOT ANYTHING WITH MORE PACKAGING? MORE STYRO-FOAM...?

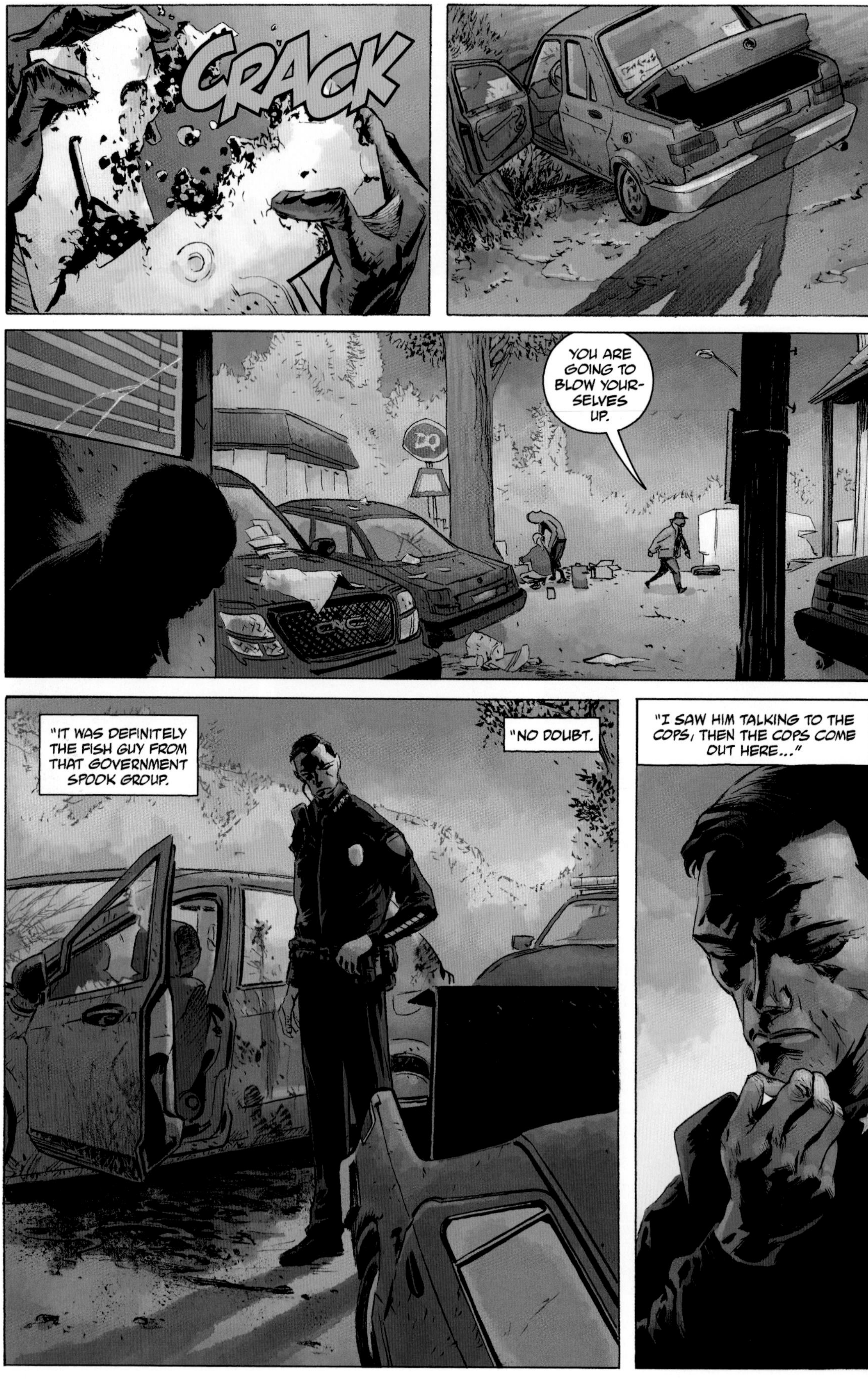
CRACK
YOU ARE GOING TO BLOW YOURSELVES UP.
"IT WAS DEFINITELY THE FISH GUY FROM THAT GOVERNMENT SPOOK GROUP.
"NO DOUBT.
"I SAW HIM TALKING TO THE COPS, THEN THE COPS COME OUT HERE..."

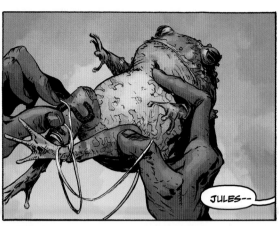

HE'S THE FISH MAN WHO GOT SHOT IN TEXAS! I HEARD HE WAS DEAD, BUT NO-- HE'S AFTER US!

JULES--

JESUS, JULES-- YOU WANT A HAND?

THEY WOULD NOT SEND ONE MAN, MORELAND.

AND I EXPECT A COOLER HEAD FROM YOU.

HE AIN'T A MAN!

WE SHOULD SPLIT. SCREW IT, WE--

NO. AND WE WILL NOT DELAY.

DID THIS FISH MAN SEE YOU?

FIND OUT WHY HE IS HERE.

HELL NO.

CRACK

I DO NOT BELIEVE IT'S FOR US.

GO ON. PUT ON A BANK SHIRT--CLEAN YOURSELF UP.

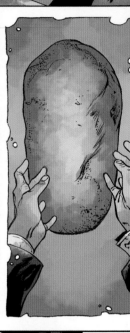

LOOKIT HIM...!

FIRST TIME YOU WALKED INTO THIS PLACE, SUZE, TYLER HERE WAS AT THE BAR--HE CALLED ME UP, SAID, DAD, YOU GET DOWN HERE, I JUST SEEN MY NEXT STEP-MOM!

Huh. LAST TIME YOU TOLD THE STORY, *MIKE* SAID THAT.

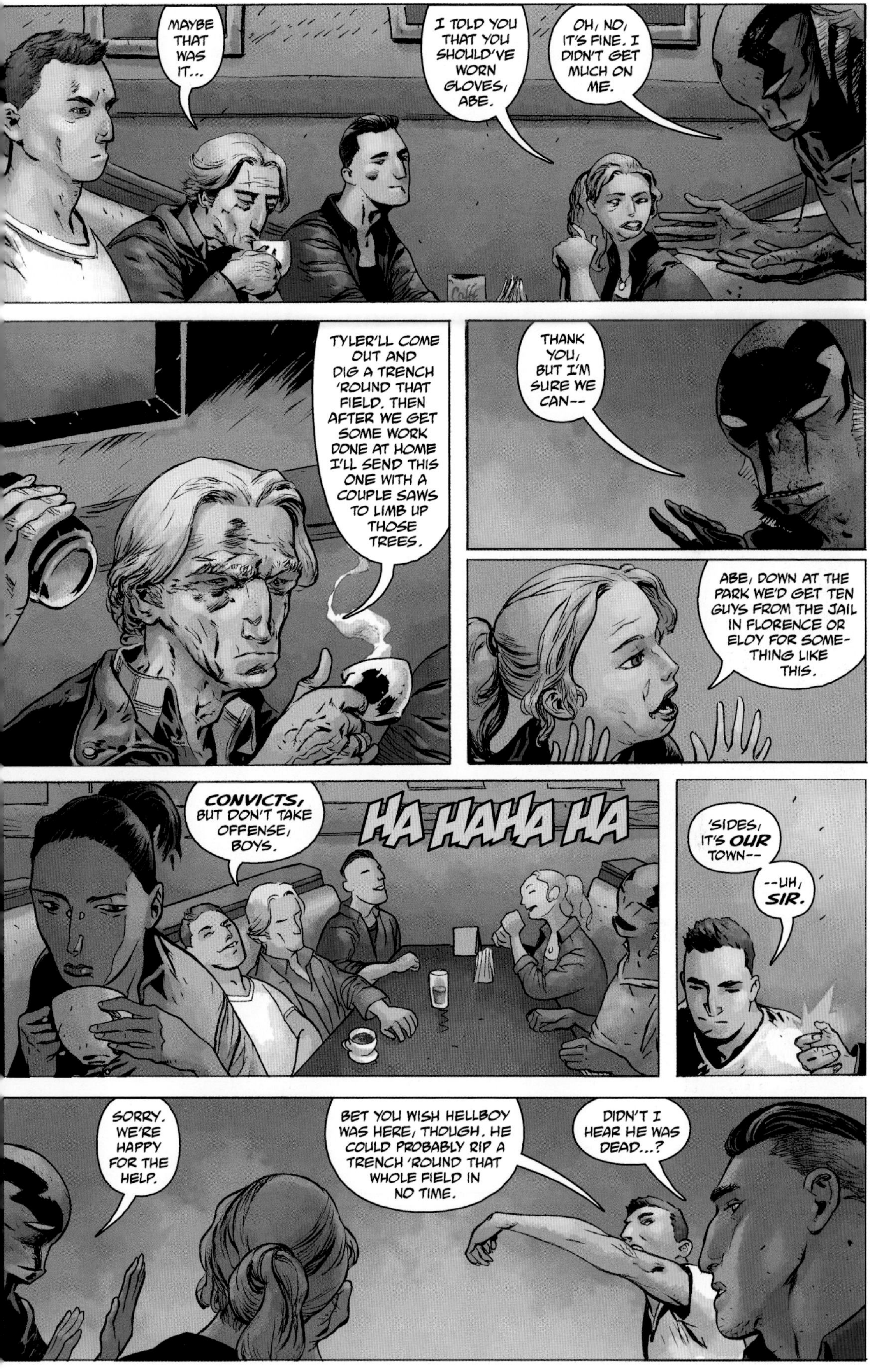
MAYBE THAT WAS IT...
I TOLD YOU THAT YOU SHOULD'VE WORN GLOVES, ABE.
OH, NO, IT'S FINE. I DIDN'T GET MUCH ON ME.
TYLER'LL COME OUT AND DIG A TRENCH 'ROUND THAT FIELD. THEN AFTER WE GET SOME WORK DONE AT HOME I'LL SEND THIS ONE WITH A COUPLE SAWS TO LIMB UP THOSE TREES.
THANK YOU, BUT I'M SURE WE CAN--
ABE, DOWN AT THE PARK WE'D GET TEN GUYS FROM THE JAIL IN FLORENCE OR ELOY FOR SOMETHING LIKE THIS.
CONVICTS, BUT DON'T TAKE OFFENSE, BOYS.
HA HAHAHA HA
'SIDES, IT'S OUR TOWN--
--UH, SIR.
SORRY. WE'RE HAPPY FOR THE HELP.
BET YOU WISH HELLBOY WAS HERE, THOUGH. HE COULD PROBABLY RIP A TRENCH 'ROUND THAT WHOLE FIELD IN NO TIME.
DIDN'T I HEAR HE WAS DEAD...?

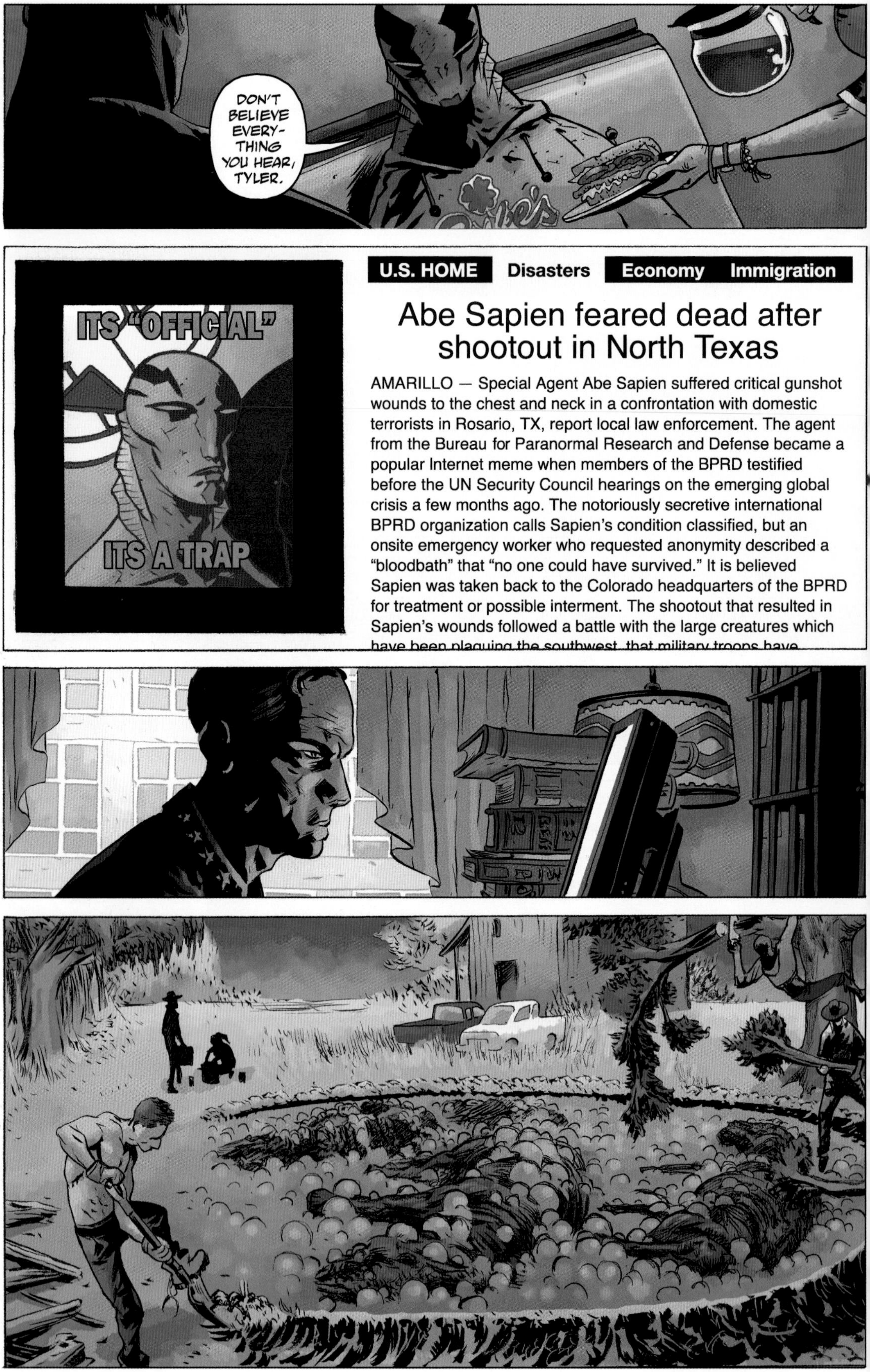

DON'T BELIEVE EVERY-THING YOU HEAR, TYLER.
U.S. HOME
Disasters
Economy
Immigration
ITS "OFFICIAL"
ITS A TRAP
Abe Sapien feared dead after shootout in North Texas
AMARILLO — Special Agent Abe Sapien suffered critical gunshot wounds to the chest and neck in a confrontation with domestic terrorists in Rosario, TX, report local law enforcement. The agent from the Bureau for Paranormal Research and Defense became a popular Internet meme when members of the BPRD testified before the UN Security Council hearings on the emerging global crisis a few months ago. The notoriously secretive international BPRD organization calls Sapien's condition classified, but an onsite emergency worker who requested anonymity described a "bloodbath" that "no one could have survived." It is believed Sapien was taken back to the Colorado headquarters of the BPRD for treatment or possible interment. The shootout that resulted in Sapien's wounds followed a battle with the large creatures which

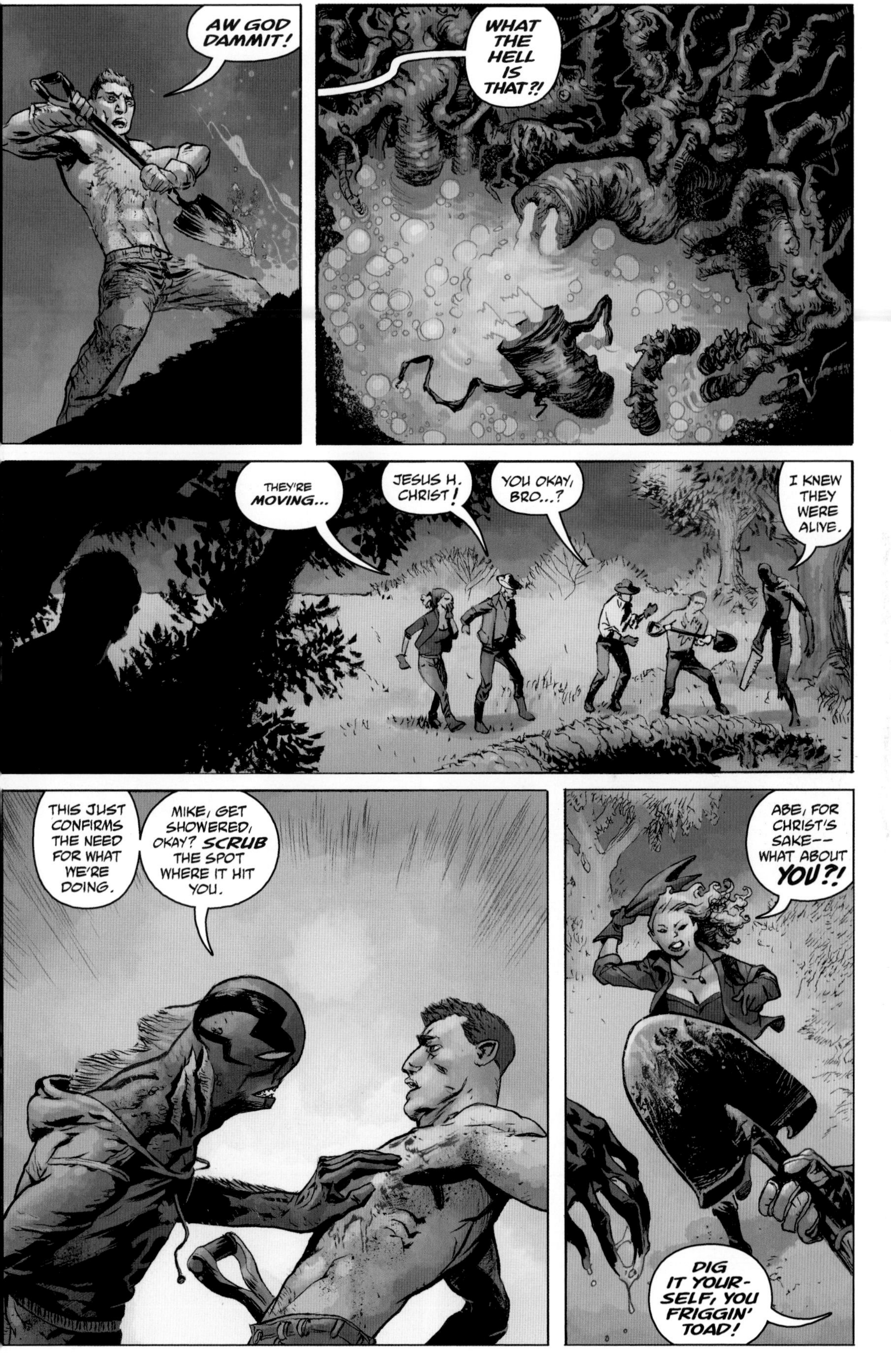
AW GOD DAMMIT!
WHAT THE HELL IS THAT?!
THEY'RE MOVING...
JESUS H. CHRIST!
YOU OKAY, BRO...?
I KNEW THEY WERE ALIVE.
THIS JUST CONFIRMS THE NEED FOR WHAT WE'RE DOING.
MIKE, GET SHOWERED, OKAY? SCRUB THE SPOT WHERE IT HIT YOU.
ABE, FOR CHRIST'S SAKE-- WHAT ABOUT YOU?!
DIG IT YOURSELF, YOU FRIGGIN' TOAD!

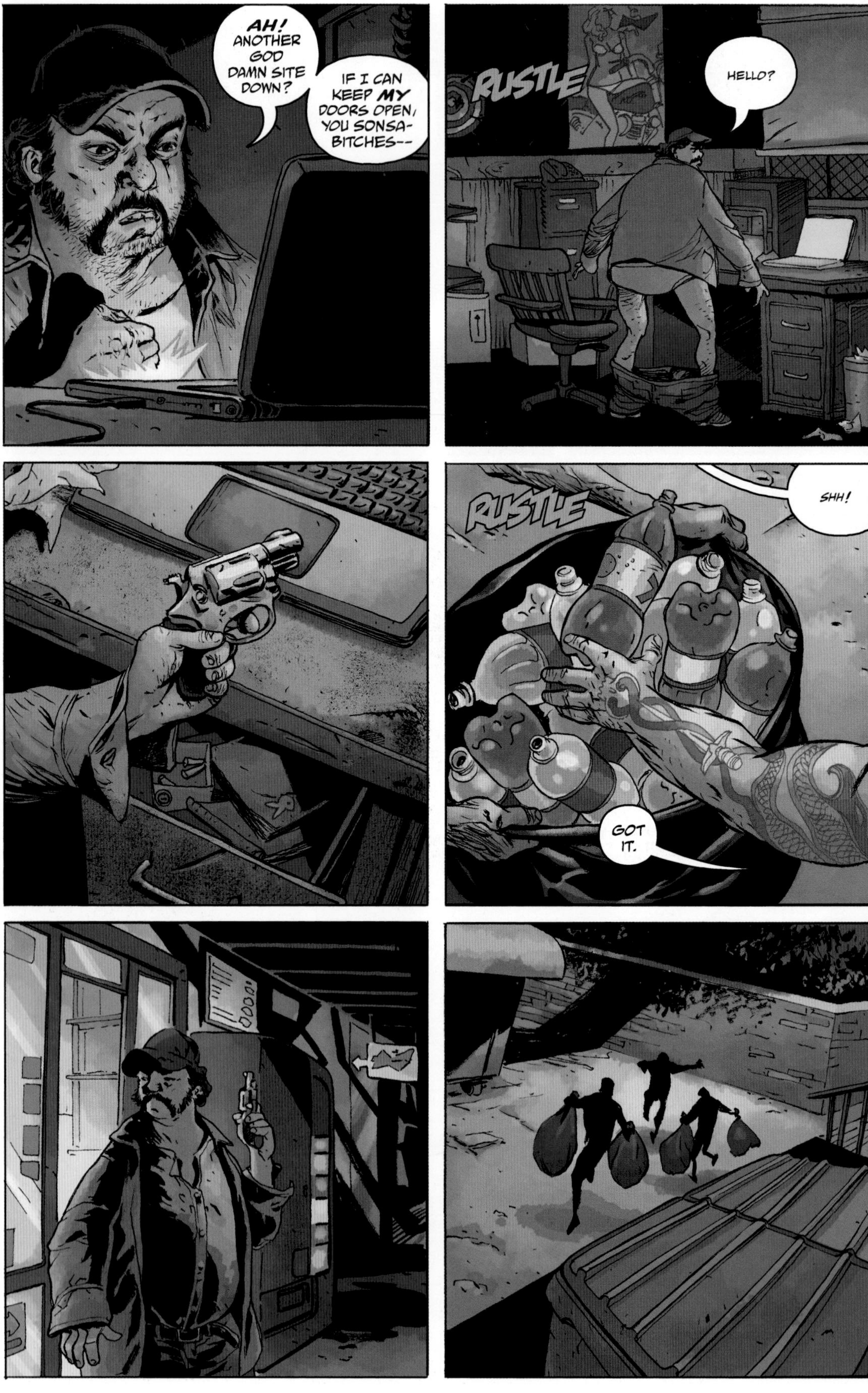
AH! ANOTHER GOD DAMN SITE DOWN?
IF I CAN KEEP MY DOORS OPEN, YOU SONSA-BITCHES--
RUSTLE
HELLO?
RUSTLE
SHH!
GOT IT.

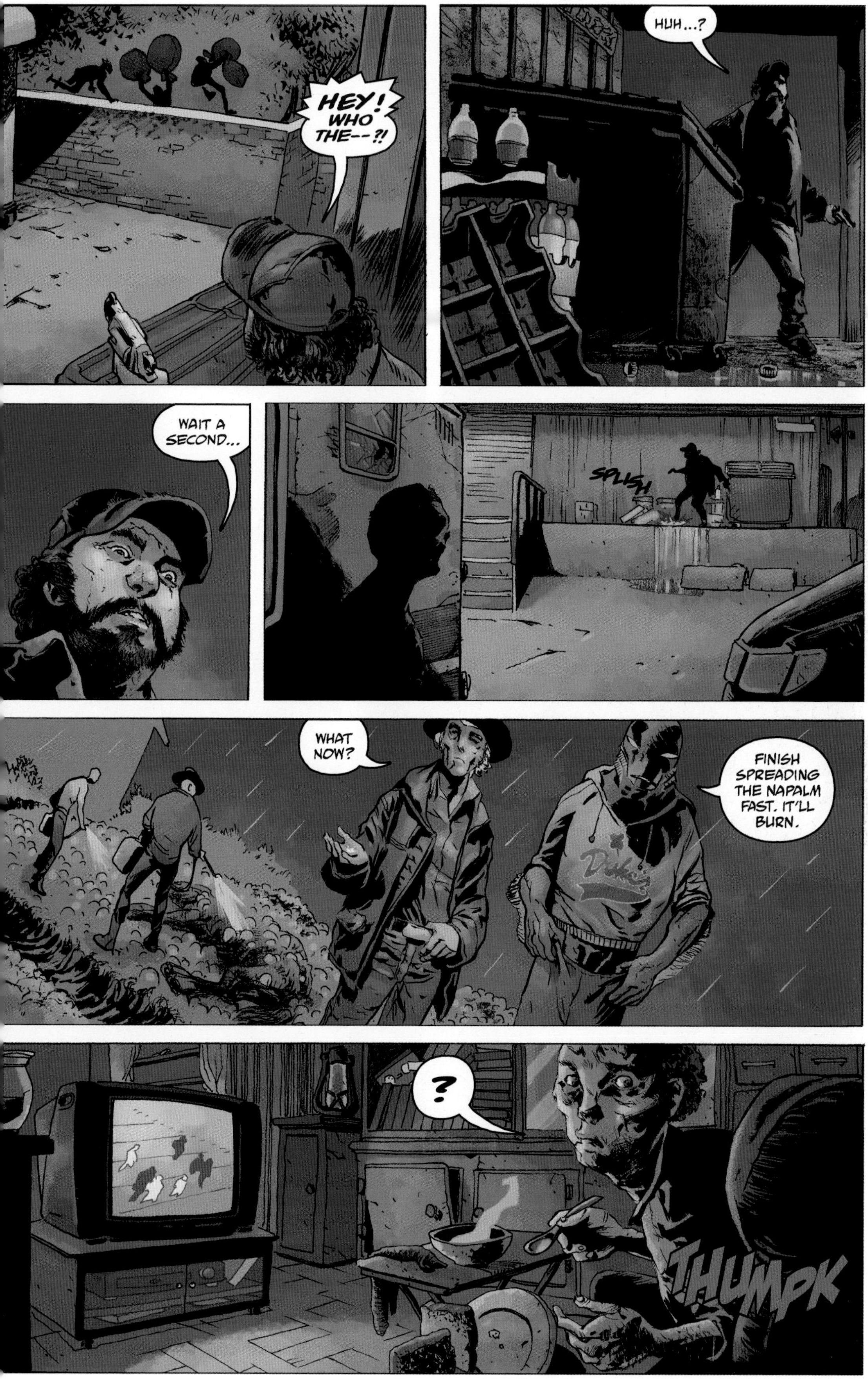
HEY! WHO THE--?!
HUH...?
WAIT A SECOND...
SPLISH
WHAT NOW?
FINISH SPREADING THE NAPALM FAST. IT'LL BURN.
?
THUMPK

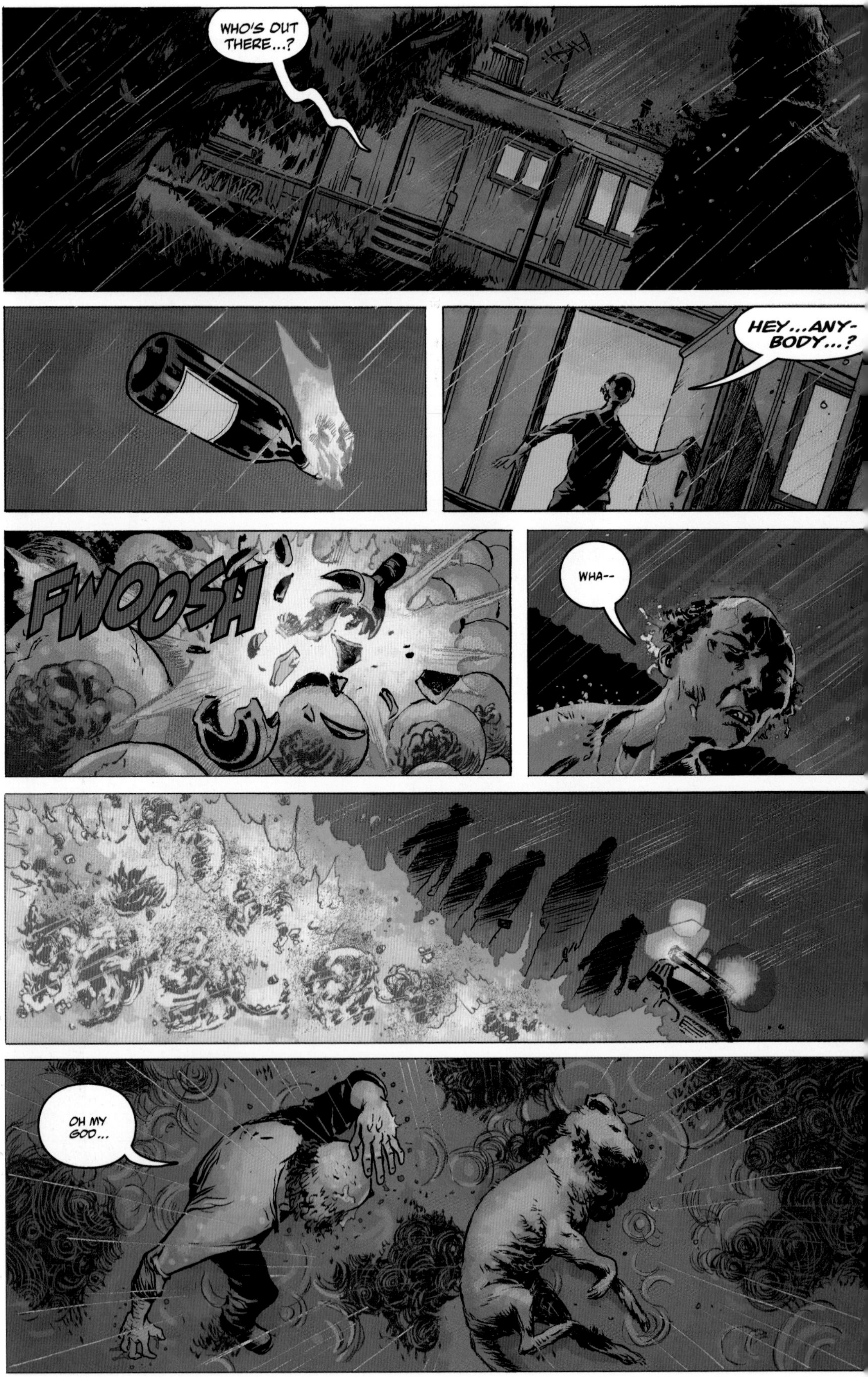
WHO'S OUT THERE...?
HEY...ANY-BODY...?
FWOOSH
WHA--
OH MY GOD...

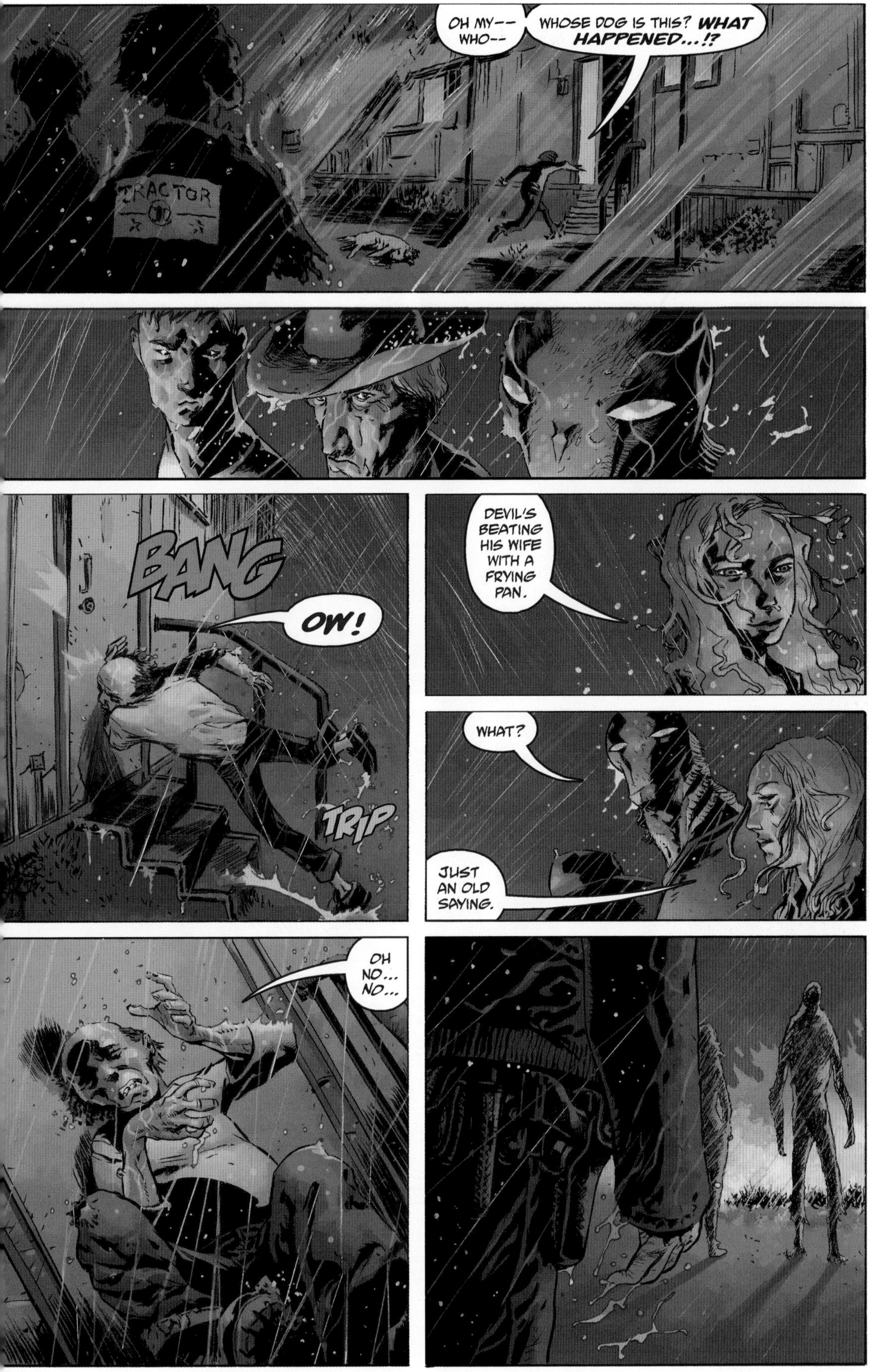
OH MY-- WHO--
WHOSE DOG IS THIS? WHAT HAPPENED...!?
TRACTOR
BANG
OW!
TRIP
DEVIL'S BEATING HIS WIFE WITH A FRYING PAN.
WHAT?
JUST AN OLD SAYING.
OH NO... NO...

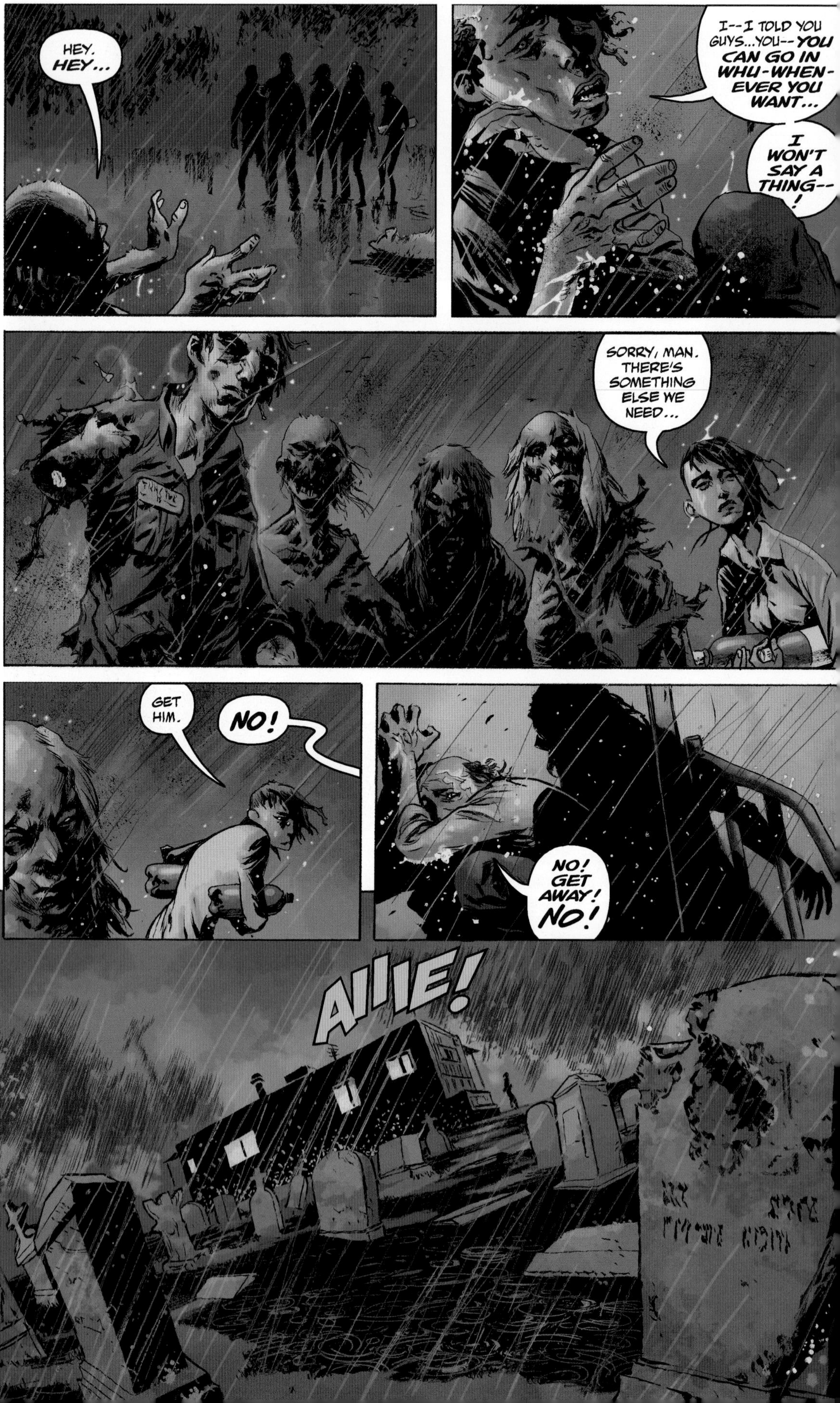
HEY. HEY...
I--I TOLD YOU GUYS...YOU--YOU CAN GO IN WHU-WHEN-EVER YOU WANT...
I WON'T SAY A THING--!
SORRY, MAN. THERE'S SOMETHING ELSE WE NEED...
GET HIM.
NO!
NO! GET AWAY! NO!
AIIIE!

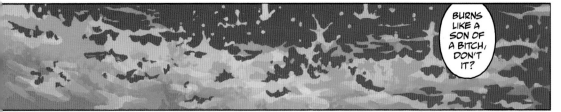

BURNS LIKE A SON OF A BITCH, DON'T IT?

YUP. IT'S BASICALLY NAPALM, WITH A LITTLE KICK WE IMPROVISED.

Y'KNOW, YOU HIKE YOUR PANTS UP JUST LIKE MY DAD USED TO.

I LOOK LIKE I'M WEARING A MIDRIFF SHIRT...!

I THOUGHT YOU WERE ABOUT TYLER'S SIZE, BUT EVEN HE'S A SHRIMP NEXT TO YOU!

PARDON THE EXPRESSION!

WELL, IT'S WORKING. NOTHING EXPLODED, AND THEY AIN'T CHEWING ON US.

YEAH...

I'VE SEEN FIRE TAKE CARE OF THIS SORT OF THING BEFORE...

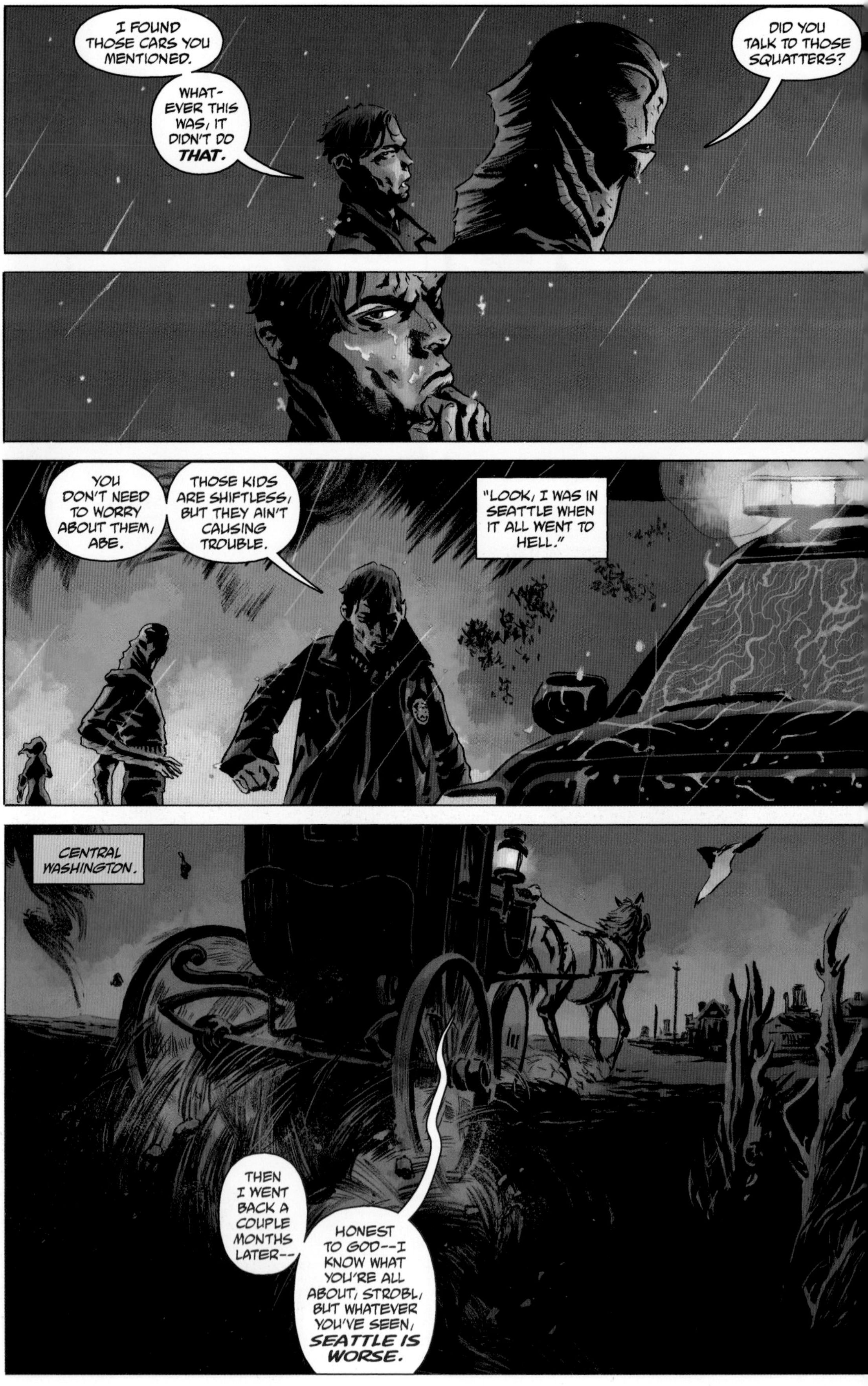

I FOUND THOSE CARS YOU MENTIONED.
WHAT-EVER THIS WAS, IT DIDN'T DO **THAT.**
DID YOU TALK TO THOSE SQUATTERS?
YOU DON'T NEED TO WORRY ABOUT THEM, ABE.
THOSE KIDS ARE SHIFTLESS, BUT THEY AIN'T CAUSING TROUBLE.
"LOOK, I WAS IN SEATTLE WHEN IT ALL WENT TO HELL."
CENTRAL WASHINGTON.
THEN I WENT BACK A COUPLE MONTHS LATER--
HONEST TO GOD--I KNOW WHAT YOU'RE ALL ABOUT, STROBL, BUT WHATEVER YOU'VE SEEN, **SEATTLE IS WORSE.**

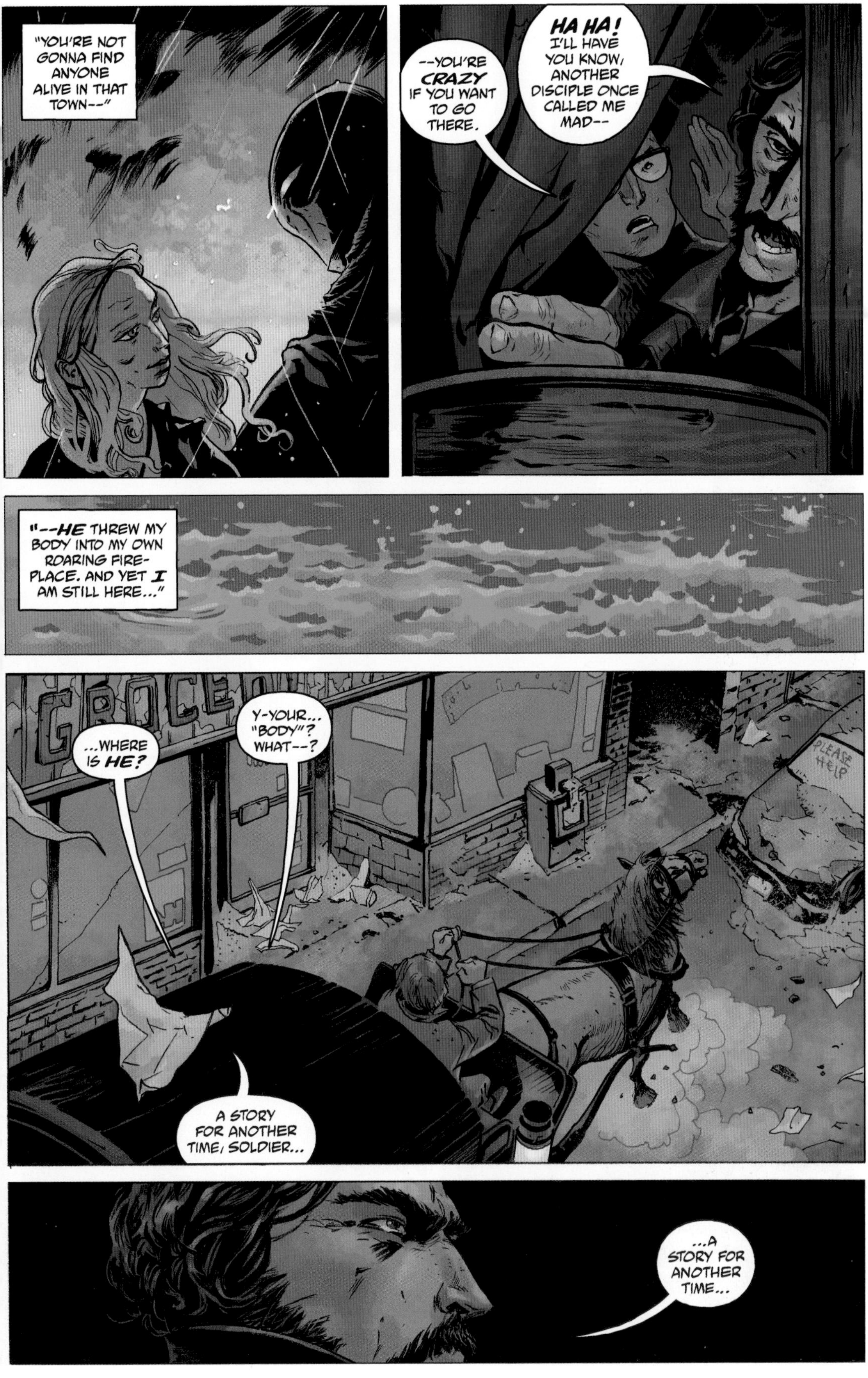
"YOU'RE NOT GONNA FIND ANYONE ALIVE IN THAT TOWN--"
--YOU'RE CRAZY IF YOU WANT TO GO THERE.
HA HA! I'LL HAVE YOU KNOW, ANOTHER DISCIPLE ONCE CALLED ME MAD--
"--HE THREW MY BODY INTO MY OWN ROARING FIRE-PLACE. AND YET I AM STILL HERE..."
GROCE
...WHERE IS HE?
Y-YOUR... "BODY"? WHAT--?
PLEASE HELP
A STORY FOR ANOTHER TIME, SOLDIER...
...A STORY FOR ANOTHER TIME...

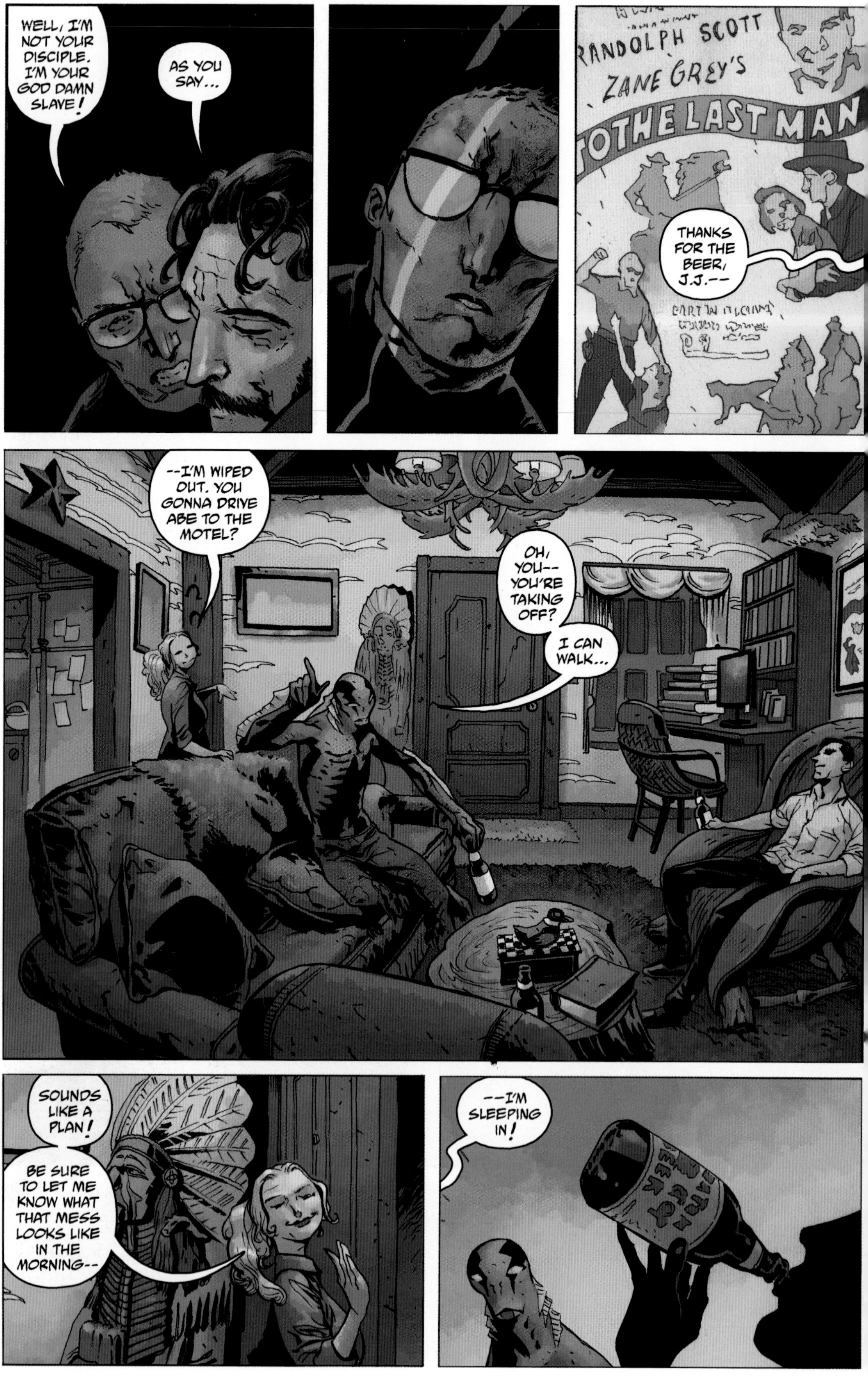
WELL, I'M NOT YOUR DISCIPLE. I'M YOUR GOD DAMN SLAVE!
AS YOU SAY...
RANDOLPH SCOTT
ZANE GREY'S
TO THE LAST MAN
THANKS FOR THE BEER, J.J.--
--I'M WIPED OUT. YOU GONNA DRIVE ABE TO THE MOTEL?
OH, YOU-- YOU'RE TAKING OFF?
I CAN WALK...
SOUNDS LIKE A PLAN!
BE SURE TO LET ME KNOW WHAT THAT MESS LOOKS LIKE IN THE MORNING--
--I'M SLEEPING IN!

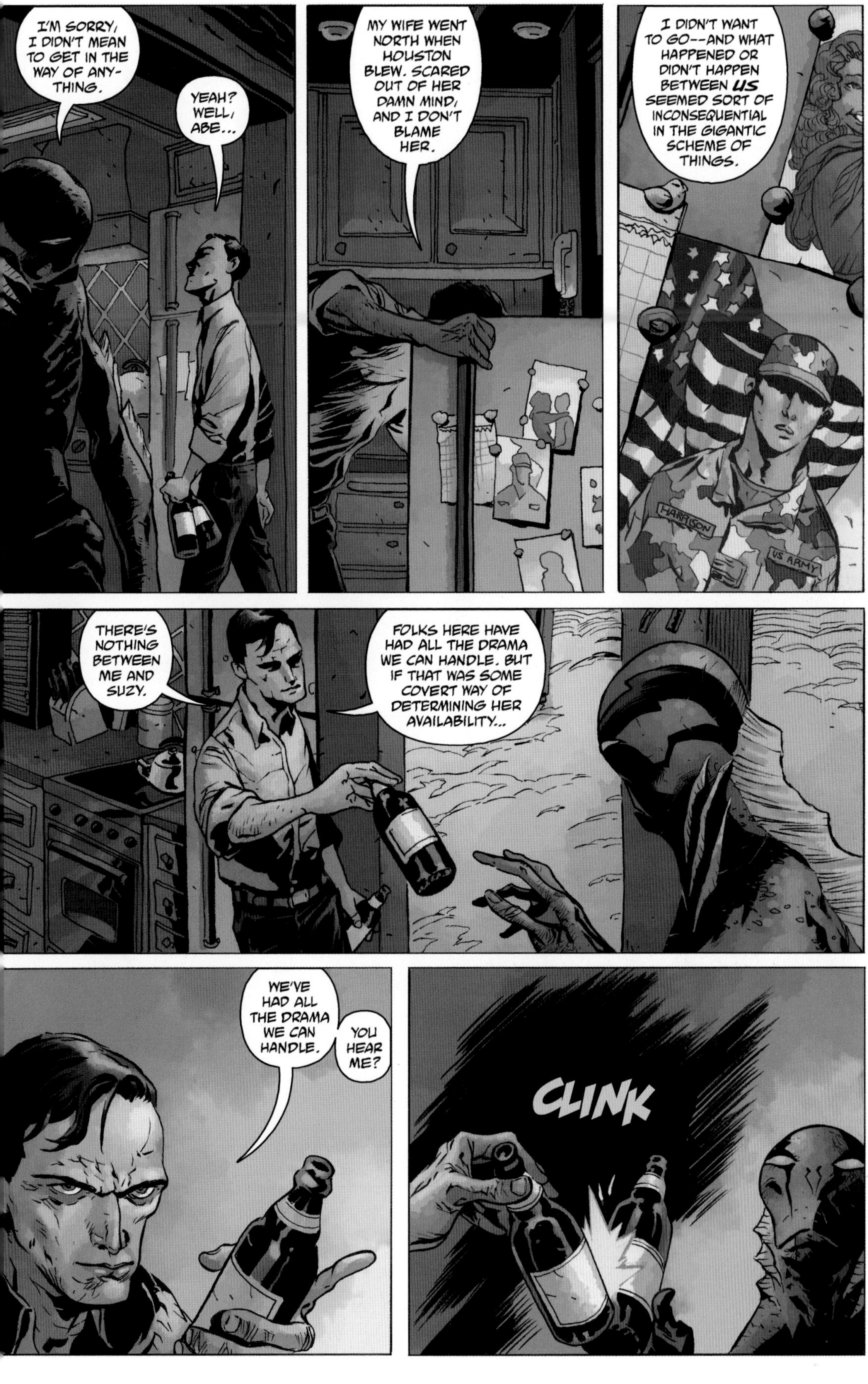
I'M SORRY, I DIDN'T MEAN TO GET IN THE WAY OF ANY-THING.
YEAH? WELL, ABE...
MY WIFE WENT NORTH WHEN HOUSTON BLEW. SCARED OUT OF HER DAMN MIND, AND I DON'T BLAME HER.
I DIDN'T WANT TO GO--AND WHAT HAPPENED OR DIDN'T HAPPEN BETWEEN US SEEMED SORT OF INCONSEQUENTIAL IN THE GIGANTIC SCHEME OF THINGS.
HARRISON
US ARMY
THERE'S NOTHING BETWEEN ME AND SUZY.
FOLKS HERE HAVE HAD ALL THE DRAMA WE CAN HANDLE. BUT IF THAT WAS SOME COVERT WAY OF DETERMINING HER AVAILABILITY...
WE'VE HAD ALL THE DRAMA WE CAN HANDLE.
YOU HEAR ME?
CLINK

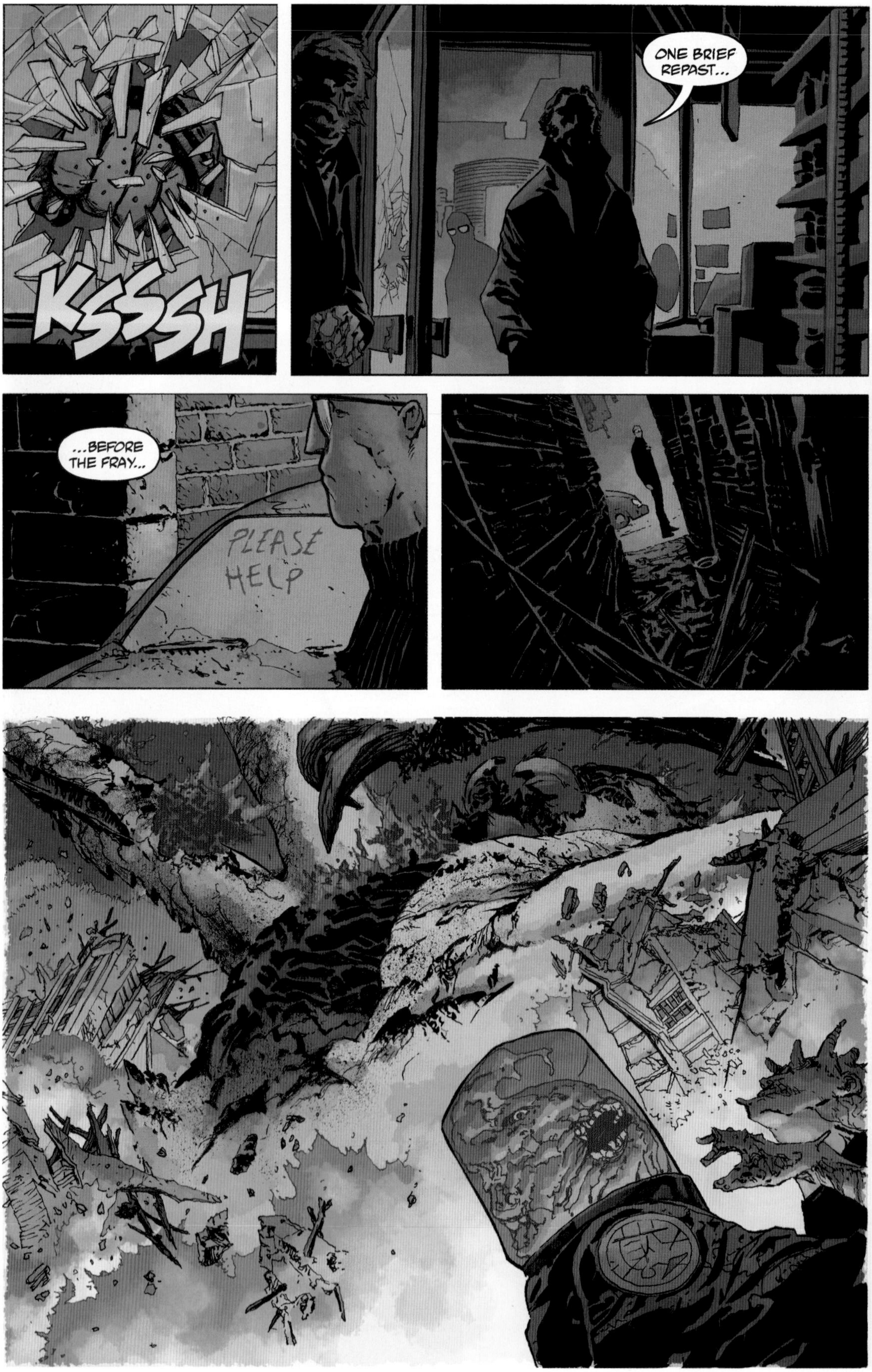
KSSSH
ONE BRIEF REPAST...
...BEFORE THE FRAY...
PLEASE HELP

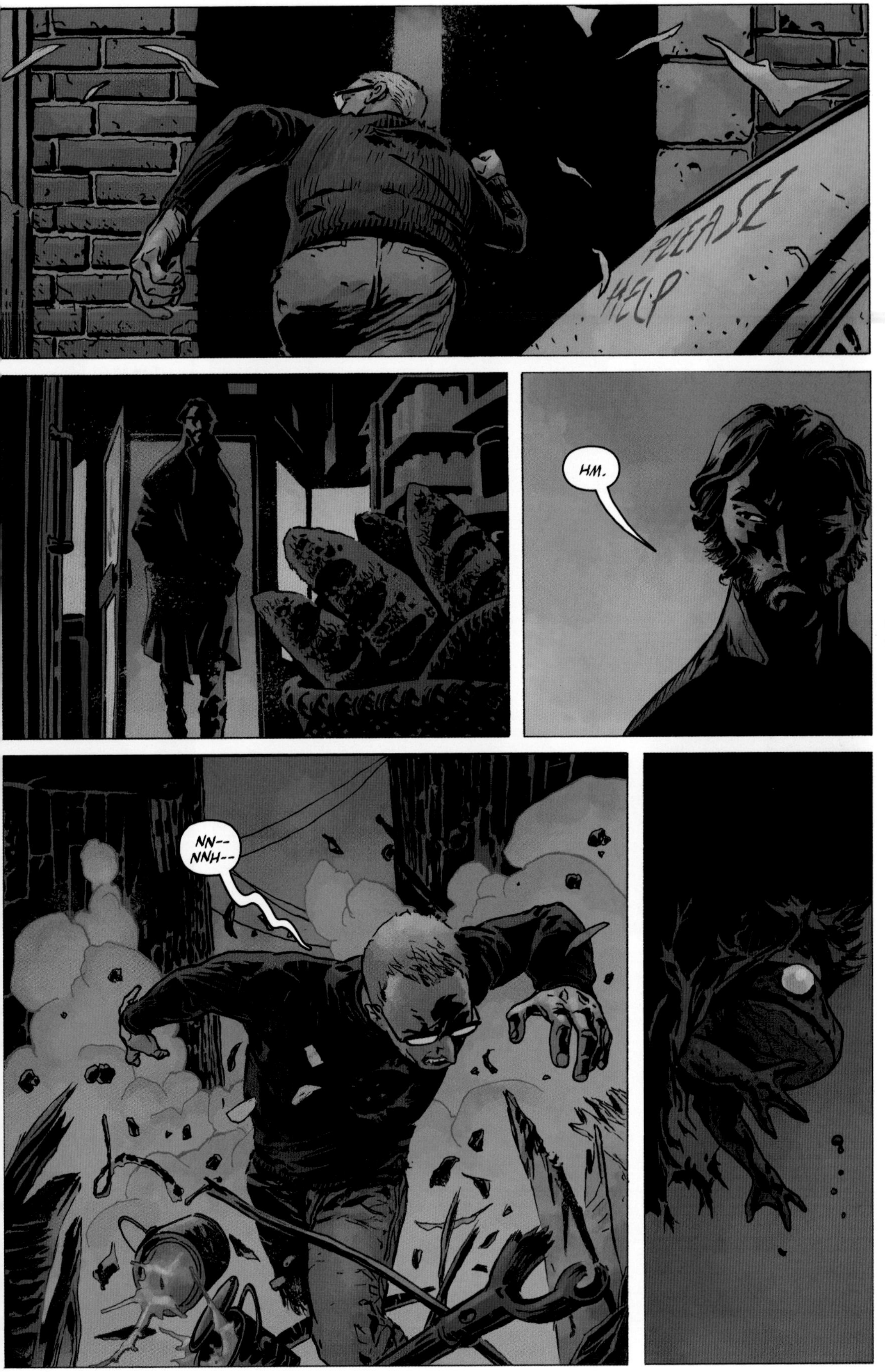
PLEASE HELP
HM.
NN--
NNH--

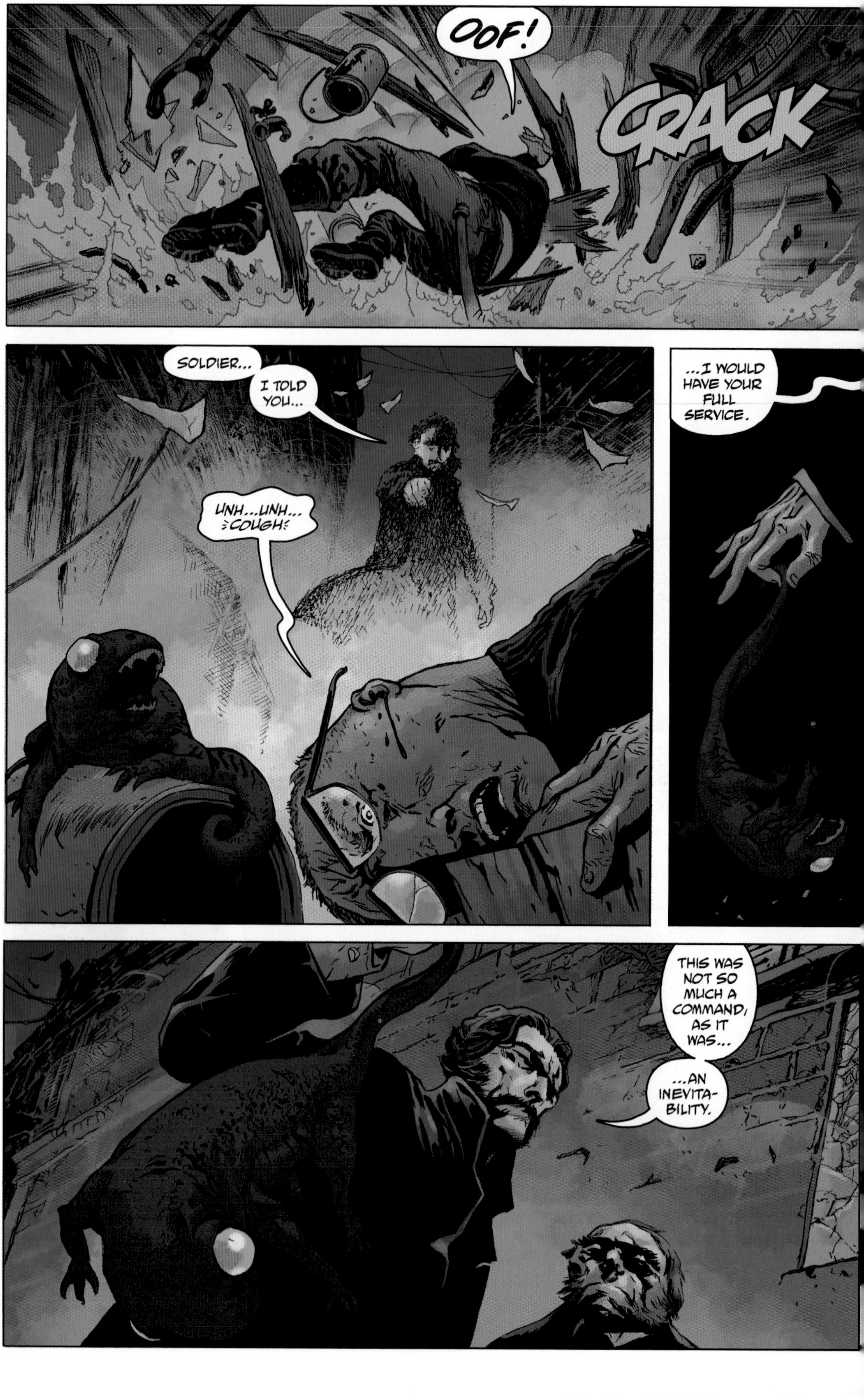
OOF!
CRACK
SOLDIER...
I TOLD YOU...
UNH...UNH... ≈COUGH≈
...I WOULD HAVE YOUR FULL SERVICE.
THIS WAS NOT SO MUCH A COMMAND, AS IT WAS...
...AN INEVITA-BILITY.

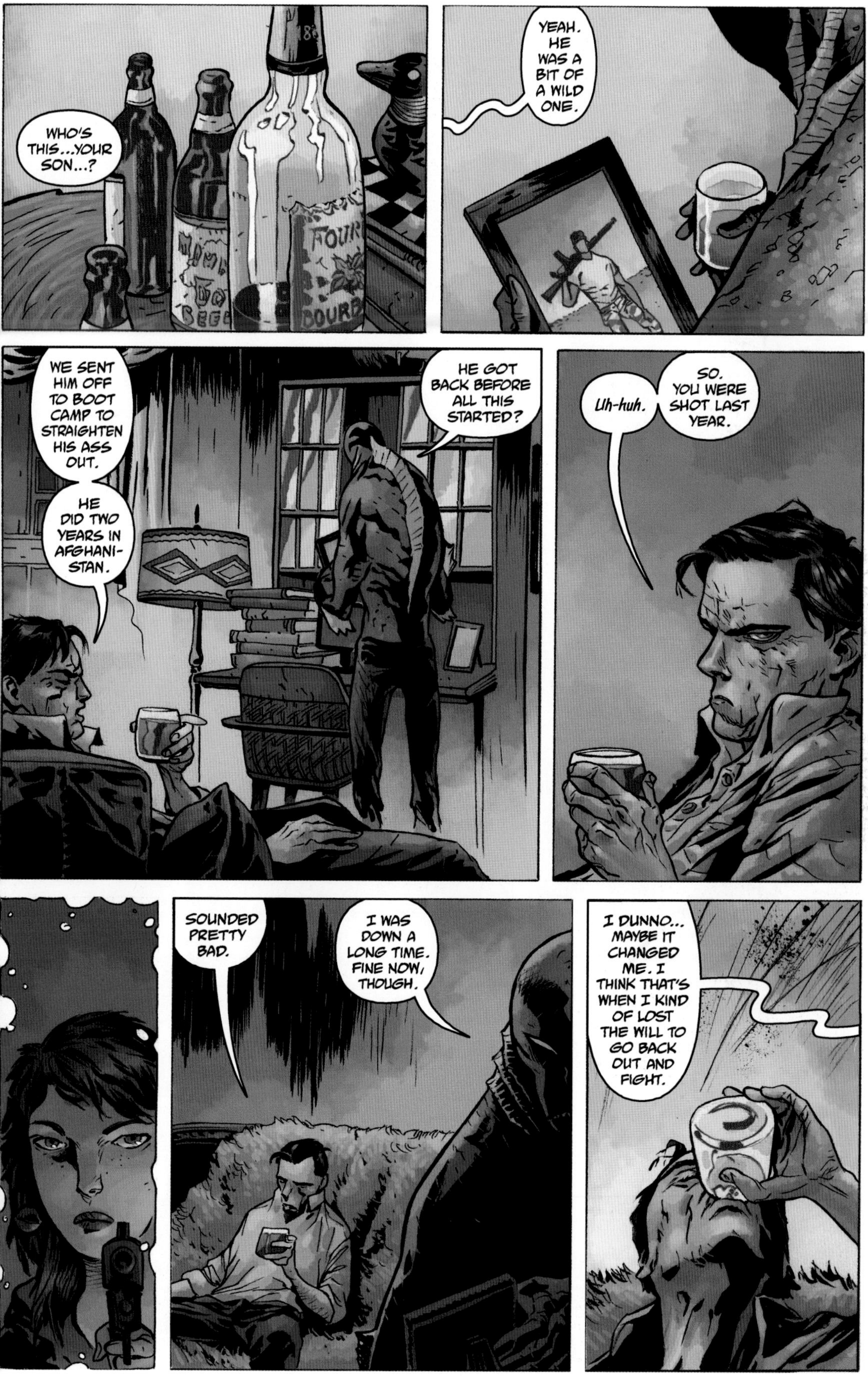
WHO'S THIS...YOUR SON...?
YEAH. HE WAS A BIT OF A WILD ONE.
WE SENT HIM OFF TO BOOT CAMP TO STRAIGHTEN HIS ASS OUT.
HE DID TWO YEARS IN AFGHANI-STAN.
HE GOT BACK BEFORE ALL THIS STARTED?
SO. YOU WERE SHOT LAST YEAR.
Uh-huh.
SOUNDED PRETTY BAD.
I WAS DOWN A LONG TIME. FINE NOW, THOUGH.
I DUNNO... MAYBE IT CHANGED ME. I THINK THAT'S WHEN I KIND OF LOST THE WILL TO GO BACK OUT AND FIGHT.

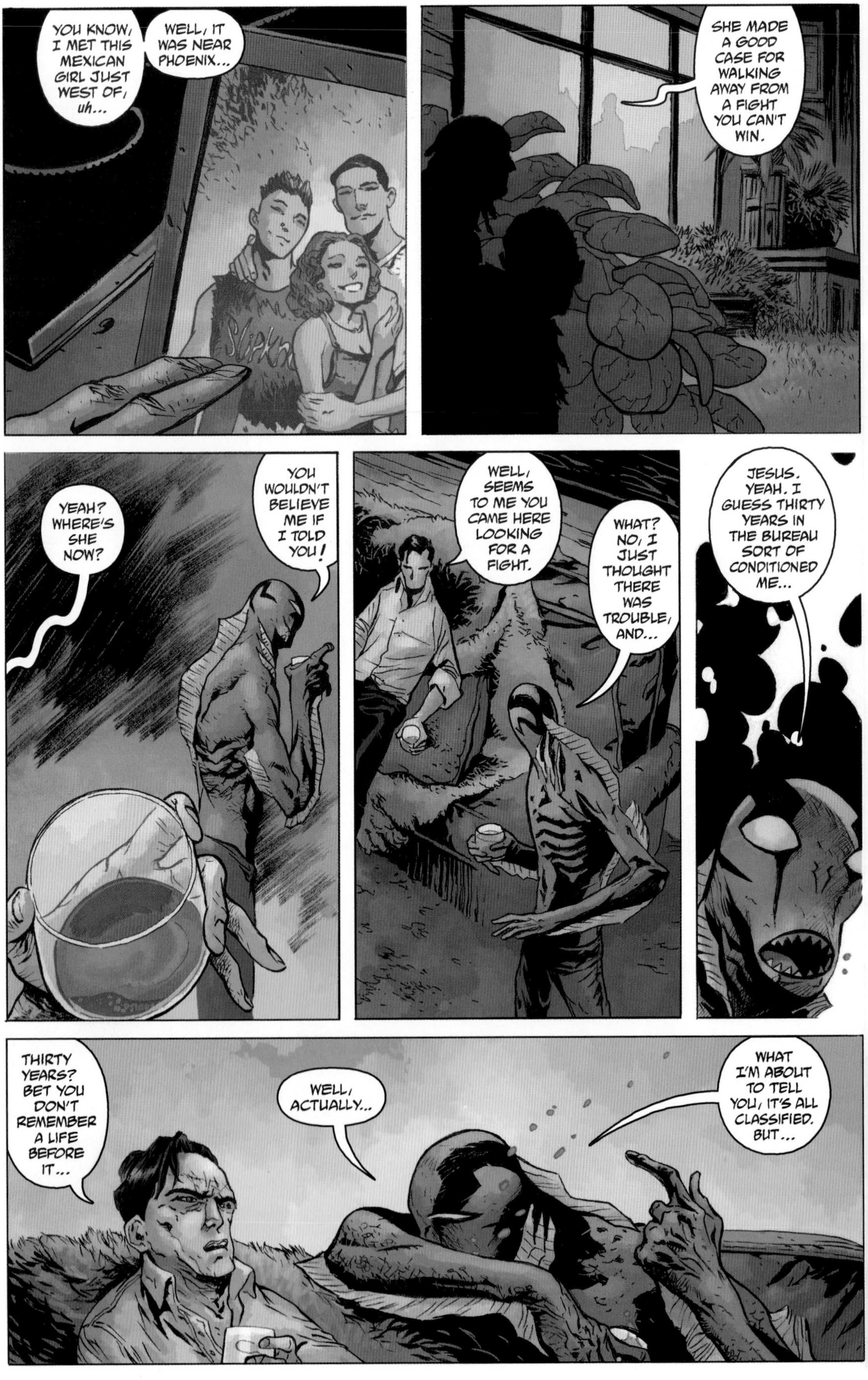
YOU KNOW, I MET THIS MEXICAN GIRL JUST WEST OF, uh...
WELL, IT WAS NEAR PHOENIX...
SHE MADE A GOOD CASE FOR WALKING AWAY FROM A FIGHT YOU CAN'T WIN.
YEAH? WHERE'S SHE NOW?
YOU WOULDN'T BELIEVE ME IF I TOLD YOU!
WELL, SEEMS TO ME YOU CAME HERE LOOKING FOR A FIGHT.
WHAT? NO, I JUST THOUGHT THERE WAS TROUBLE, AND...
JESUS. YEAH. I GUESS THIRTY YEARS IN THE BUREAU SORT OF CONDITIONED ME...
THIRTY YEARS? BET YOU DON'T REMEMBER A LIFE BEFORE IT...
WELL, ACTUALLY...
WHAT I'M ABOUT TO TELL YOU, IT'S ALL CLASSIFIED. BUT...

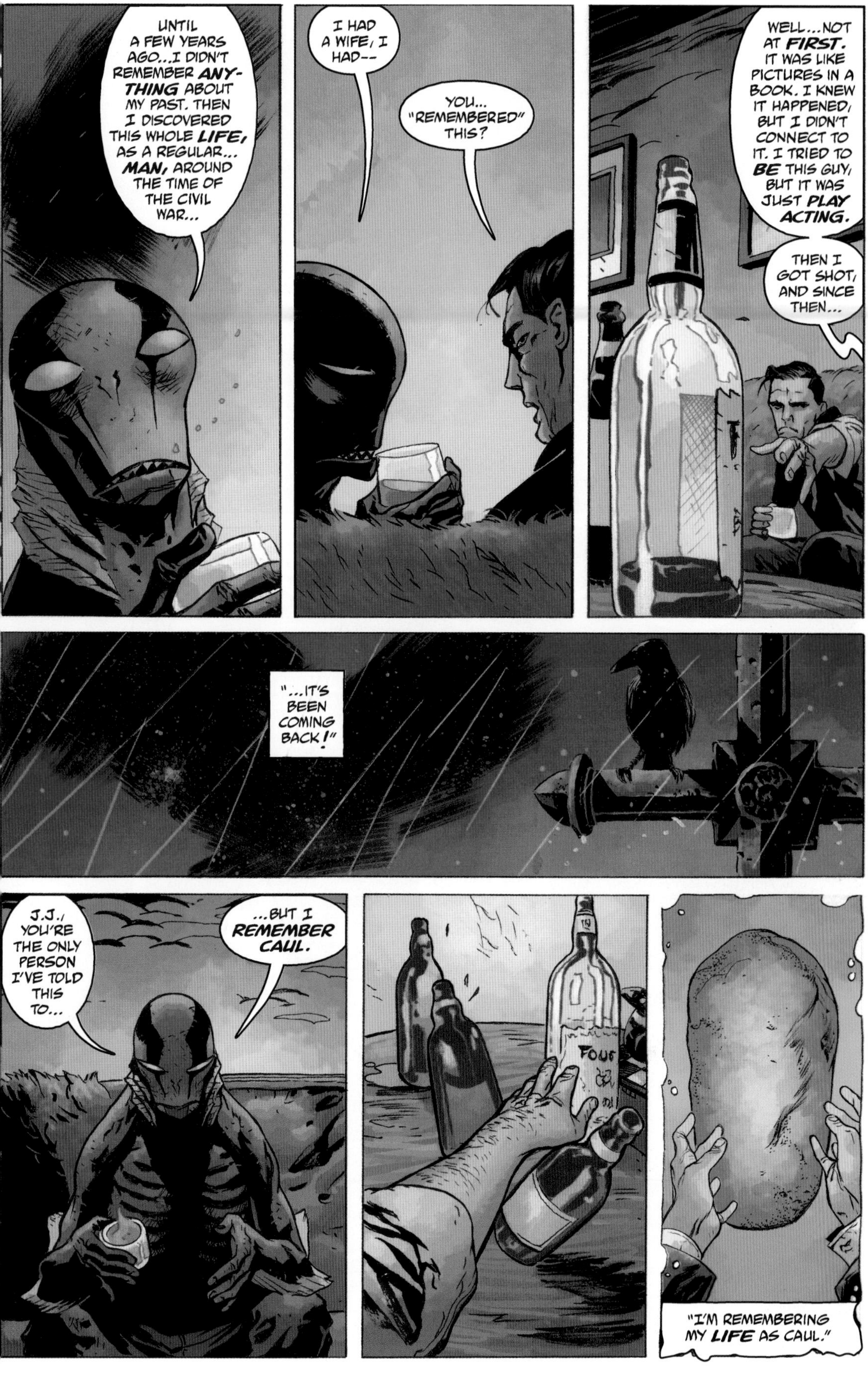

UNTIL A FEW YEARS AGO...I DIDN'T REMEMBER ANYTHING ABOUT MY PAST. THEN I DISCOVERED THIS WHOLE LIFE, AS A REGULAR... MAN, AROUND THE TIME OF THE CIVIL WAR...
I HAD A WIFE, I HAD--
YOU... "REMEMBERED" THIS?
WELL...NOT AT FIRST. IT WAS LIKE PICTURES IN A BOOK. I KNEW IT HAPPENED, BUT I DIDN'T CONNECT TO IT. I TRIED TO BE THIS GUY, BUT IT WAS JUST PLAY ACTING.
THEN I GOT SHOT, AND SINCE THEN...
"...IT'S BEEN COMING BACK!"
J.J., YOU'RE THE ONLY PERSON I'VE TOLD THIS TO...
...BUT I REMEMBER CAUL.
"I'M REMEMBERING MY LIFE AS CAUL."

ANNE
BODAYLA
May 11 1871
Jan 17 1884

MARY
BODAYLA
May 11 1871
Jan 17 1884

THAT'S WEIRD.

SEE? THEY WERE BURIED TOGETHER UNDER ONE GRAVE-STONE.

YOU THINK *THAT'S* WHAT'S WEIRD?

LOOK, BARB. SAME BIRTH DATES-- *AND* DEATH DATES...

THEIR POOR PARENTS...

WE HAVE TO GO.

MEXICO, I MEAN.

WE HAVE TO GO NOW, BEN.

WHOA, *LISTEN.* I WANT TO, BUT WE NEED A *LOT* MORE MONEY. EVERYTHING'S BLACK MARKET OUT THERE NOW.

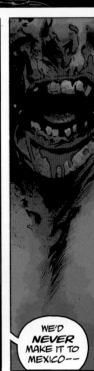

WE'D *NEVER* MAKE IT TO MEXICO--

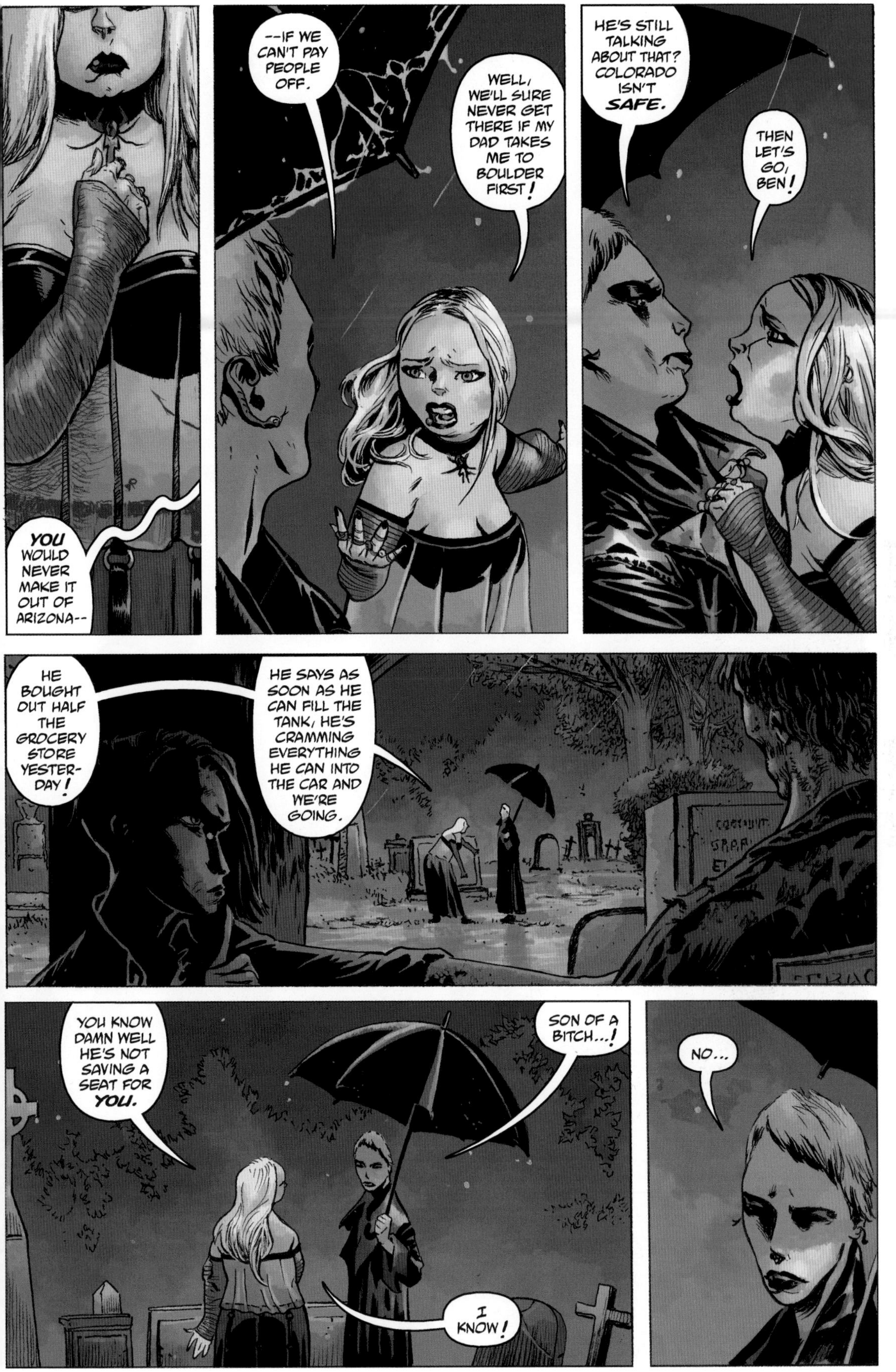

YOU WOULD NEVER MAKE IT OUT OF ARIZONA--
--IF WE CAN'T PAY PEOPLE OFF.
WELL, WE'LL SURE NEVER GET THERE IF MY DAD TAKES ME TO BOULDER FIRST!
HE'S STILL TALKING ABOUT THAT? COLORADO ISN'T SAFE.
THEN LET'S GO, BEN!
HE BOUGHT OUT HALF THE GROCERY STORE YESTER-DAY!
HE SAYS AS SOON AS HE CAN FILL THE TANK, HE'S CRAMMING EVERYTHING HE CAN INTO THE CAR AND WE'RE GOING.
YOU KNOW DAMN WELL HE'S NOT SAVING A SEAT FOR YOU.
SON OF A BITCH...!
I KNOW!
NO...

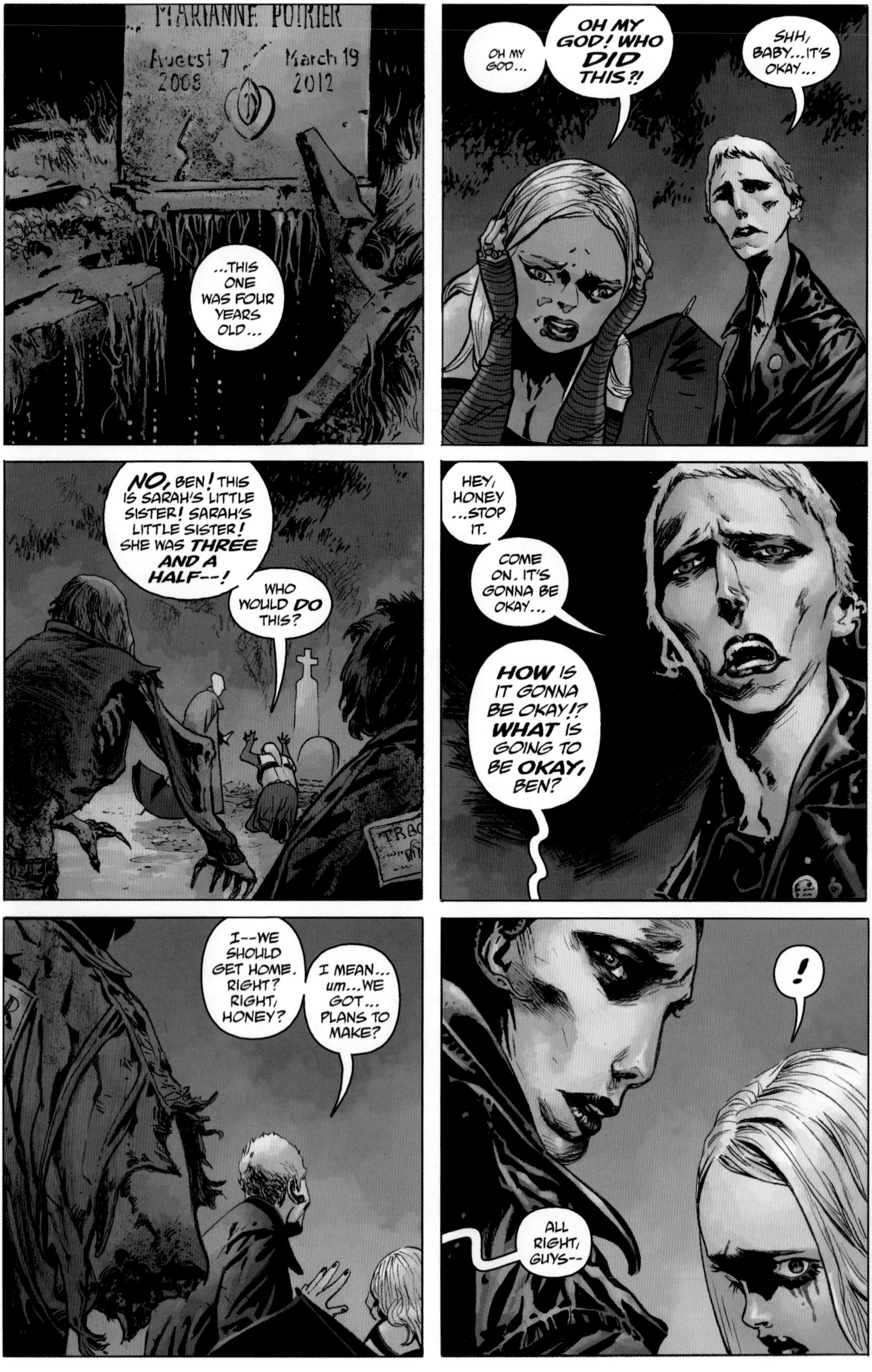
MARIANNE POIRIER
August 7 2008
March 19 2012
...THIS ONE WAS FOUR YEARS OLD...
OH MY GOD...
OH MY GOD! WHO DID THIS?!
SHH, BABY... IT'S OKAY...
NO, BEN! THIS IS SARAH'S LITTLE SISTER! SARAH'S LITTLE SISTER! SHE WAS THREE AND A HALF--!
WHO WOULD DO THIS?
HEY, HONEY ...STOP IT.
COME ON. IT'S GONNA BE OKAY...
HOW IS IT GONNA BE OKAY!? WHAT IS GOING TO BE OKAY, BEN?
I--WE SHOULD GET HOME. RIGHT? RIGHT, HONEY?
I MEAN... um...WE GOT... PLANS TO MAKE?
!
ALL RIGHT, GUYS--

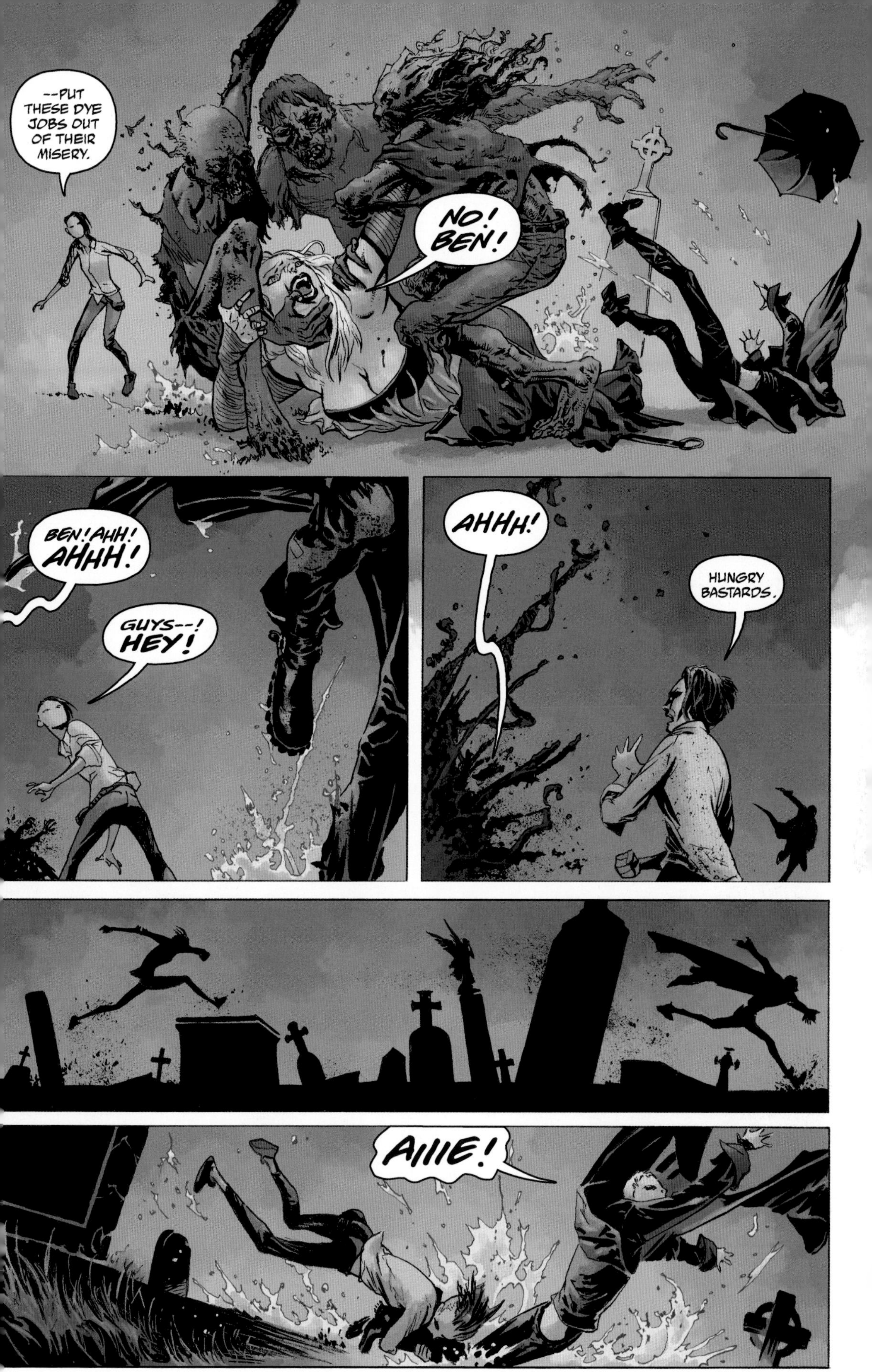
--PUT THESE DYE JOBS OUT OF THEIR MISERY.
NO! BEN!
BEN! AHH! AHHH!
GUYS--! HEY!
AHHH!
HUNGRY BASTARDS.
AIIIE!

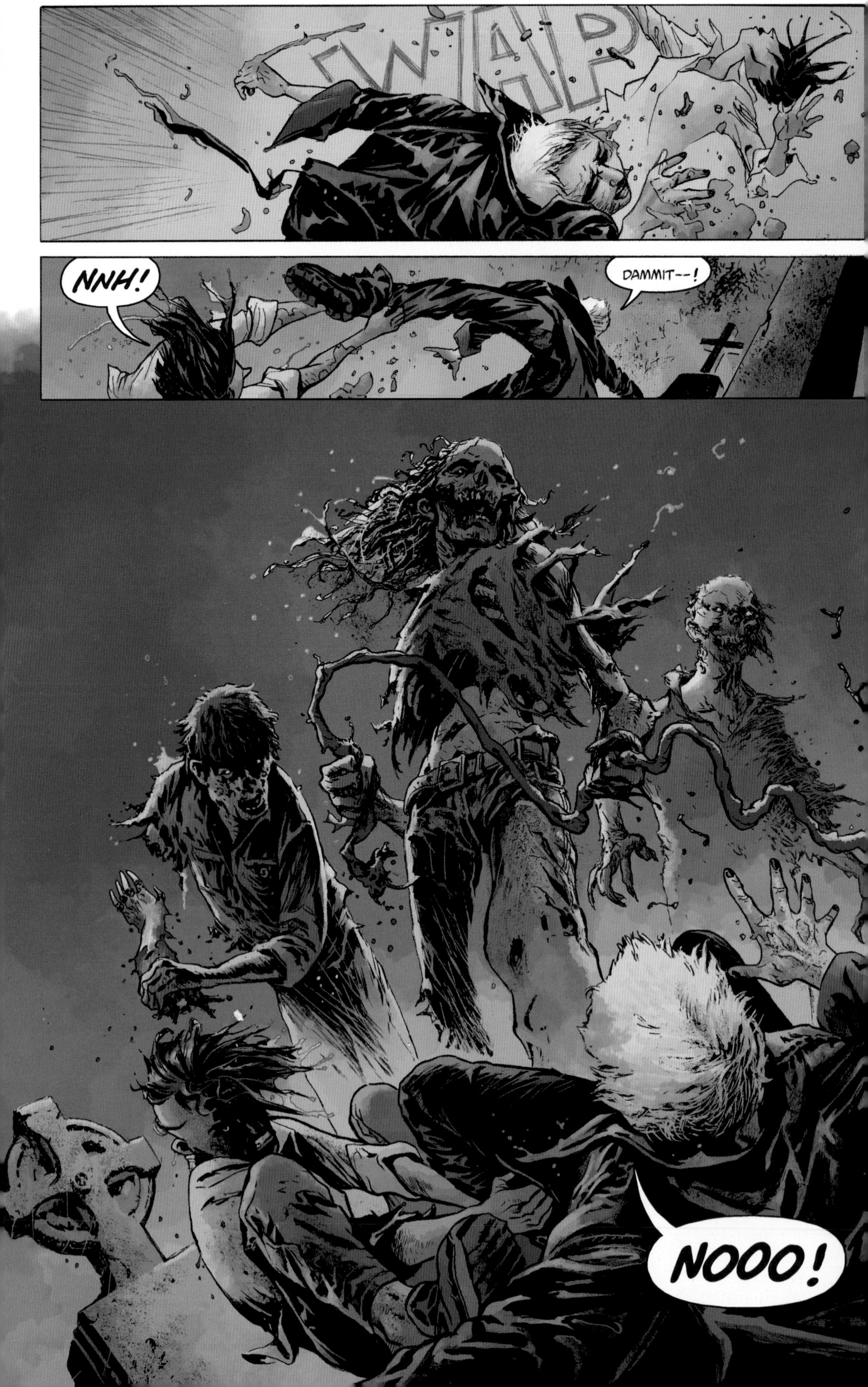
WAP
NNH!
DAMMIT--!
NOOO!

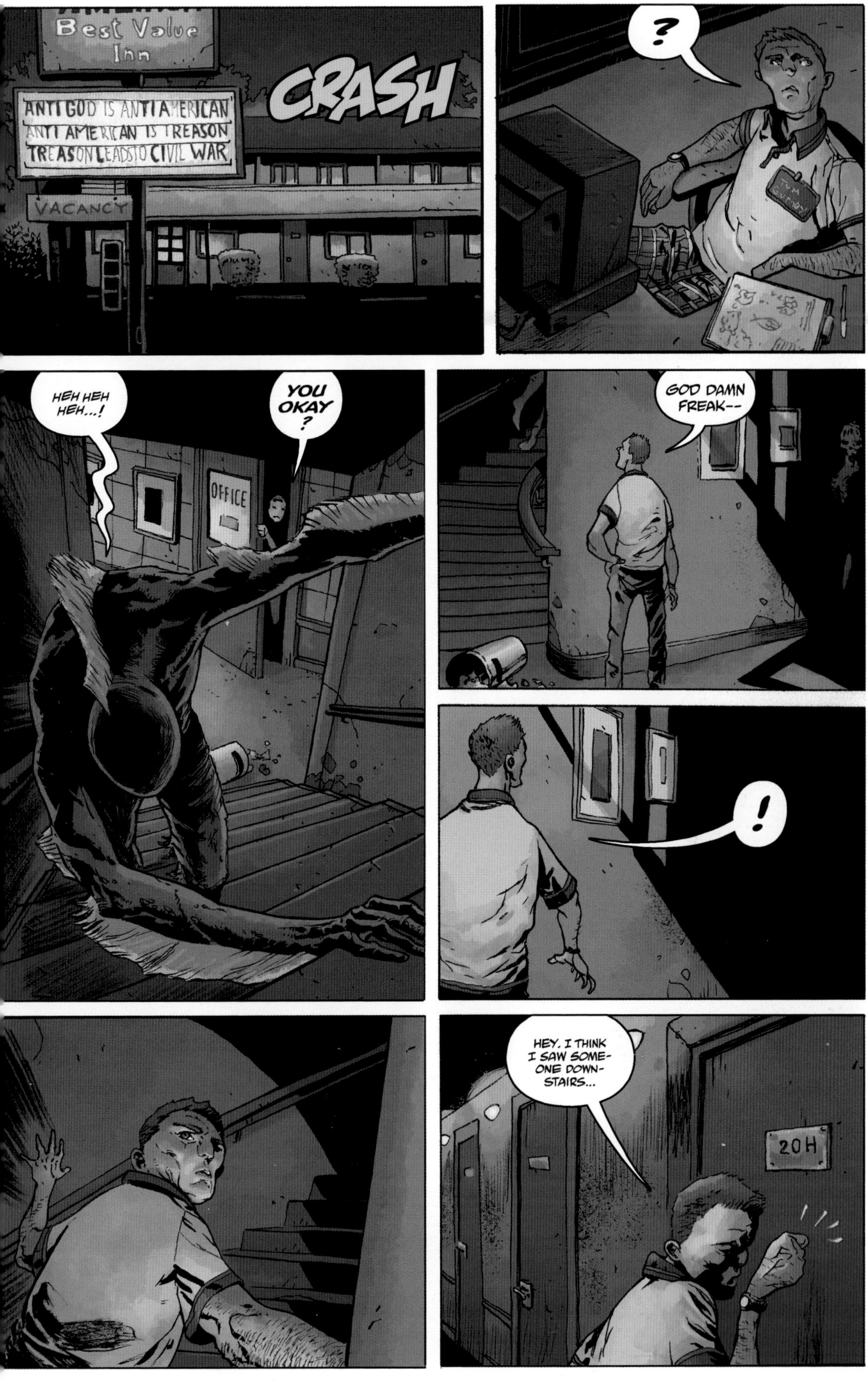

Best Value
Inn
ANTI GOD IS ANTI AMERICAN
ANTI AMERICAN IS TREASON
TREASON LEADS TO CIVIL WAR
VACANCY
CRASH
?
HEH HEH
HEH...!
YOU
OKAY
?
OFFICE
GOD DAMN
FREAK--
!
HEY. I THINK
I SAW SOME-
ONE DOWN-
STAIRS...
20H

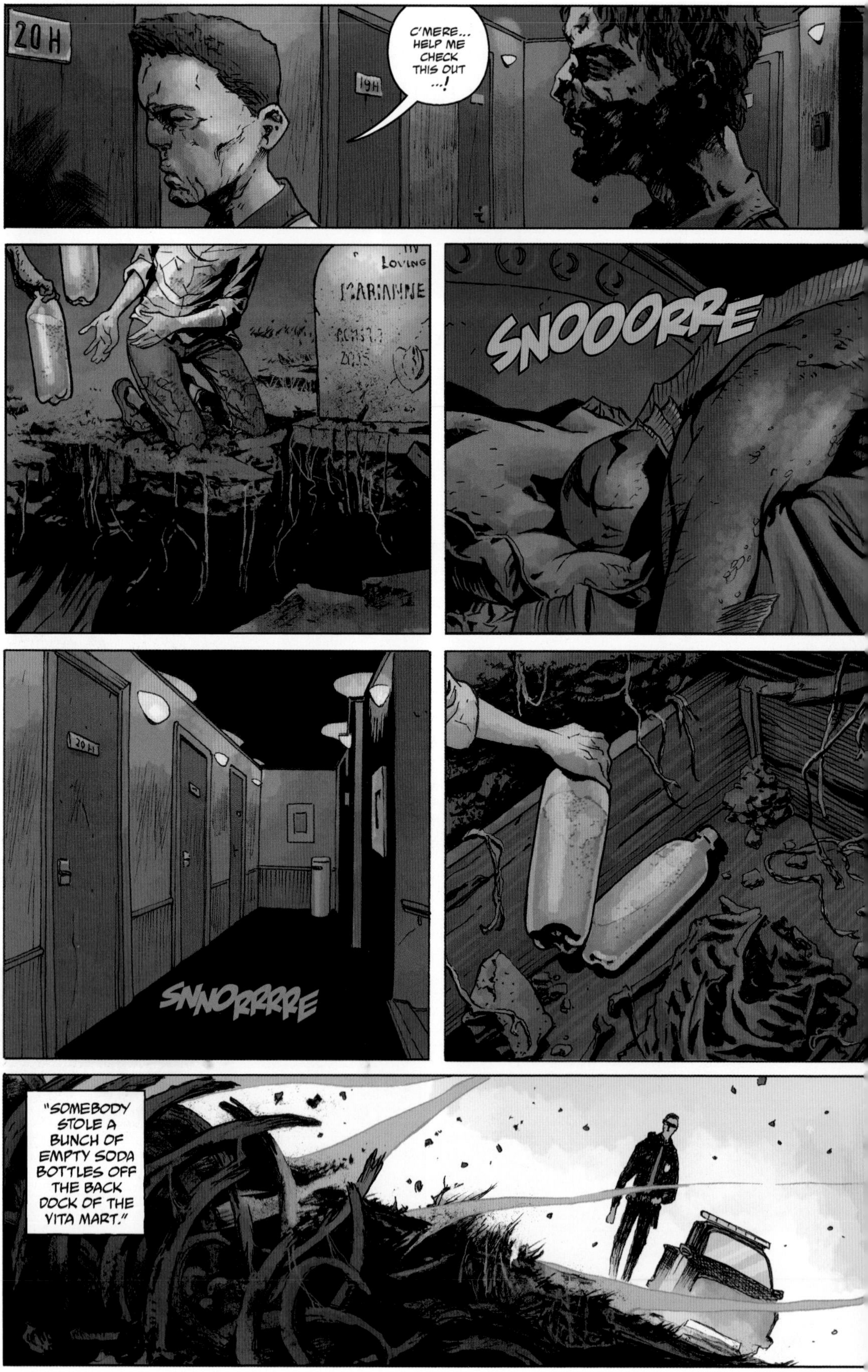

20 H
19 H
C'MERE... HELP ME CHECK THIS OUT ...!
IN LOVING
MARIANNE
SNOOORRE
20 H
SNNORRRRE
"SOMEBODY STOLE A BUNCH OF EMPTY SODA BOTTLES OFF THE BACK DOCK OF THE VITA MART."

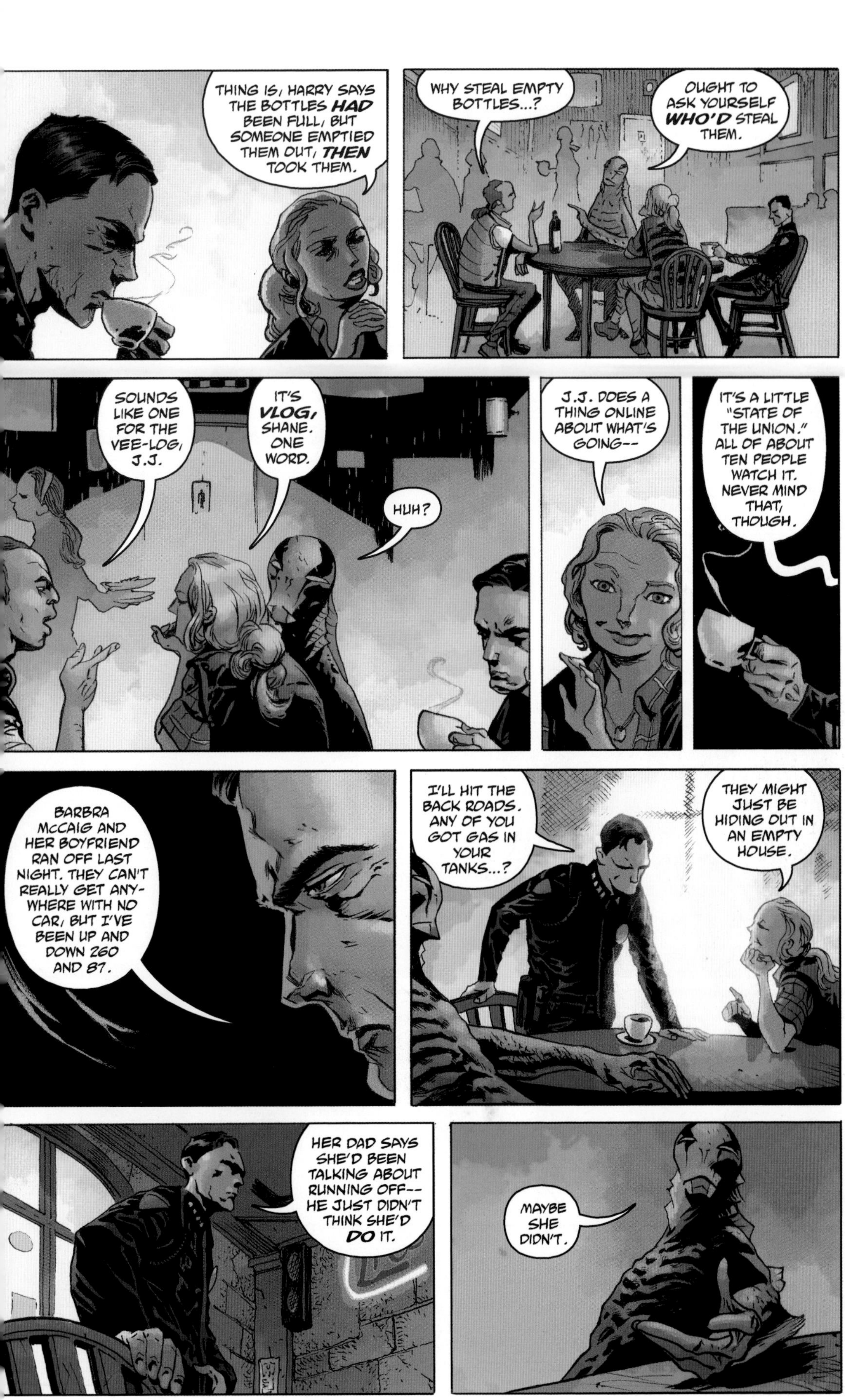
THING IS, HARRY SAYS THE BOTTLES HAD BEEN FULL, BUT SOMEONE EMPTIED THEM OUT, THEN TOOK THEM.
WHY STEAL EMPTY BOTTLES...?
OUGHT TO ASK YOURSELF WHO'D STEAL THEM.
SOUNDS LIKE ONE FOR THE VEE-LOG, J.J.
IT'S VLOG, SHANE. ONE WORD.
HUH?
J.J. DOES A THING ONLINE ABOUT WHAT'S GOING--
IT'S A LITTLE "STATE OF THE UNION." ALL OF ABOUT TEN PEOPLE WATCH IT. NEVER MIND THAT, THOUGH.
BARBRA McCAIG AND HER BOYFRIEND RAN OFF LAST NIGHT. THEY CAN'T REALLY GET ANY-WHERE WITH NO CAR, BUT I'VE BEEN UP AND DOWN 260 AND 87.
I'LL HIT THE BACK ROADS. ANY OF YOU GOT GAS IN YOUR TANKS...?
THEY MIGHT JUST BE HIDING OUT IN AN EMPTY HOUSE.
HER DAD SAYS SHE'D BEEN TALKING ABOUT RUNNING OFF-- HE JUST DIDN'T THINK SHE'D DO IT.
MAYBE SHE DIDN'T.

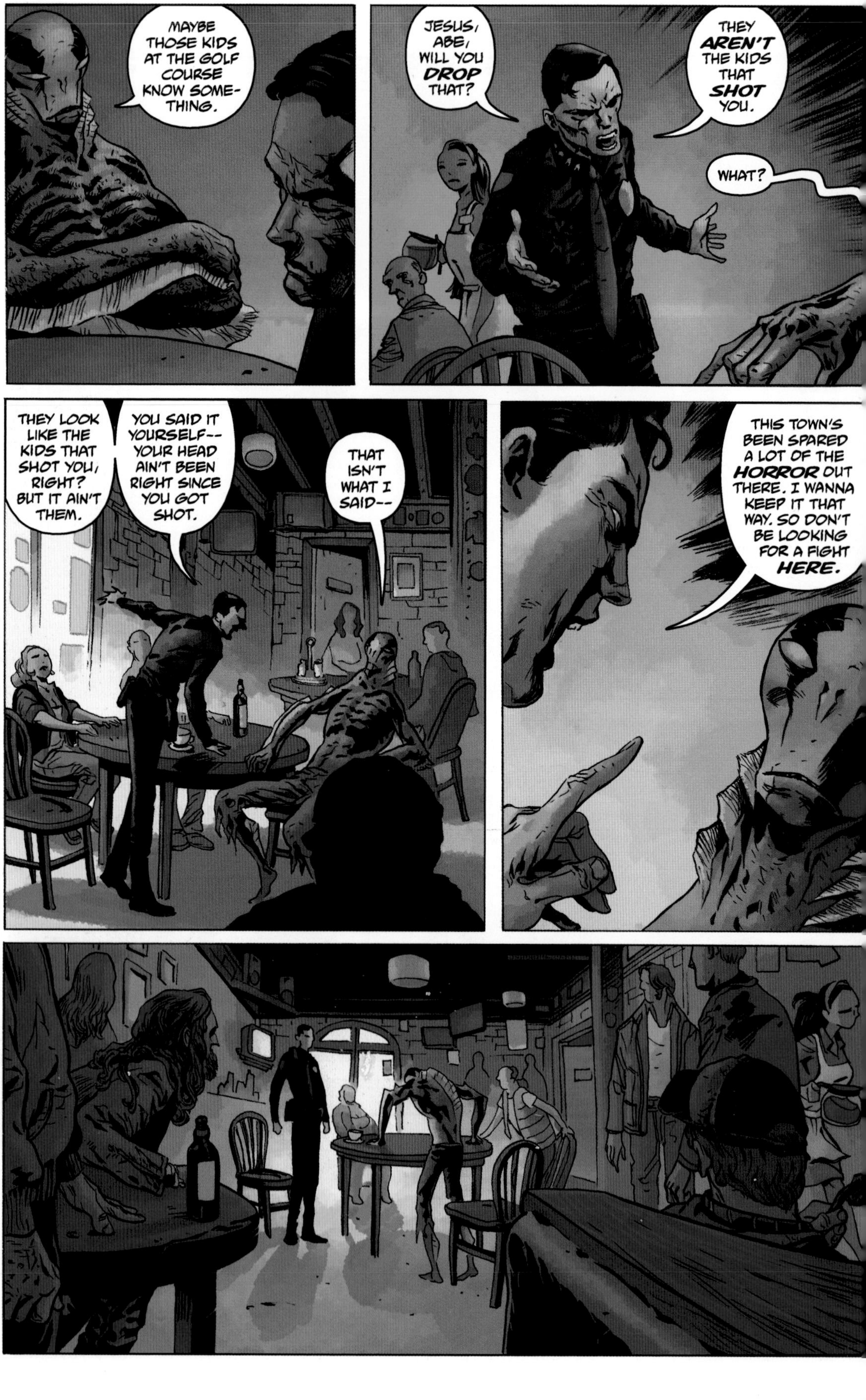

MAYBE THOSE KIDS AT THE GOLF COURSE KNOW SOME-THING.
JESUS, ABE, WILL YOU DROP THAT?
THEY AREN'T THE KIDS THAT SHOT YOU.
WHAT?
THEY LOOK LIKE THE KIDS THAT SHOT YOU, RIGHT? BUT IT AIN'T THEM.
YOU SAID IT YOURSELF-- YOUR HEAD AIN'T BEEN RIGHT SINCE YOU GOT SHOT.
THAT ISN'T WHAT I SAID--
THIS TOWN'S BEEN SPARED A LOT OF THE HORROR OUT THERE. I WANNA KEEP IT THAT WAY. SO DON'T BE LOOKING FOR A FIGHT HERE.

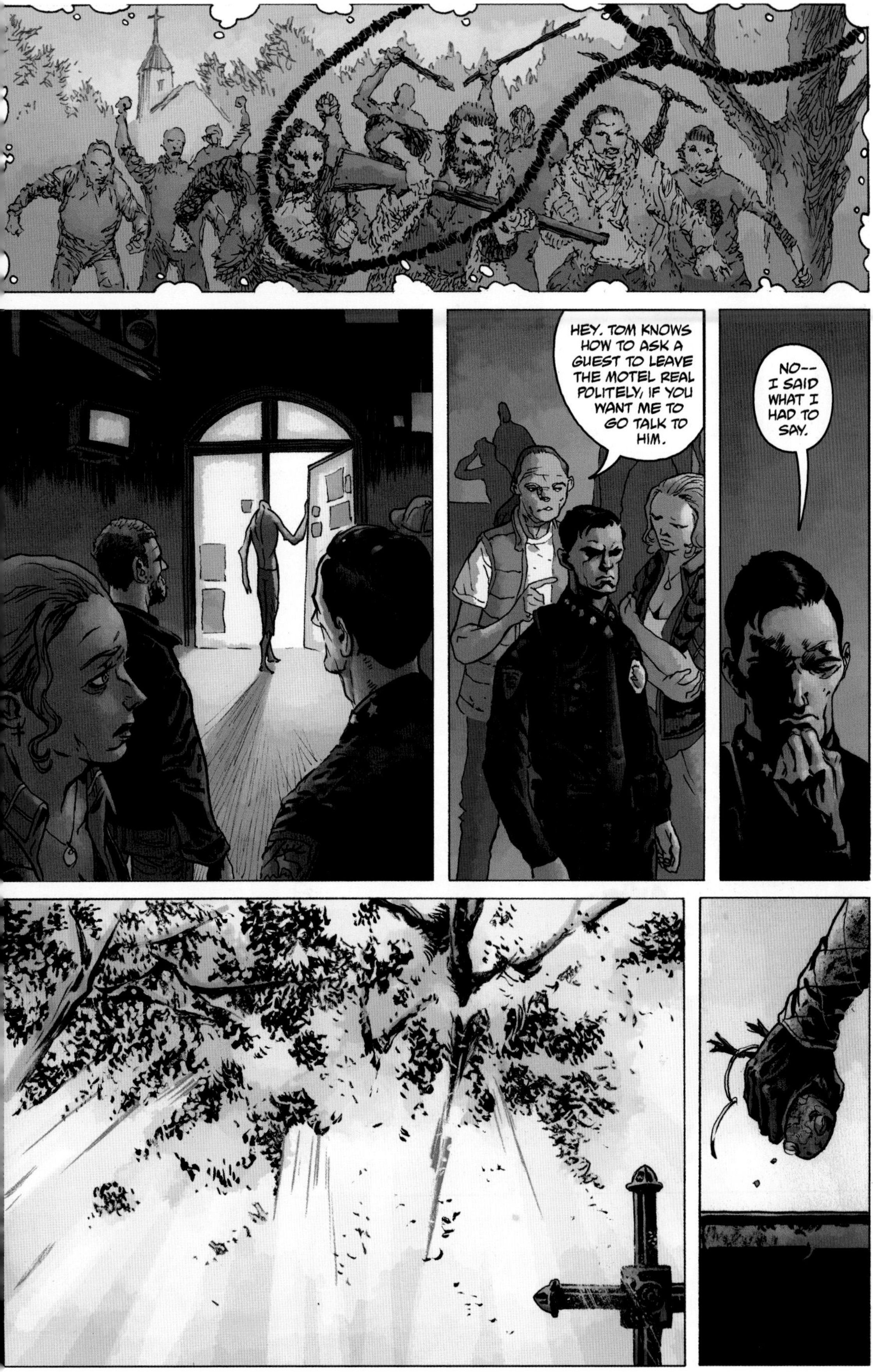
HEY. TOM KNOWS HOW TO ASK A GUEST TO LEAVE THE MOTEL REAL POLITELY, IF YOU WANT ME TO GO TALK TO HIM.
NO-- I SAID WHAT I HAD TO SAY.

"J.J.! HEY, J.J., HOLD UP A SEC..."

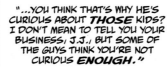

SO WHAT WAS THAT ABOUT ABE GETTING SHOT...?

NEVER MIND THAT.

WHAT? I'M JUST ASKING. SOME STREET KID SHOT HIM...

"...YOU THINK THAT'S WHY HE'S CURIOUS ABOUT *THOSE* KIDS? I DON'T MEAN TO TELL YOU YOUR BUSINESS, J.J., BUT SOME OF THE GUYS THINK YOU'RE NOT CURIOUS *ENOUGH.*"

YOU KNOW-- ABOUT THOSE KIDS.

REALLY?

YOU WANT ME TO GIVE THOSE KIDS A HARD TIME? WHAT DO YOU THINK IT'S LIKE, BEING TWENTY, TWENTY-FIVE YEARS OLD--

"--TRYING TO IMAGINE SOME KINDA FUTURE WITH THE WORLD ENDING AROUND YOU? YOU THINK THEY GOT IT EASY?"

NO ONE HAS IT EASY ANYMORE. SO I'M A LITTLE NERVOUS ABOUT A BUNCH OF GYPSIES CAMPED IN MY TOWN.

AND FOR SOME REASON THE CHIEF OF POLICE ISN'T!

IT JUST SEEMS LIKE YOU'RE... SOFT ON, WELL, WILD KIDS...

I CANNOT BELIEVE YOU'RE SAYING THAT TO ME.

"J.J., YOU SAVED YOUR SON FROM A HARD LIFE, AND THEN--"

NO. HE SAVED HIMSELF. THE *ARMY* SAVED HIM.

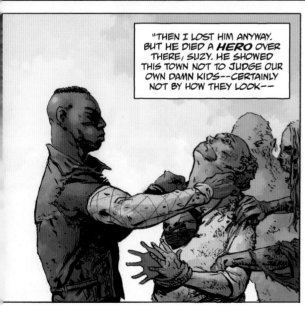

"THEN I LOST HIM ANYWAY. BUT HE DIED A *HERO* OVER THERE, SUZY. HE SHOWED THIS TOWN NOT TO JUDGE OUR OWN DAMN KIDS--CERTAINLY NOT BY HOW THEY LOOK--"

"--AND THAT IS *JUST* WHAT ABE IS DOING."

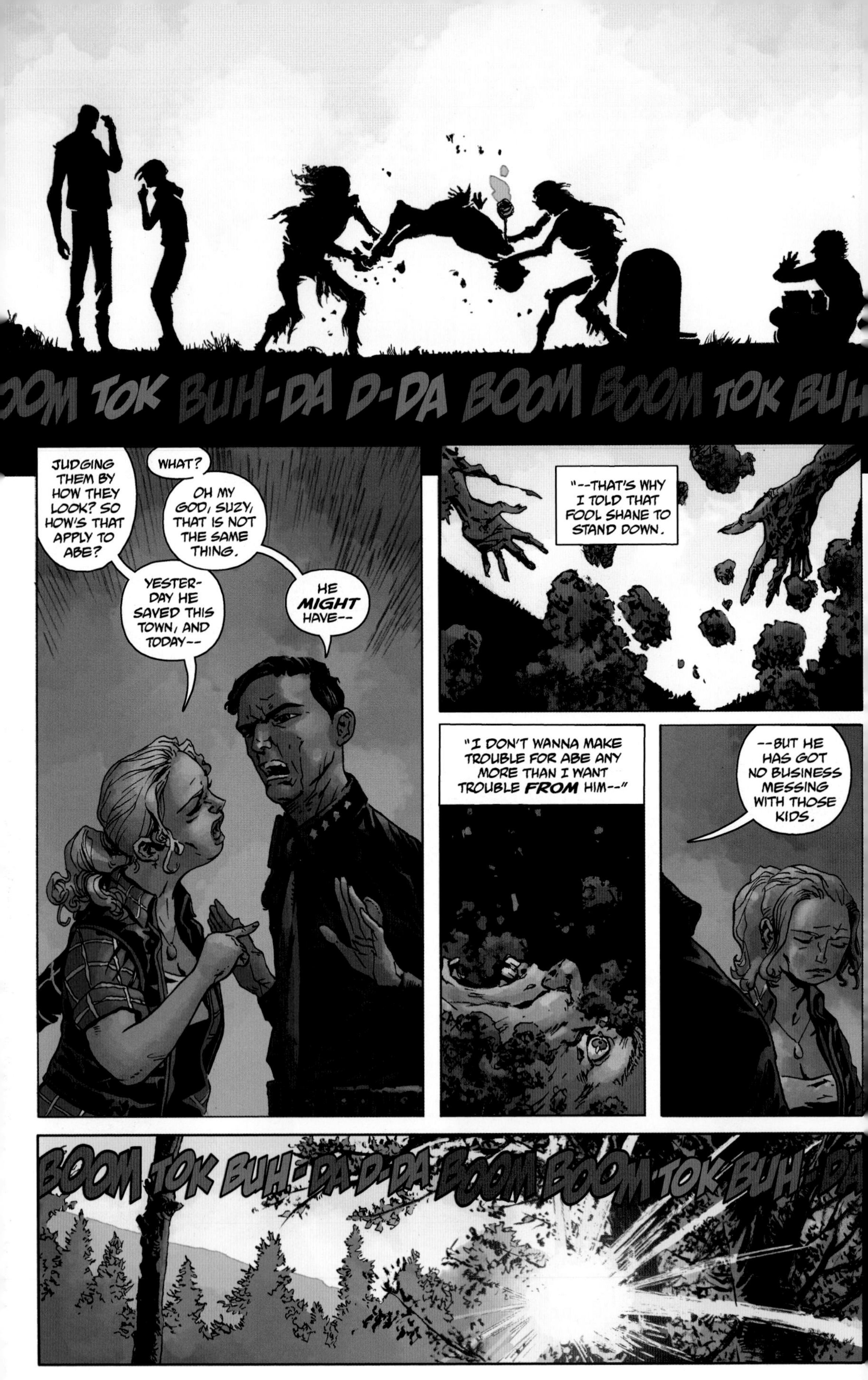

BOOM TOK BUH-DA D-DA BOOM BOOM TOK BUH
JUDGING THEM BY HOW THEY LOOK? SO HOW'S THAT APPLY TO ABE?
WHAT?
OH MY GOD, SUZY, THAT IS NOT THE SAME THING.
YESTER-DAY HE SAVED THIS TOWN, AND TODAY--
HE MIGHT HAVE--
"--THAT'S WHY I TOLD THAT FOOL SHANE TO STAND DOWN.
"I DON'T WANNA MAKE TROUBLE FOR ABE ANY MORE THAN I WANT TROUBLE FROM HIM--"
--BUT HE HAS GOT NO BUSINESS MESSING WITH THOSE KIDS.
BOOM TOK BUH-DA D-DA BOOM BOOM TOK BUH-DA

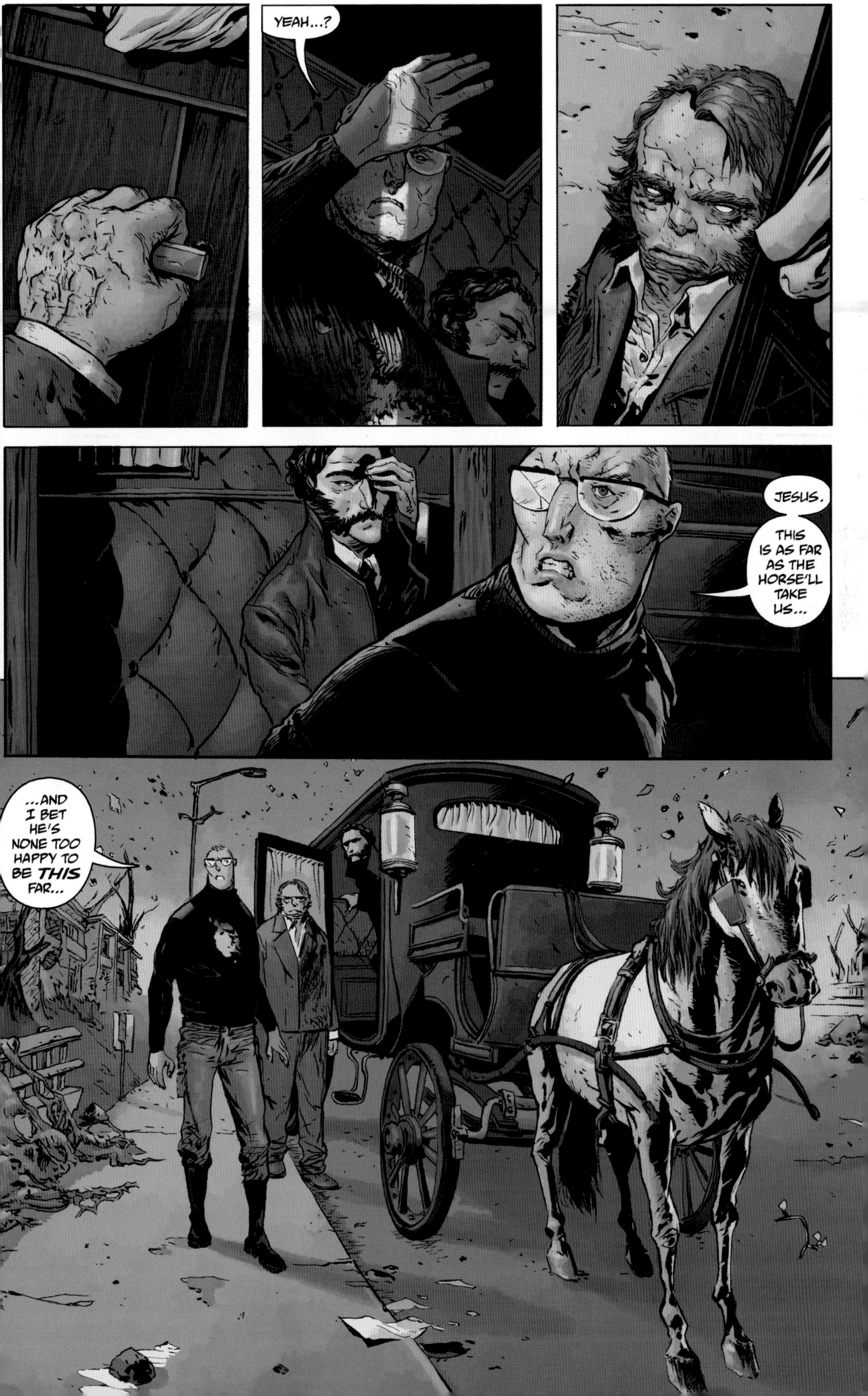

YEAH...?
JESUS.
THIS IS AS FAR AS THE HORSE'LL TAKE US...
...AND I BET HE'S NONE TOO HAPPY TO BE ***THIS*** FAR...

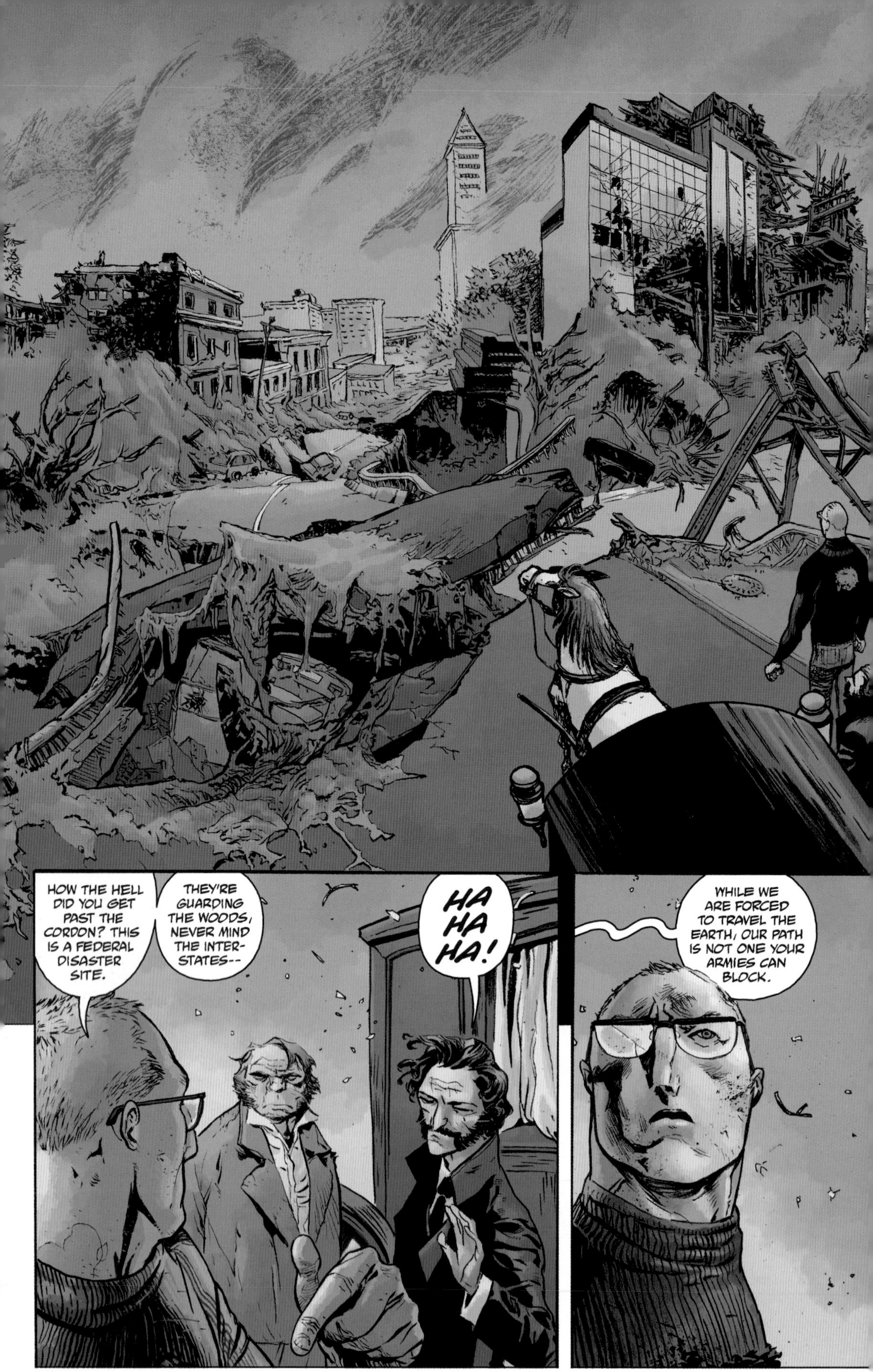
HOW THE HELL DID YOU GET PAST THE CORDON? THIS IS A FEDERAL DISASTER SITE.
THEY'RE GUARDING THE WOODS, NEVER MIND THE INTER-STATES--
HA HA HA!
WHILE WE ARE FORCED TO TRAVEL THE EARTH, OUR PATH IS NOT ONE YOUR ARMIES CAN BLOCK.

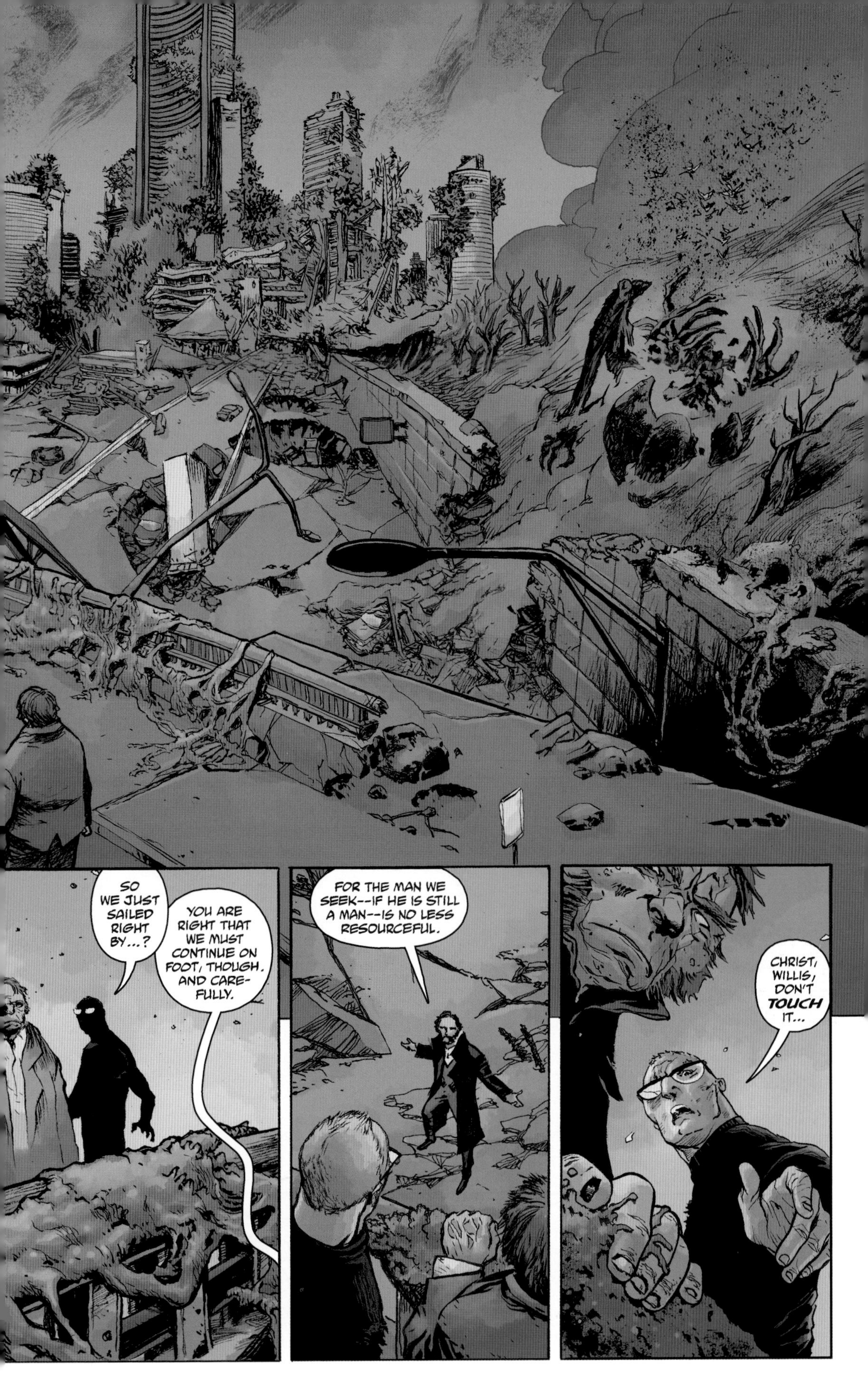
SO WE JUST SAILED RIGHT BY...?
YOU ARE RIGHT THAT WE MUST CONTINUE ON FOOT, THOUGH. AND CAREFULLY.
FOR THE MAN WE SEEK--IF HE IS STILL A MAN--IS NO LESS RESOURCEFUL.
CHRIST, WILLIS, DON'T *TOUCH* IT...

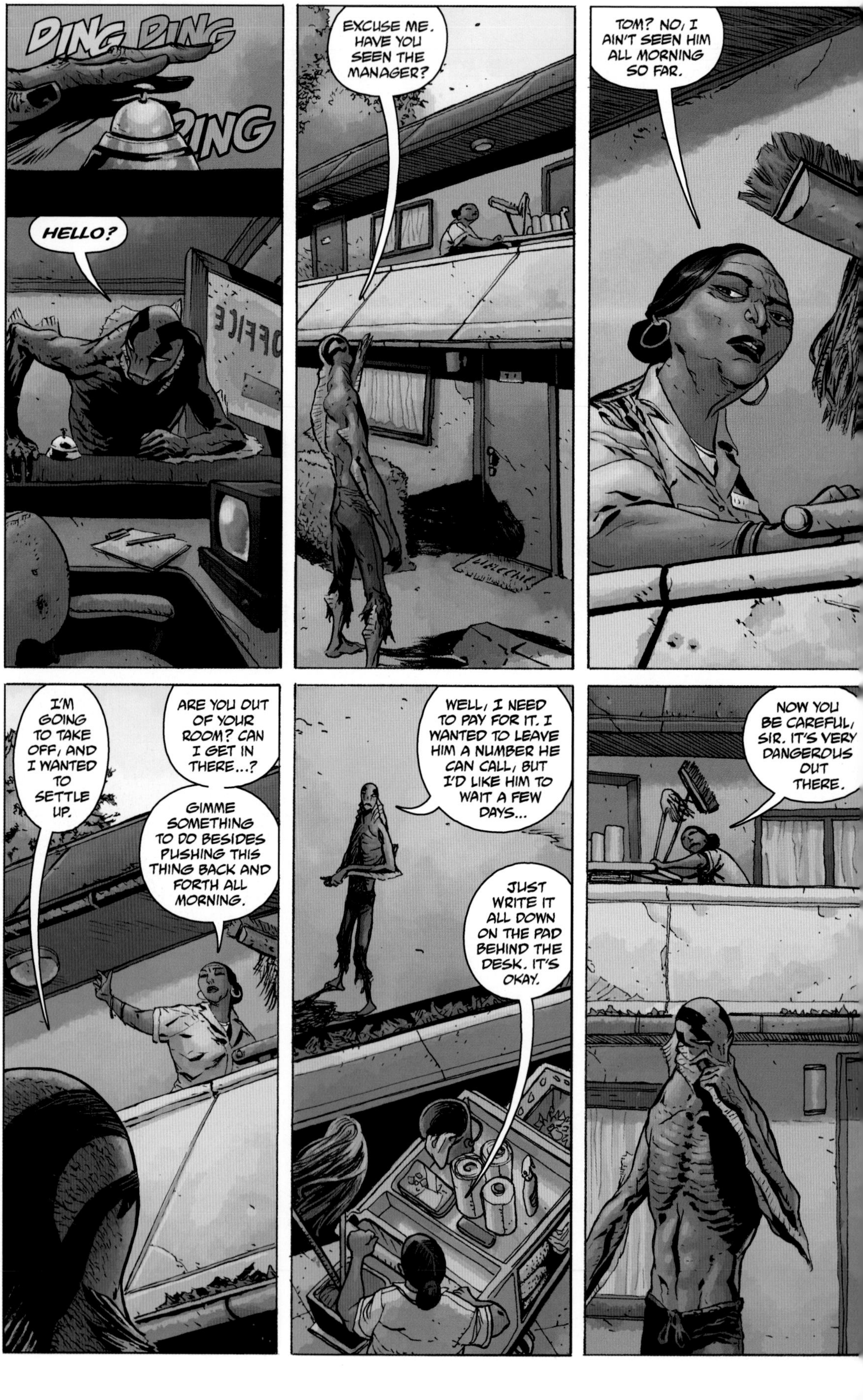
DING DING
DING
HELLO?
OFFICE
EXCUSE ME. HAVE YOU SEEN THE MANAGER?
TOM? NO, I AIN'T SEEN HIM ALL MORNING SO FAR.
I'M GOING TO TAKE OFF, AND I WANTED TO SETTLE UP.
ARE YOU OUT OF YOUR ROOM? CAN I GET IN THERE...?
GIMME SOMETHING TO DO BESIDES PUSHING THIS THING BACK AND FORTH ALL MORNING.
WELL, I NEED TO PAY FOR IT. I WANTED TO LEAVE HIM A NUMBER HE CAN CALL, BUT I'D LIKE HIM TO WAIT A FEW DAYS...
JUST WRITE IT ALL DOWN ON THE PAD BEHIND THE DESK. IT'S OKAY.
NOW YOU BE CAREFUL, SIR. IT'S VERY DANGEROUS OUT THERE.

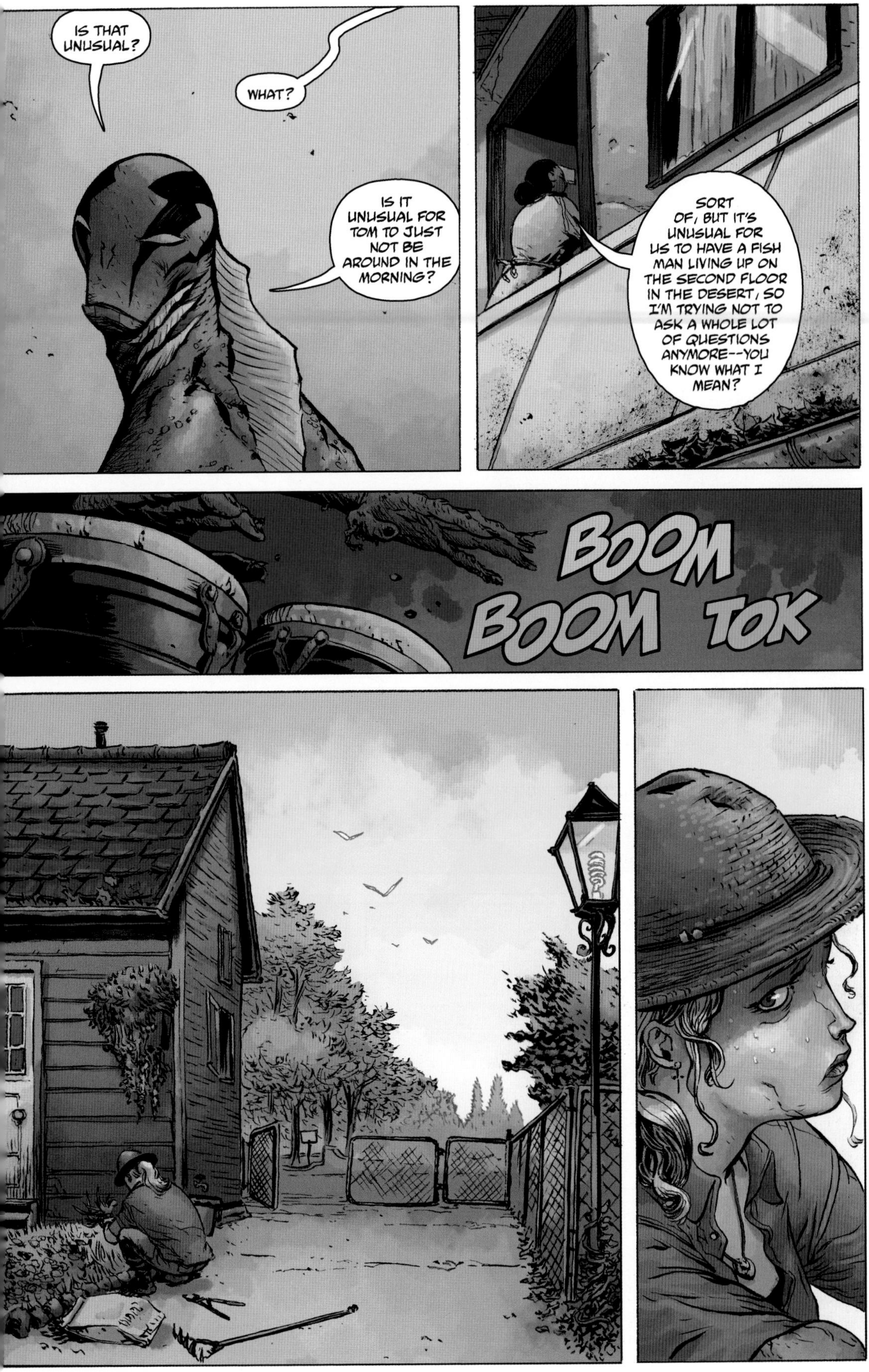
IS THAT UNUSUAL?
WHAT?
IS IT UNUSUAL FOR TOM TO JUST NOT BE AROUND IN THE MORNING?
SORT OF, BUT IT'S UNUSUAL FOR US TO HAVE A FISH MAN LIVING UP ON THE SECOND FLOOR IN THE DESERT, SO I'M TRYING NOT TO ASK A WHOLE LOT OF QUESTIONS ANYMORE--YOU KNOW WHAT I MEAN?
BOOM
BOOM TOK

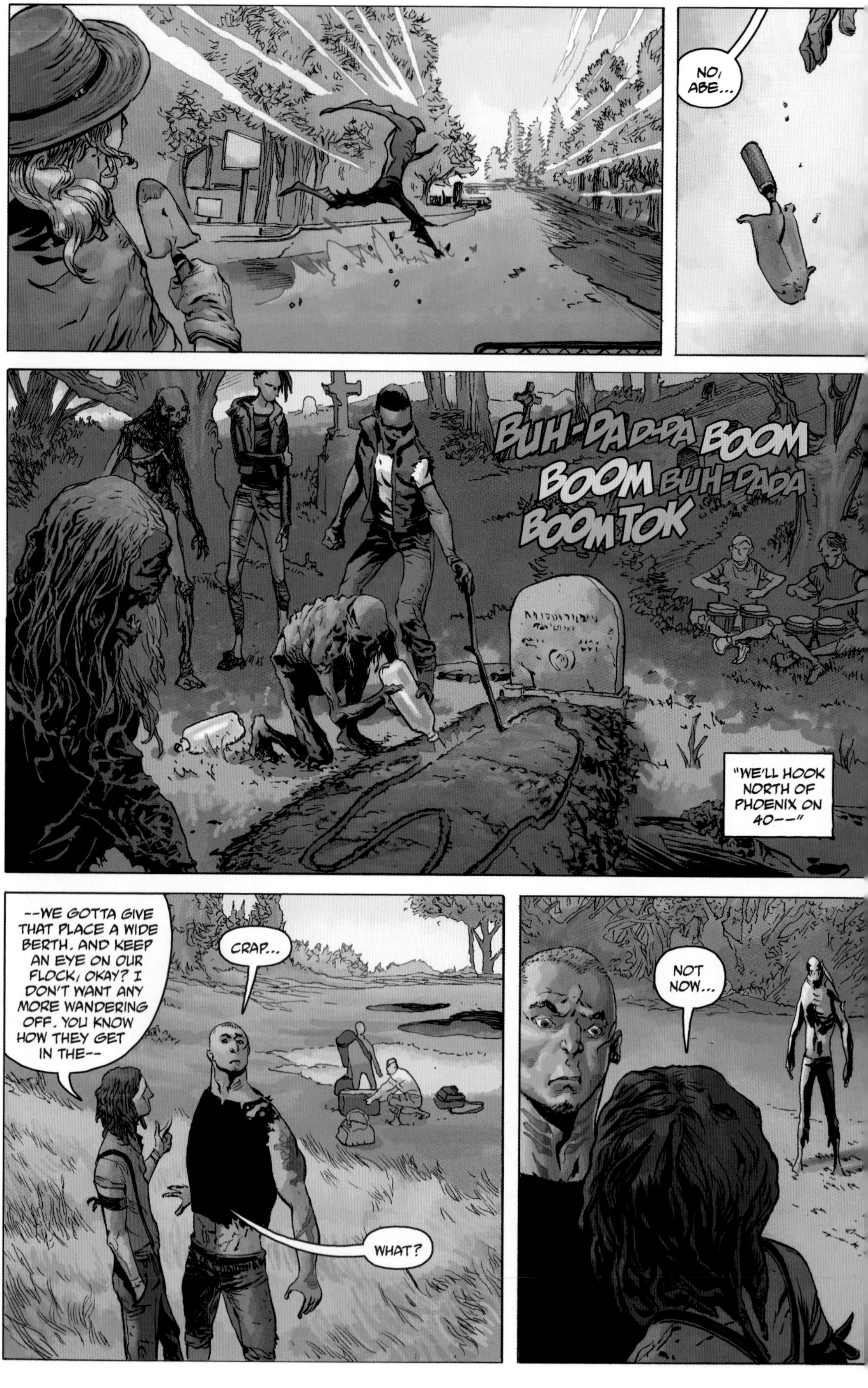
NO, ABE...
BUH-DAD-DA BOOM BOOM BUH-DADA BOOM TOK
"WE'LL HOOK NORTH OF PHOENIX ON 40--"
--WE GOTTA GIVE THAT PLACE A WIDE BERTH. AND KEEP AN EYE ON OUR FLOCK, OKAY? I DON'T WANT ANY MORE WANDERING OFF. YOU KNOW HOW THEY GET IN THE--
CRAP...
WHAT?
NOT NOW...

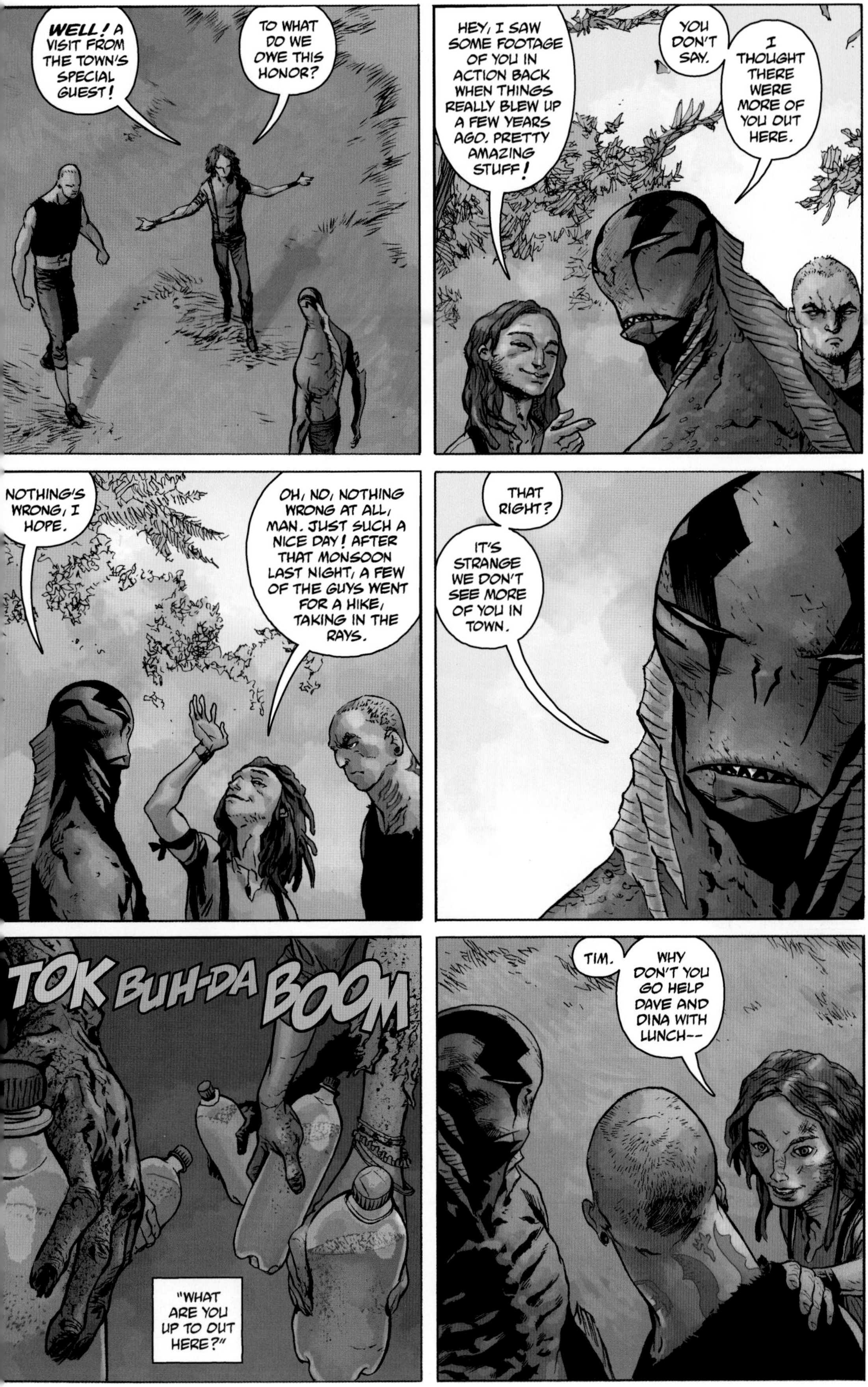
WELL! A VISIT FROM THE TOWN'S SPECIAL GUEST!
TO WHAT DO WE OWE THIS HONOR?
HEY, I SAW SOME FOOTAGE OF YOU IN ACTION BACK WHEN THINGS REALLY BLEW UP A FEW YEARS AGO. PRETTY AMAZING STUFF!
YOU DON'T SAY.
I THOUGHT THERE WERE MORE OF YOU OUT HERE.
NOTHING'S WRONG, I HOPE.
OH, NO, NOTHING WRONG AT ALL, MAN. JUST SUCH A NICE DAY! AFTER THAT MONSOON LAST NIGHT, A FEW OF THE GUYS WENT FOR A HIKE, TAKING IN THE RAYS.
THAT RIGHT?
IT'S STRANGE WE DON'T SEE MORE OF YOU IN TOWN.
TOK BUH-DA BOOM
"WHAT ARE YOU UP TO OUT HERE?"
TIM.
WHY DON'T YOU GO HELP DAVE AND DINA WITH LUNCH--

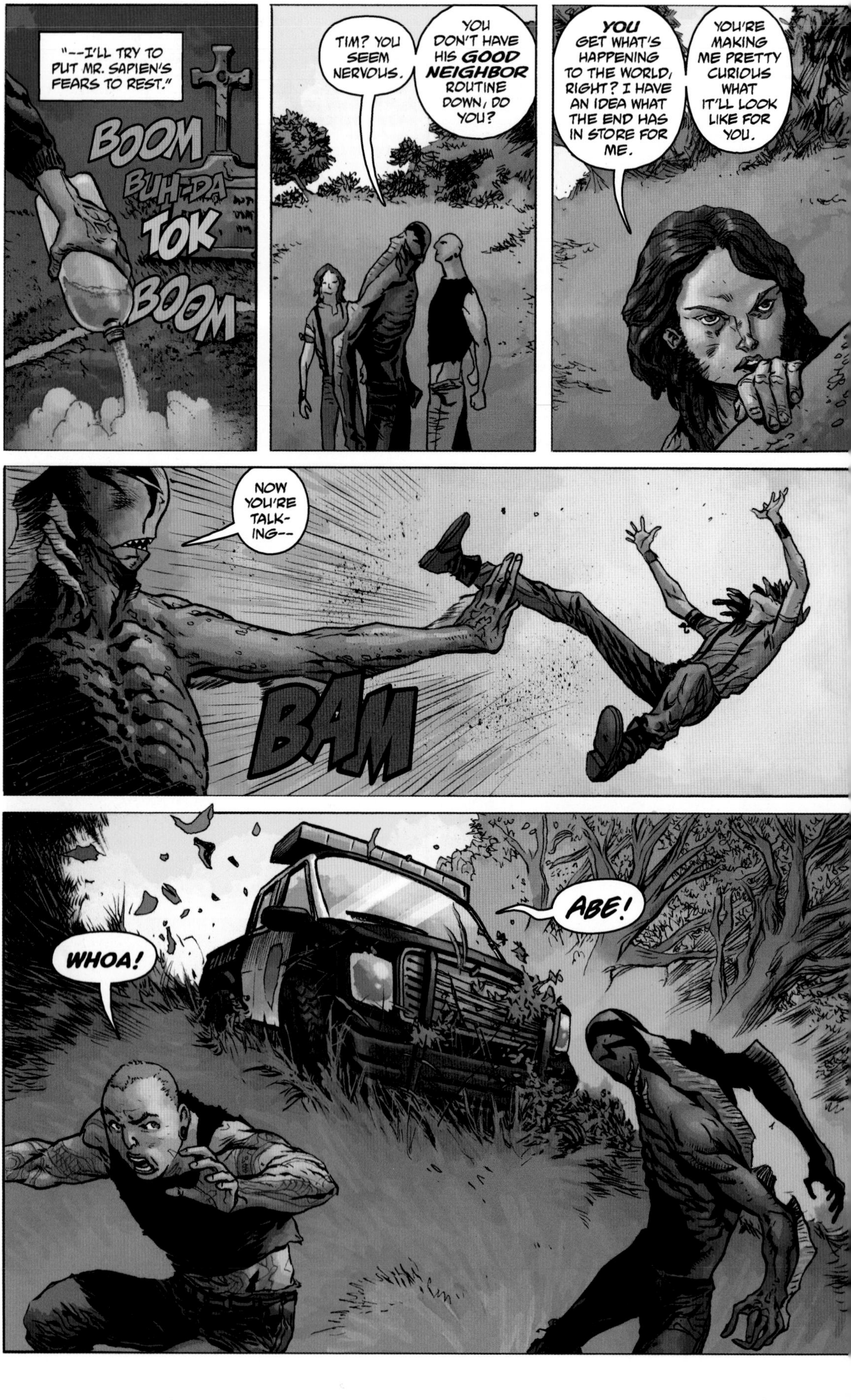
"--I'LL TRY TO PUT MR. SAPIEN'S FEARS TO REST."
BOOM
BUH-DA
TOK
BOOM
TIM? YOU SEEM NERVOUS.
YOU DON'T HAVE HIS GOOD NEIGHBOR ROUTINE DOWN, DO YOU?
YOU GET WHAT'S HAPPENING TO THE WORLD, RIGHT? I HAVE AN IDEA WHAT THE END HAS IN STORE FOR ME.
YOU'RE MAKING ME PRETTY CURIOUS WHAT IT'LL LOOK LIKE FOR YOU.
NOW YOU'RE TALKING--
BAM
WHOA!
ABE!

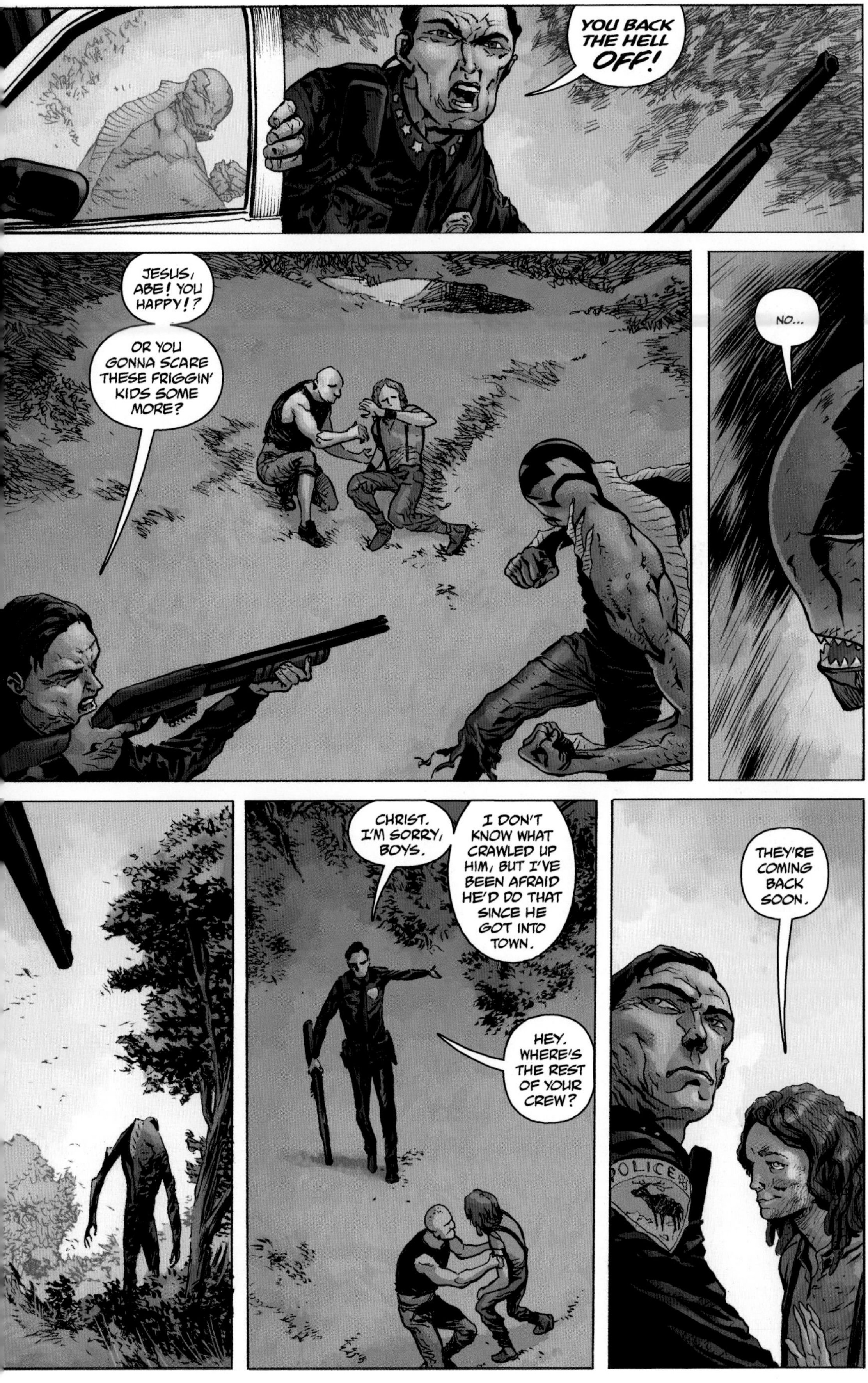
YOU BACK THE HELL OFF!
JESUS, ABE! YOU HAPPY!?
OR YOU GONNA SCARE THESE FRIGGIN' KIDS SOME MORE?
NO...
CHRIST. I'M SORRY, BOYS.
I DON'T KNOW WHAT CRAWLED UP HIM, BUT I'VE BEEN AFRAID HE'D DO THAT SINCE HE GOT INTO TOWN.
HEY. WHERE'S THE REST OF YOUR CREW?
THEY'RE COMING BACK SOON.
POLICE

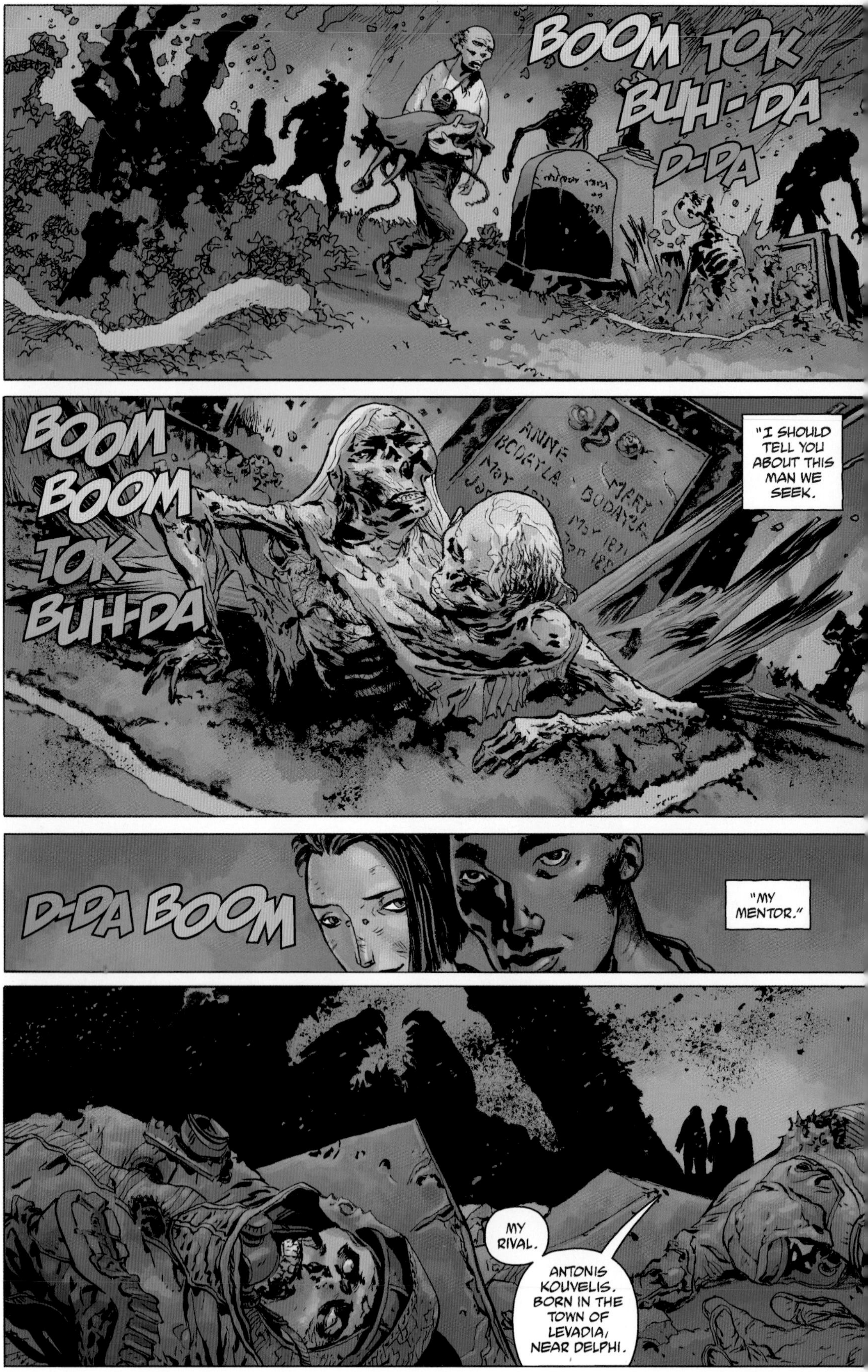
BOOM TOK BUH-DA D-DA
BOOM BOOM TOK BUH-DA
"I SHOULD TELL YOU ABOUT THIS MAN WE SEEK.
D-DA BOOM
"MY MENTOR."
MY RIVAL.
ANTONIS KOUVELIS. BORN IN THE TOWN OF LEVADIA, NEAR DELPHI.

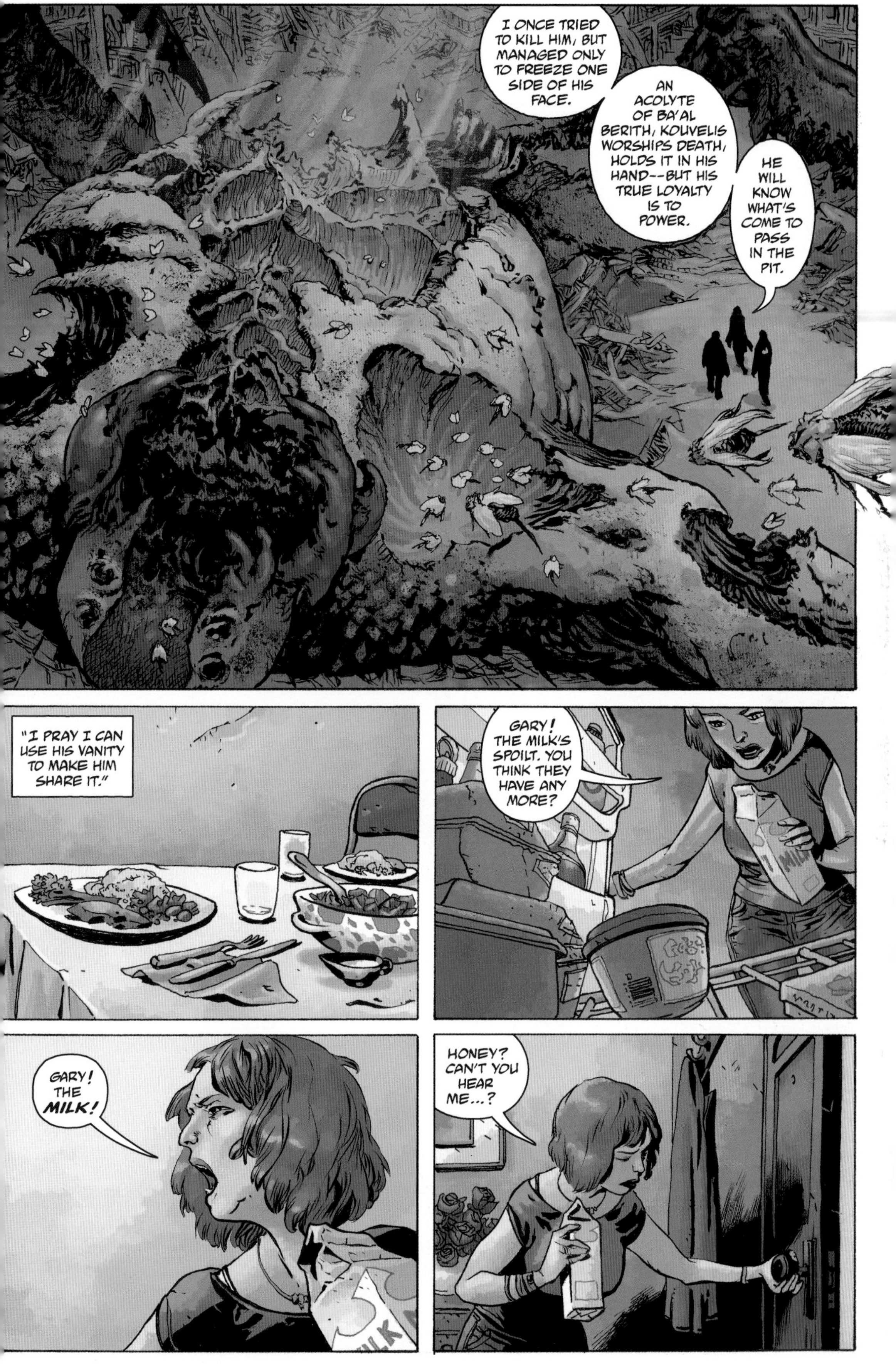

I ONCE TRIED TO KILL HIM, BUT MANAGED ONLY TO FREEZE ONE SIDE OF HIS FACE.
AN ACOLYTE OF BA'AL BERITH, KOUVELIS WORSHIPS DEATH, HOLDS IT IN HIS HAND--BUT HIS TRUE LOYALTY IS TO POWER.
HE WILL KNOW WHAT'S COME TO PASS IN THE PIT.
"I PRAY I CAN USE HIS VANITY TO MAKE HIM SHARE IT."
GARY! THE MILK'S SPOILT. YOU THINK THEY HAVE ANY MORE?
MILK
GARY! THE *MILK!*
HONEY? CAN'T YOU HEAR ME...?

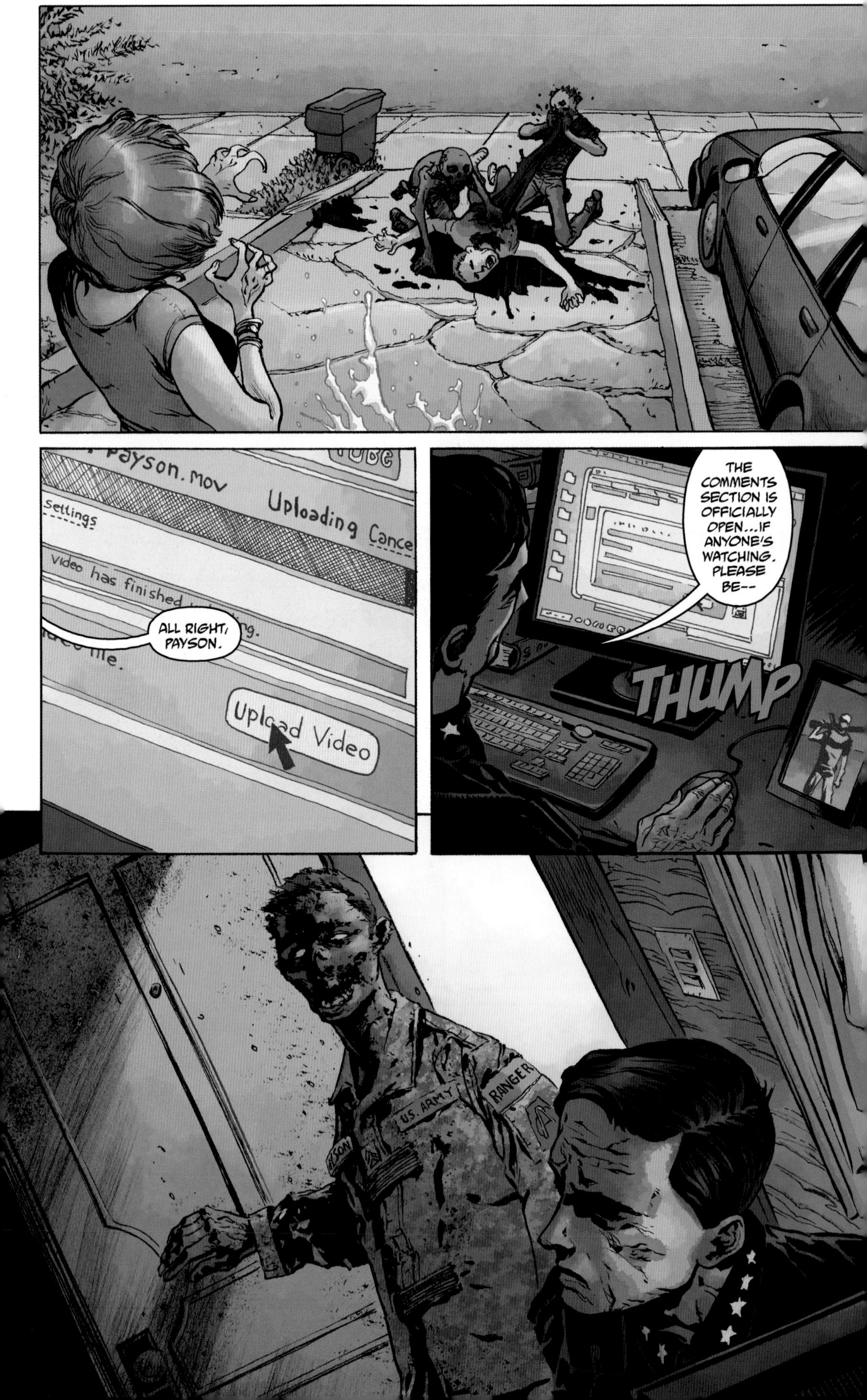

payson.mov
Uploading
Settings
ALL RIGHT, PAYSON.
Upload Video
THE COMMENTS SECTION IS OFFICIALLY OPEN...IF ANYONE'S WATCHING. PLEASE BE--
THUMP
U.S. ARMY
RANGER

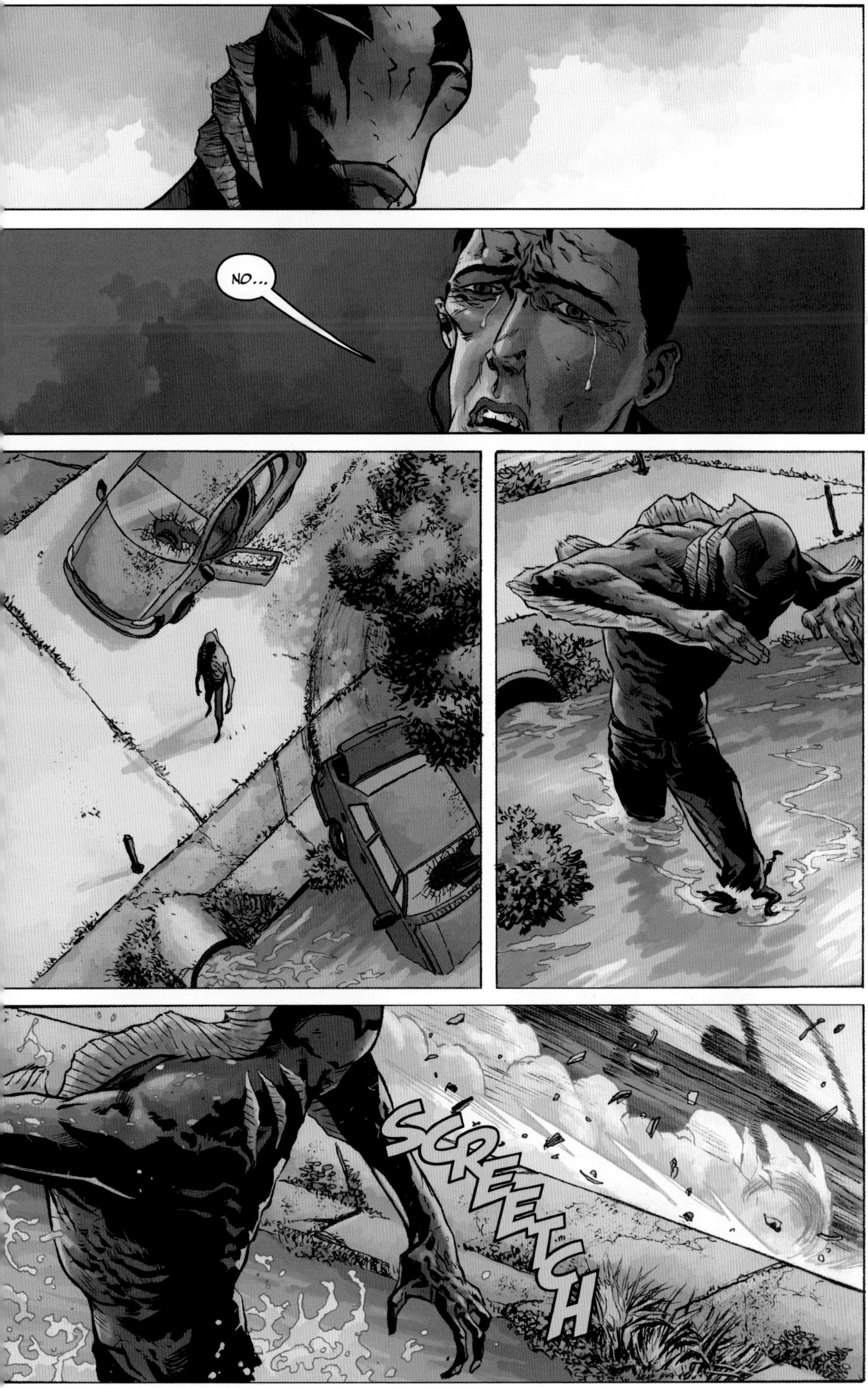
NO...
SCREECH

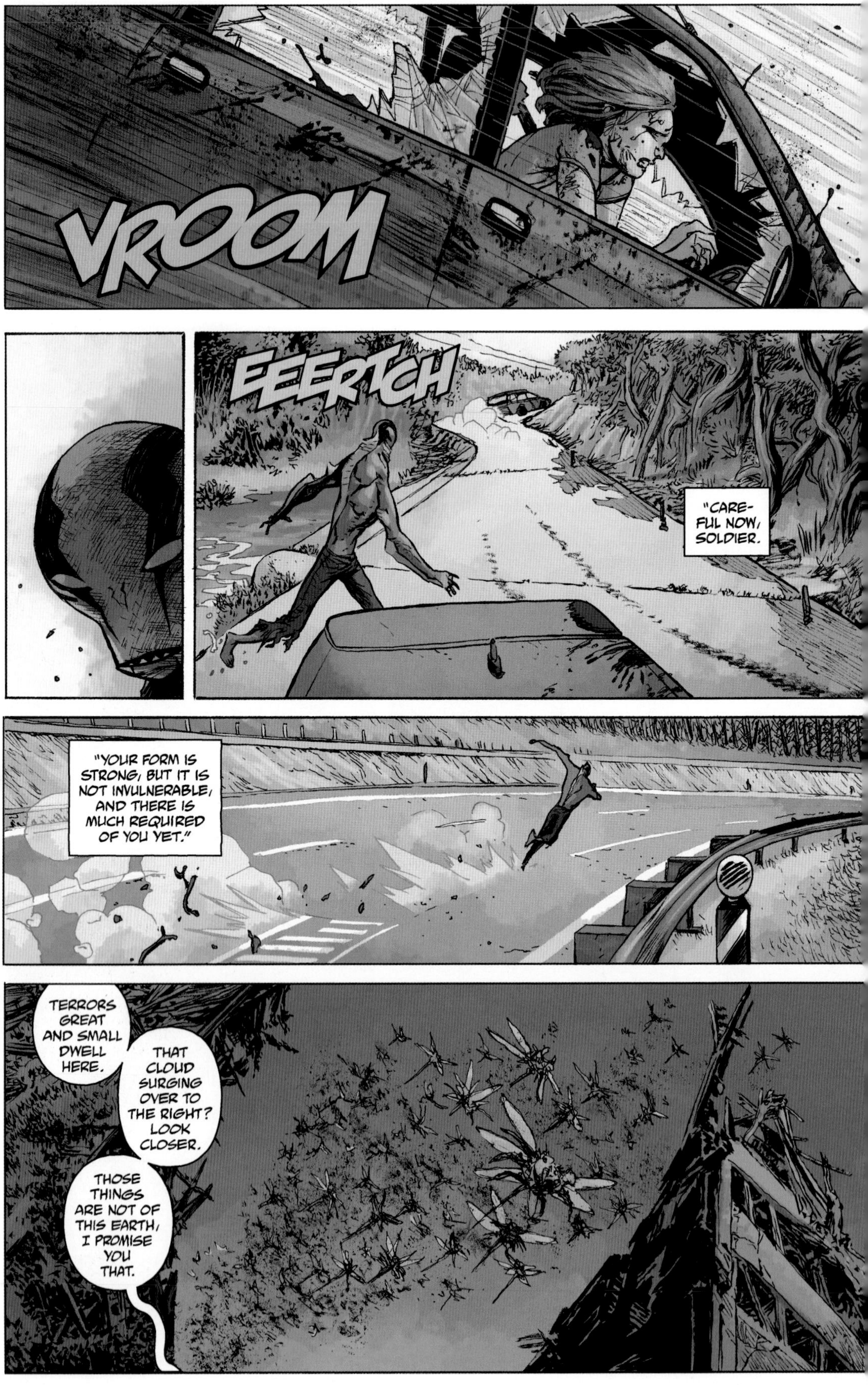
VROOM
EEERTCH
"CARE-FUL NOW, SOLDIER.
"YOUR FORM IS STRONG, BUT IT IS NOT INVULNERABLE, AND THERE IS MUCH REQUIRED OF YOU YET."
TERRORS GREAT AND SMALL DWELL HERE.
THAT CLOUD SURGING OVER TO THE RIGHT? LOOK CLOSER.
THOSE THINGS ARE NOT OF THIS EARTH, I PROMISE YOU THAT.

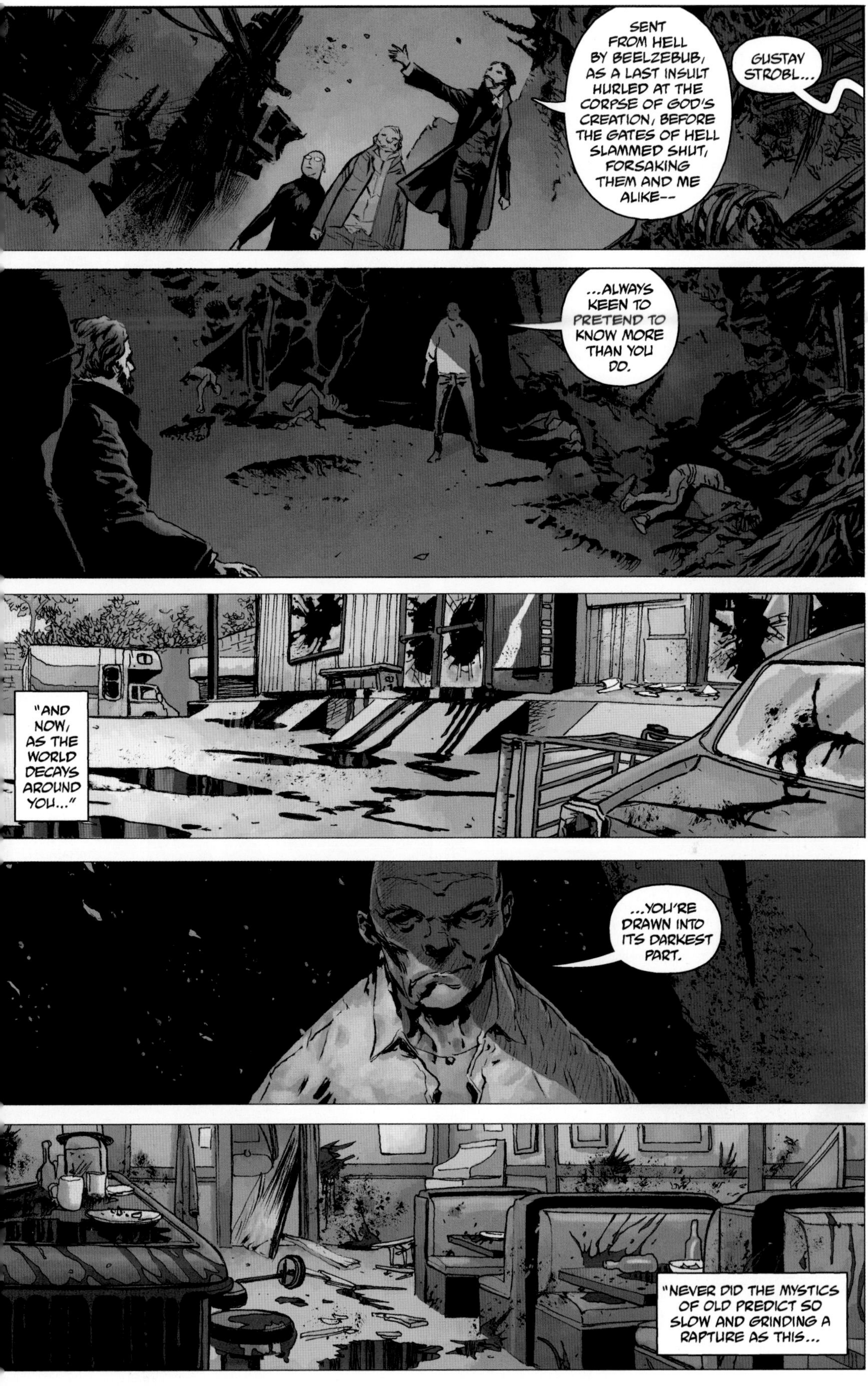
SENT FROM HELL BY BEELZEBUB, AS A LAST INSULT HURLED AT THE CORPSE OF GOD'S CREATION, BEFORE THE GATES OF HELL SLAMMED SHUT, FORSAKING THEM AND ME ALIKE--
GUSTAV STROBL...
...ALWAYS KEEN TO PRETEND TO KNOW MORE THAN YOU DO.
"AND NOW, AS THE WORLD DECAYS AROUND YOU..."
...YOU'RE DRAWN INTO ITS DARKEST PART.
"NEVER DID THE MYSTICS OF OLD PREDICT SO SLOW AND GRINDING A RAPTURE AS THIS...

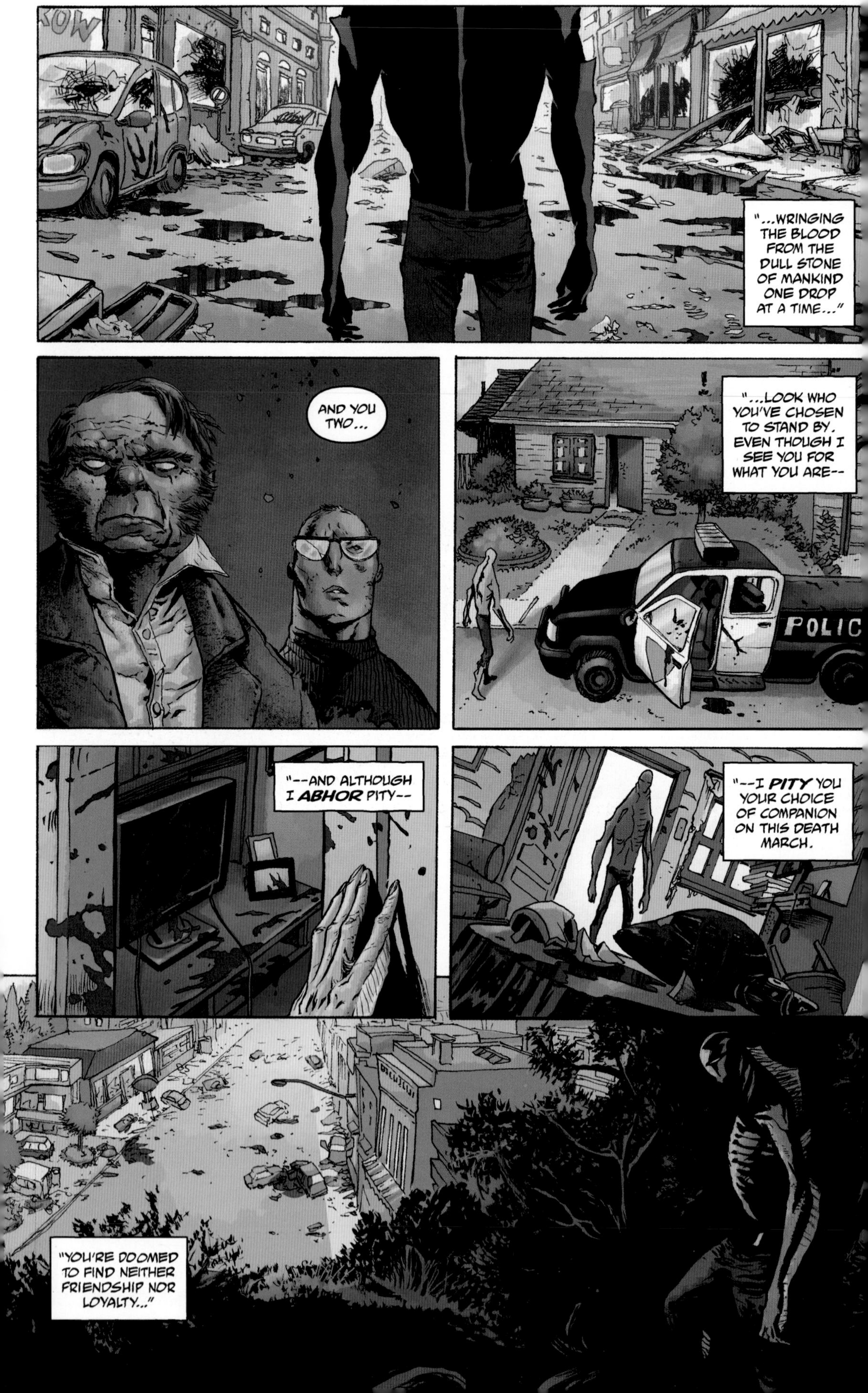

KOW
"...WRINGING THE BLOOD FROM THE DULL STONE OF MANKIND ONE DROP AT A TIME..."
AND YOU TWO...
"...LOOK WHO YOU'VE CHOSEN TO STAND BY. EVEN THOUGH I SEE YOU FOR WHAT YOU ARE--
POLIC
"--AND ALTHOUGH I ABHOR PITY--
"--I PITY YOU YOUR CHOICE OF COMPANION ON THIS DEATH MARCH.
"YOU'RE DOOMED TO FIND NEITHER FRIENDSHIP NOR LOYALTY..."

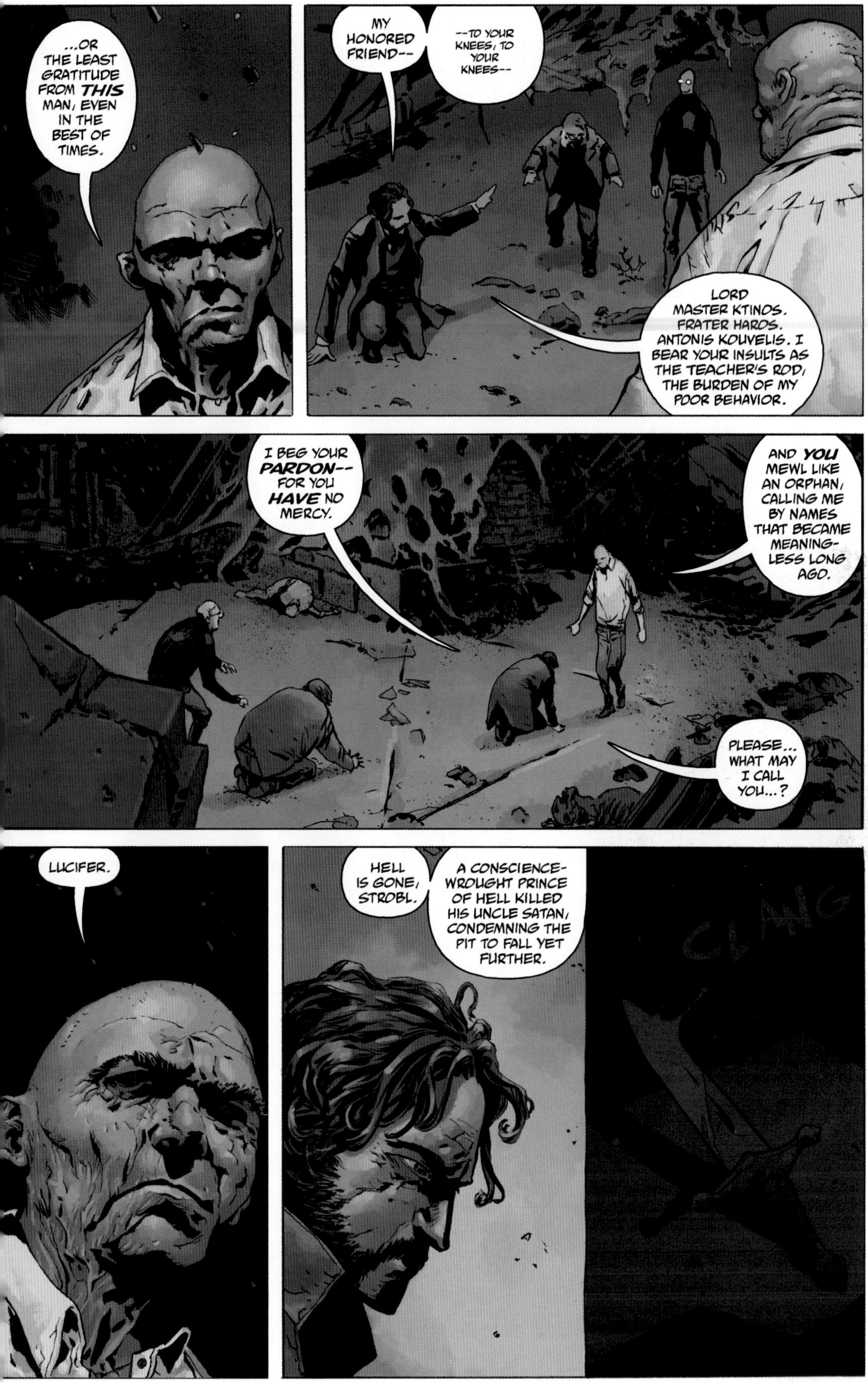
...OR THE LEAST GRATITUDE FROM THIS MAN, EVEN IN THE BEST OF TIMES.
MY HONORED FRIEND--
--TO YOUR KNEES, TO YOUR KNEES--
LORD MASTER KTINOS. FRATER HAROS. ANTONIS KOUVELIS. I BEAR YOUR INSULTS AS THE TEACHER'S ROD, THE BURDEN OF MY POOR BEHAVIOR.
I BEG YOUR PARDON-- FOR YOU HAVE NO MERCY.
AND YOU MEWL LIKE AN ORPHAN, CALLING ME BY NAMES THAT BECAME MEANINGLESS LONG AGO.
PLEASE... WHAT MAY I CALL YOU...?
LUCIFER.
HELL IS GONE, STROBL.
A CONSCIENCE-WROUGHT PRINCE OF HELL KILLED HIS UNCLE SATAN, CONDEMNING THE PIT TO FALL YET FURTHER.
CLANG

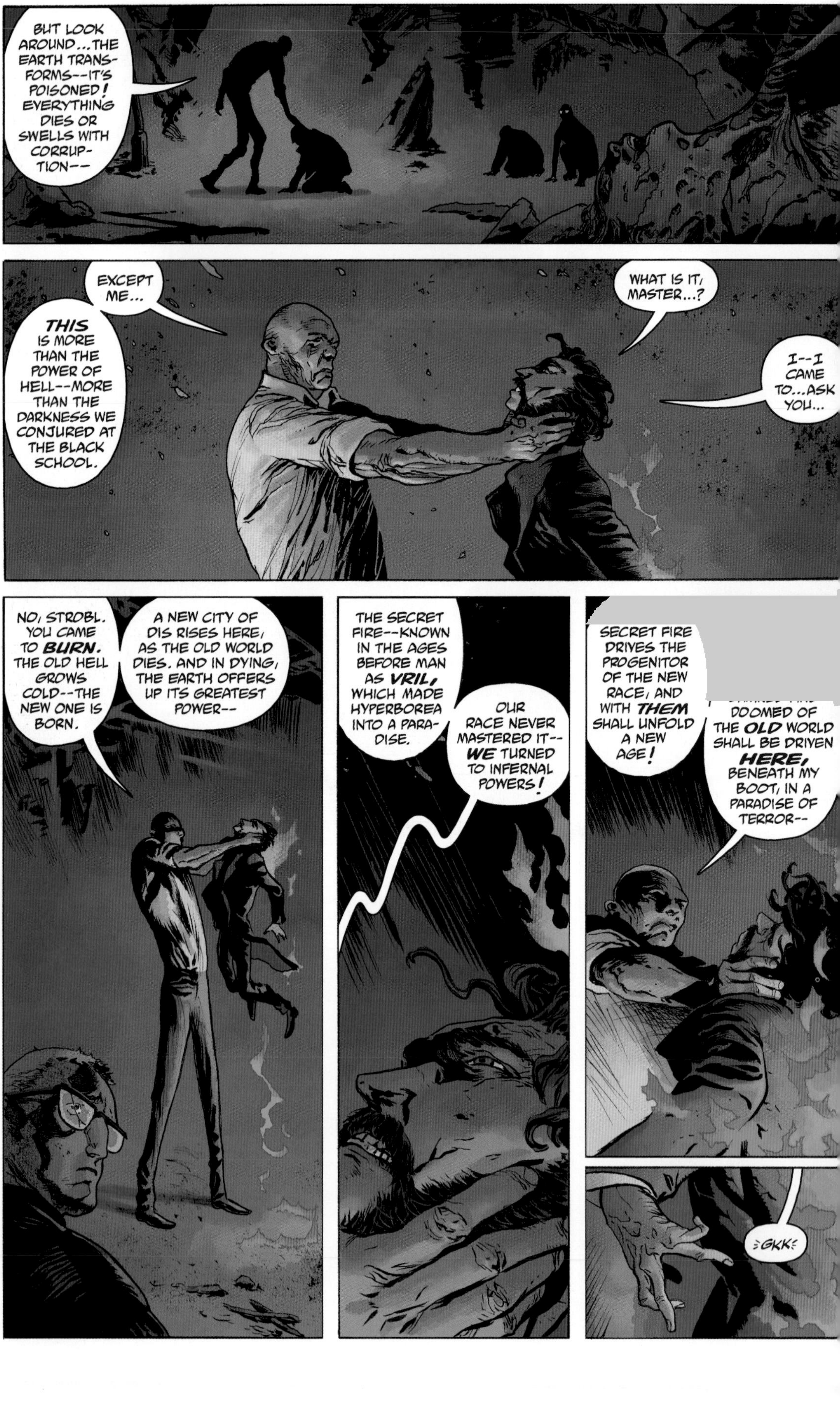

BUT LOOK AROUND... THE EARTH TRANSFORMS--IT'S POISONED! EVERYTHING DIES OR SWELLS WITH CORRUPTION--
EXCEPT ME...
THIS IS MORE THAN THE POWER OF HELL--MORE THAN THE DARKNESS WE CONJURED AT THE BLACK SCHOOL.
WHAT IS IT, MASTER...?
I--I CAME TO...ASK YOU...
NO, STROBL. YOU CAME TO BURN. THE OLD HELL GROWS COLD--THE NEW ONE IS BORN.
A NEW CITY OF DIS RISES HERE, AS THE OLD WORLD DIES. AND IN DYING, THE EARTH OFFERS UP ITS GREATEST POWER--
THE SECRET FIRE--KNOWN IN THE AGES BEFORE MAN AS VRIL, WHICH MADE HYPERBOREA INTO A PARADISE.
OUR RACE NEVER MASTERED IT--WE TURNED TO INFERNAL POWERS!
SECRET FIRE DRIVES THE PROGENITOR OF THE NEW RACE, AND WITH THEM SHALL UNFOLD A NEW AGE!
DOOMED OF THE OLD WORLD SHALL BE DRIVEN HERE, BENEATH MY BOOT, IN A PARADISE OF TERROR--
GKK

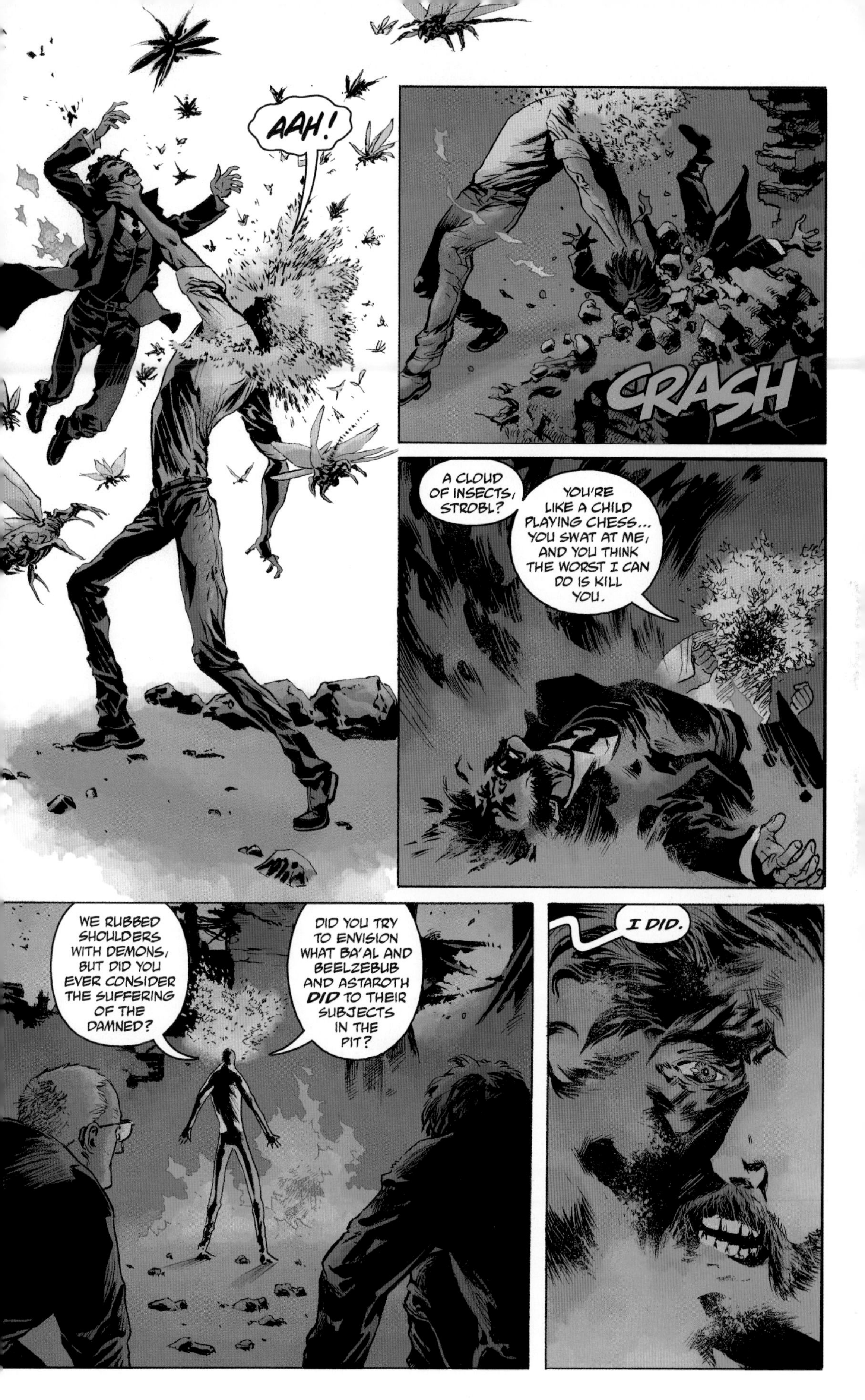
AAH!
CRASH
A CLOUD OF INSECTS, STROBL?
YOU'RE LIKE A CHILD PLAYING CHESS... YOU SWAT AT ME, AND YOU THINK THE WORST I CAN DO IS KILL YOU.
WE RUBBED SHOULDERS WITH DEMONS, BUT DID YOU EVER CONSIDER THE SUFFERING OF THE DAMNED?
DID YOU TRY TO ENVISION WHAT BA'AL AND BEELZEBUB AND ASTAROTH DID TO THEIR SUBJECTS IN THE PIT?
I DID.

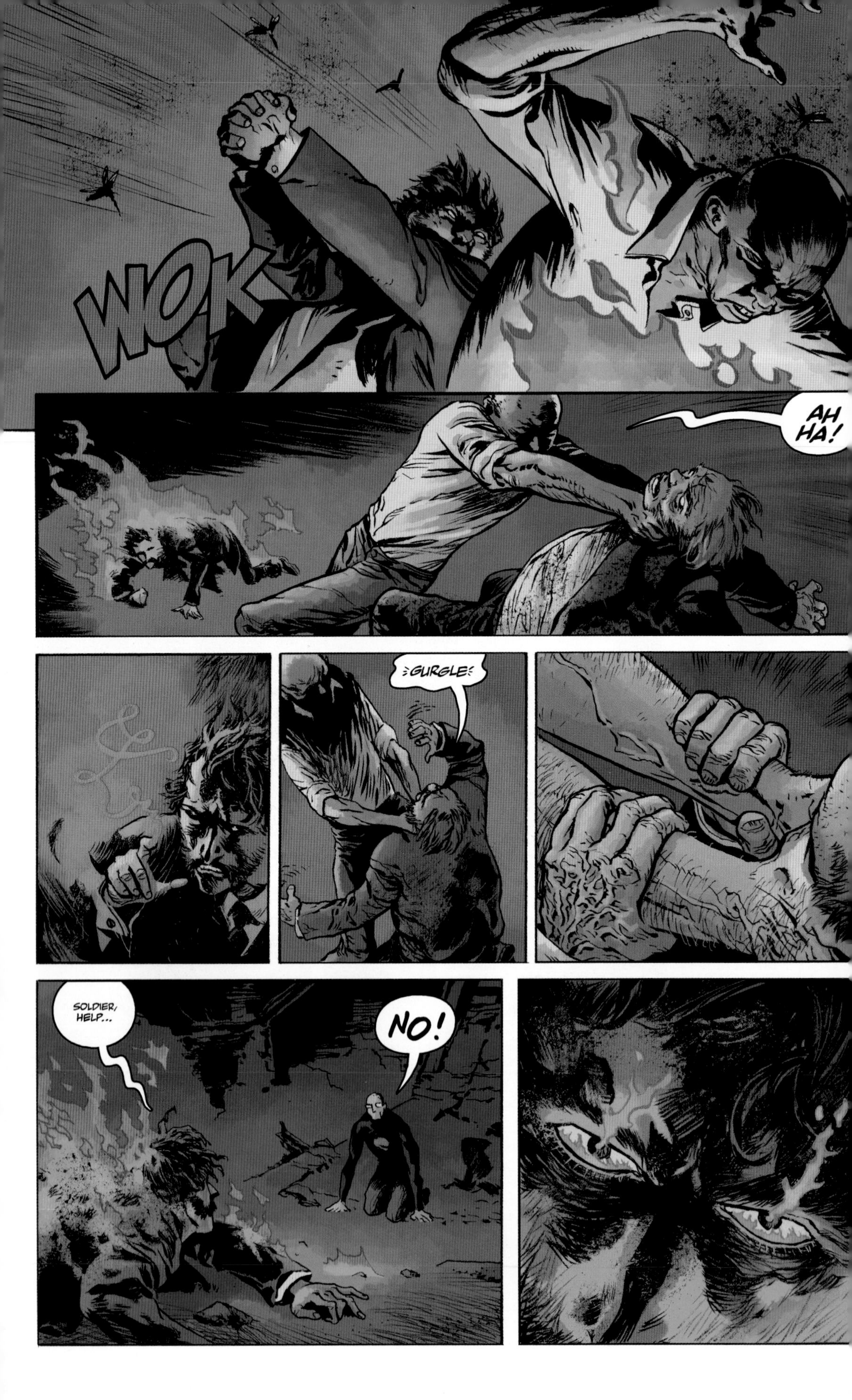
WOK
AH HA!
GURGLE
SOLDIER, HELP...
NO!

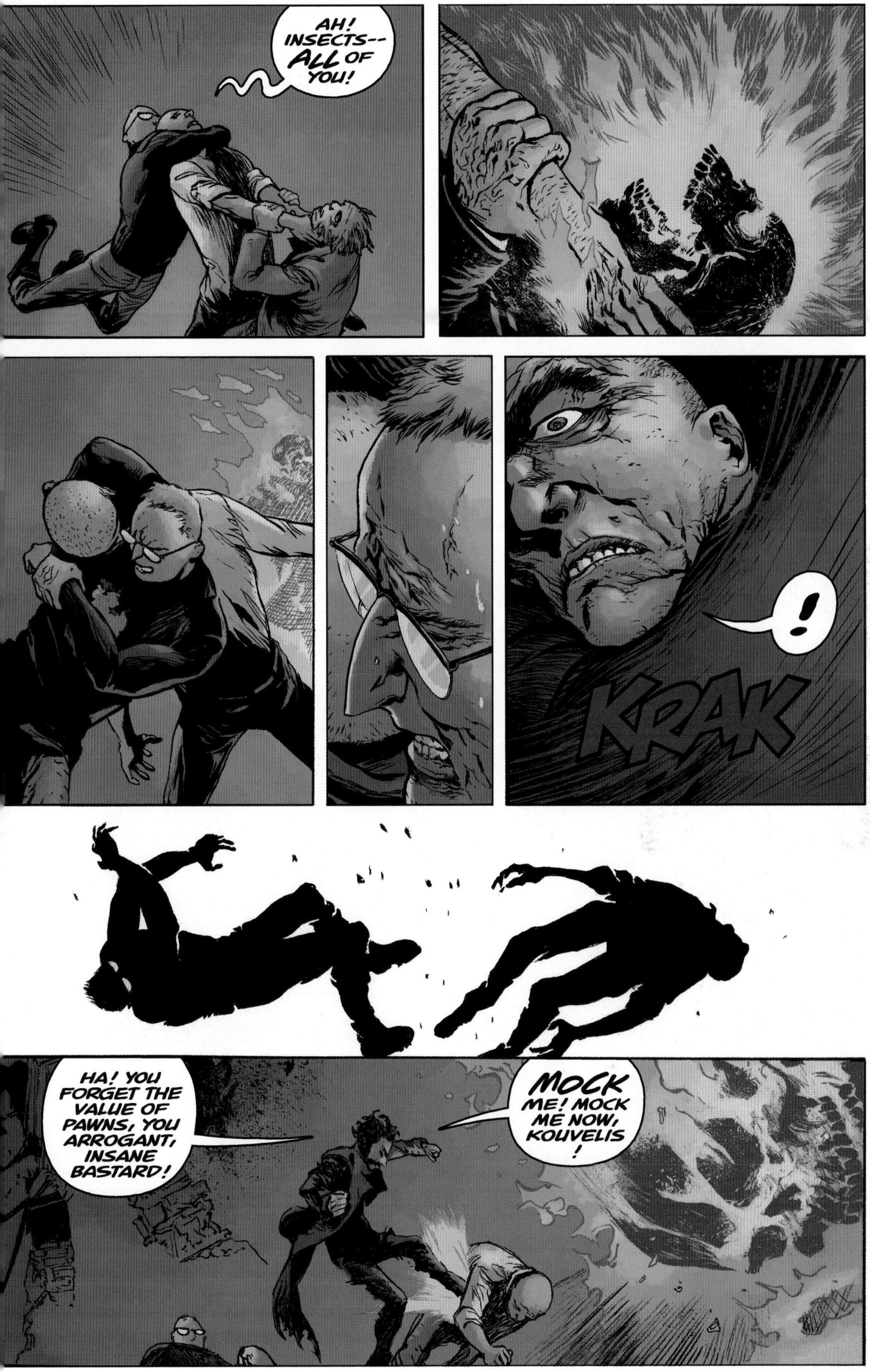
AH! INSECTS-- ALL OF YOU!
!
KRAK
HA! YOU FORGET THE VALUE OF PAWNS, YOU ARROGANT, INSANE BASTARD!
MOCK ME! MOCK ME NOW, KOUVELIS!

SHUT UP!
HOW DARE YOU!
SOLDIER... YOU ARE A FOOL, BUT YOU SERVE A PURPOSE STILL...
I NEED SOMEONE TO MIND THE HORSE...
YOU AND YOUR HORSE CAN DIE HERE FOR ALL I CARE! I'M DONE. I'M DONE WITH IT.
DON'T BE ABSURD. YOU JUST KILLED A MAN WITH WHOM YOU HAD NO QUARREL-- BECAUSE I BID IT.
I THINK YOU WILL BE MY COACH-MAN.
THE BLACK SCHOOL...?
I'D WONDERED IF YOU WERE LISTENING. YES.
WHERE...?

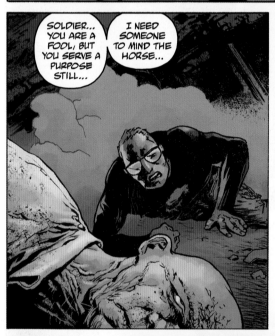

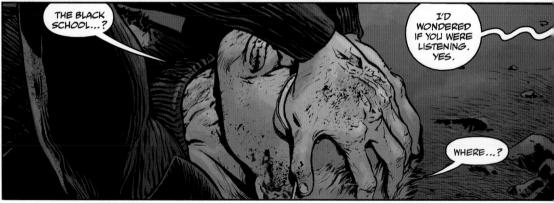

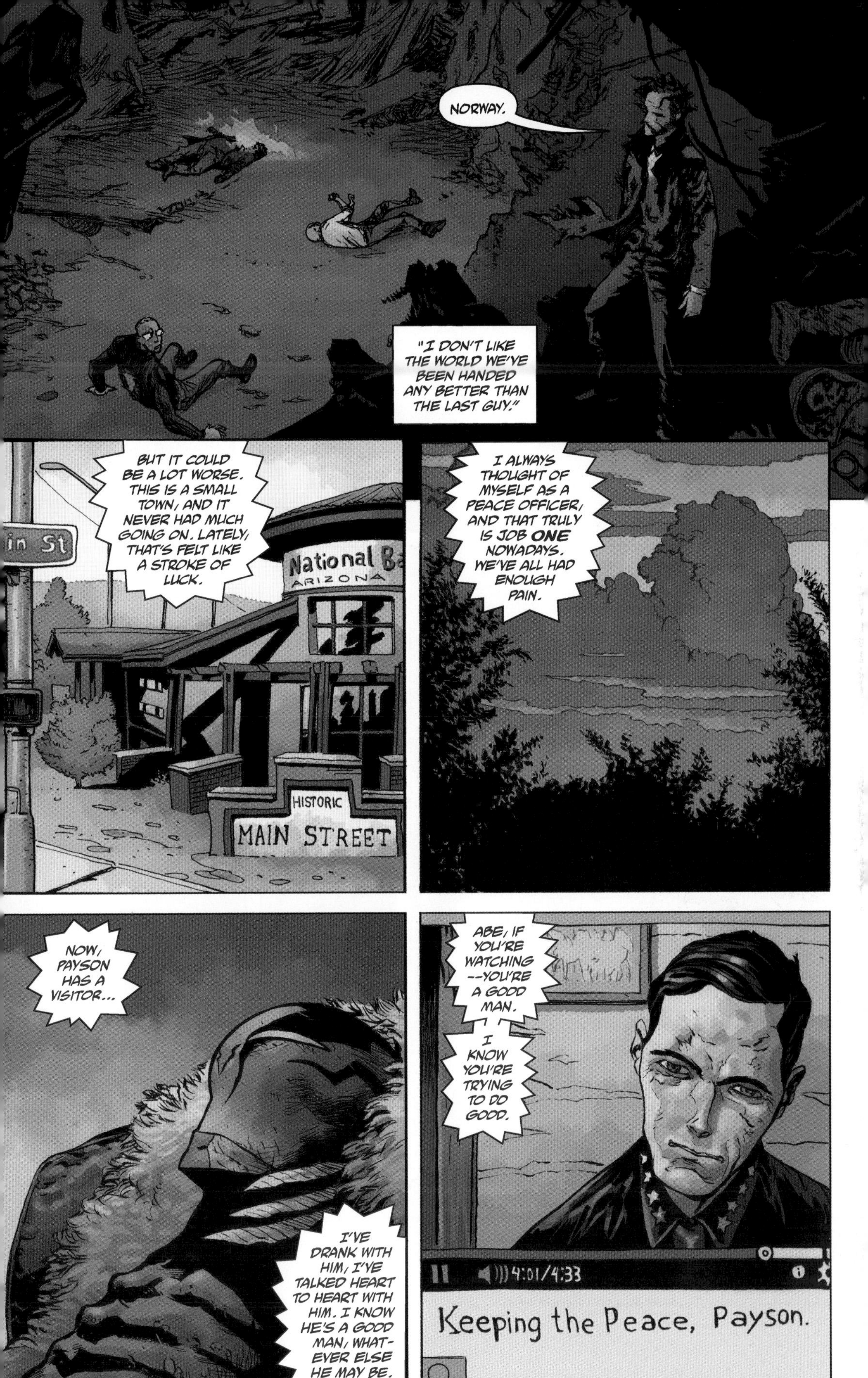
NORWAY.
"I DON'T LIKE THE WORLD WE'VE BEEN HANDED ANY BETTER THAN THE LAST GUY."
BUT IT COULD BE A LOT WORSE. THIS IS A SMALL TOWN, AND IT NEVER HAD MUCH GOING ON. LATELY, THAT'S FELT LIKE A STROKE OF LUCK.
in St
National Ba
ARIZONA
HISTORIC
MAIN STREET
I ALWAYS THOUGHT OF MYSELF AS A PEACE OFFICER, AND THAT TRULY IS JOB **ONE** NOWADAYS. WE'VE ALL HAD ENOUGH PAIN.
NOW, PAYSON HAS A VISITOR...
I'VE DRANK WITH HIM, I'VE TALKED HEART TO HEART WITH HIM. I KNOW HE'S A GOOD MAN, WHATEVER ELSE HE MAY BE.
ABE, IF YOU'RE WATCHING --YOU'RE A GOOD MAN.
I KNOW YOU'RE TRYING TO DO GOOD.
4:01/4:33
Keeping the Peace, Payson.

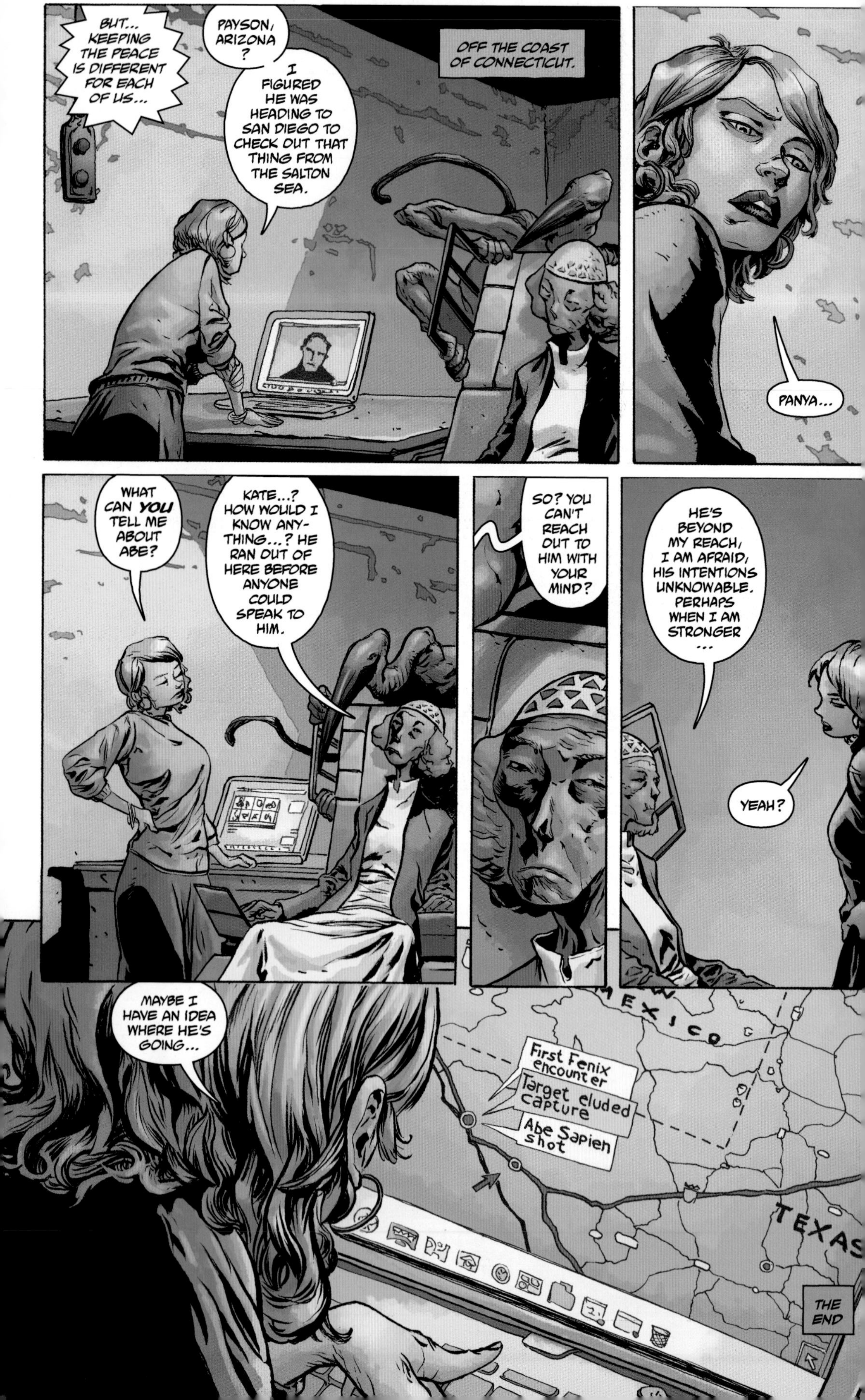
BUT... KEEPING THE PEACE IS DIFFERENT FOR EACH OF US...
PAYSON, ARIZONA?
OFF THE COAST OF CONNECTICUT.
I FIGURED HE WAS HEADING TO SAN DIEGO TO CHECK OUT THAT THING FROM THE SALTON SEA.
PANYA...
WHAT CAN YOU TELL ME ABOUT ABE?
KATE...? HOW WOULD I KNOW ANYTHING...? HE RAN OUT OF HERE BEFORE ANYONE COULD SPEAK TO HIM.
SO? YOU CAN'T REACH OUT TO HIM WITH YOUR MIND?
HE'S BEYOND MY REACH, I AM AFRAID, HIS INTENTIONS UNKNOWABLE. PERHAPS WHEN I AM STRONGER...
YEAH?
MAYBE I HAVE AN IDEA WHERE HE'S GOING...
MEXICO
First Fenix encounter
Target eluded capture
Abe Sapien shot
TEXAS
THE END

ABE SAPIEN™

Sketchbook

Notes by
Scott Allie

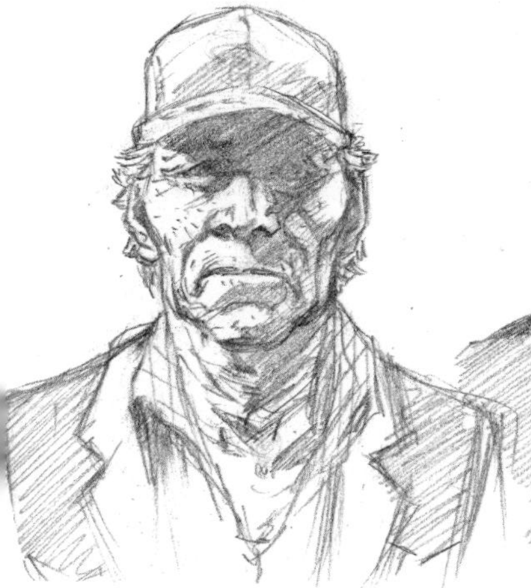

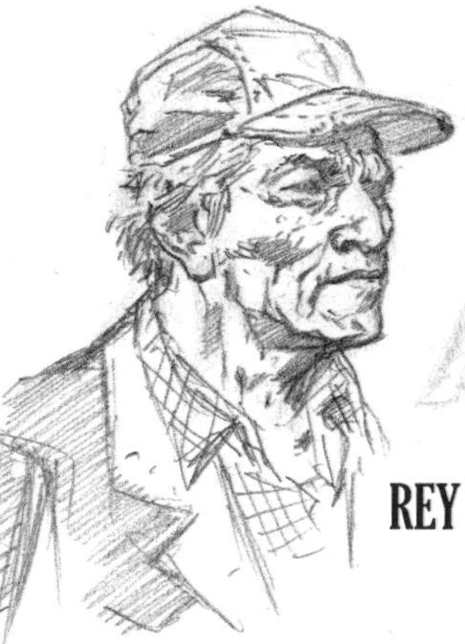

REY

PATRICK

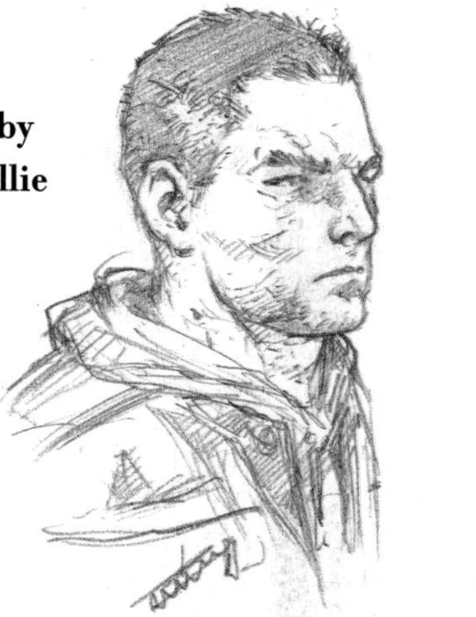

Sebastián's designs for the cast of *The Shape of Things to Come*. The militiamen were named after Dark Horse associate editors.

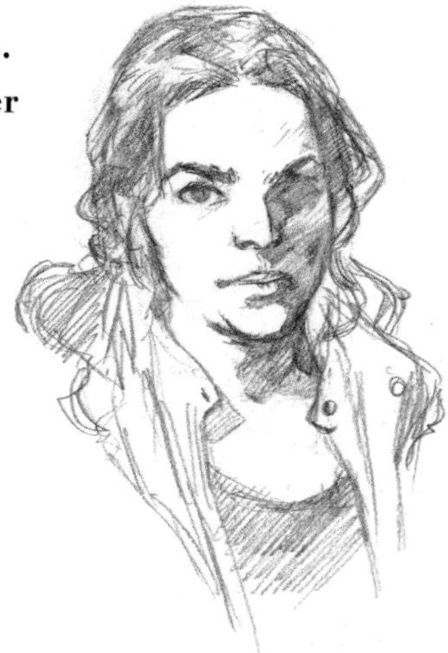

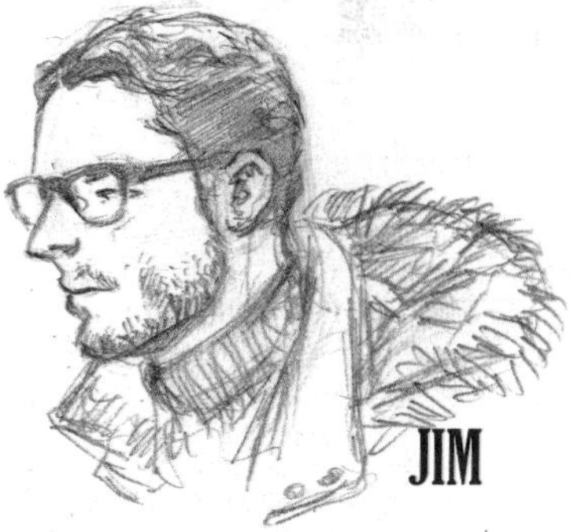

JIM

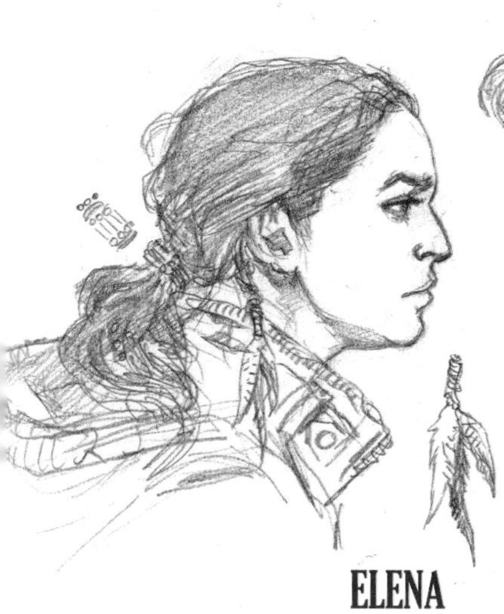

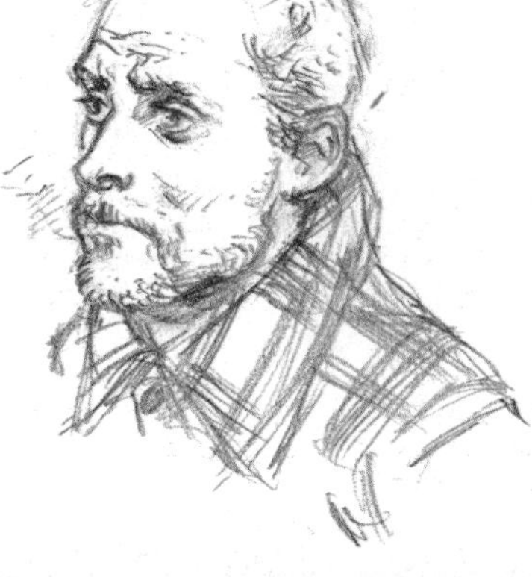

ELENA

BRENDAN

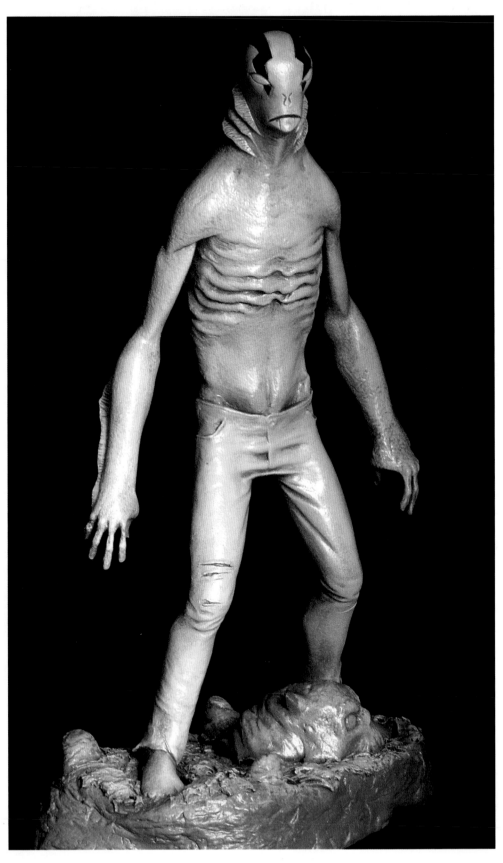

Sculpture by Pablo Blanco.
https://www.facebook.com/pabloblanco088

Although Seba drew the story, Max designed Coyolxauhqui for his incredible cover to issue #6.

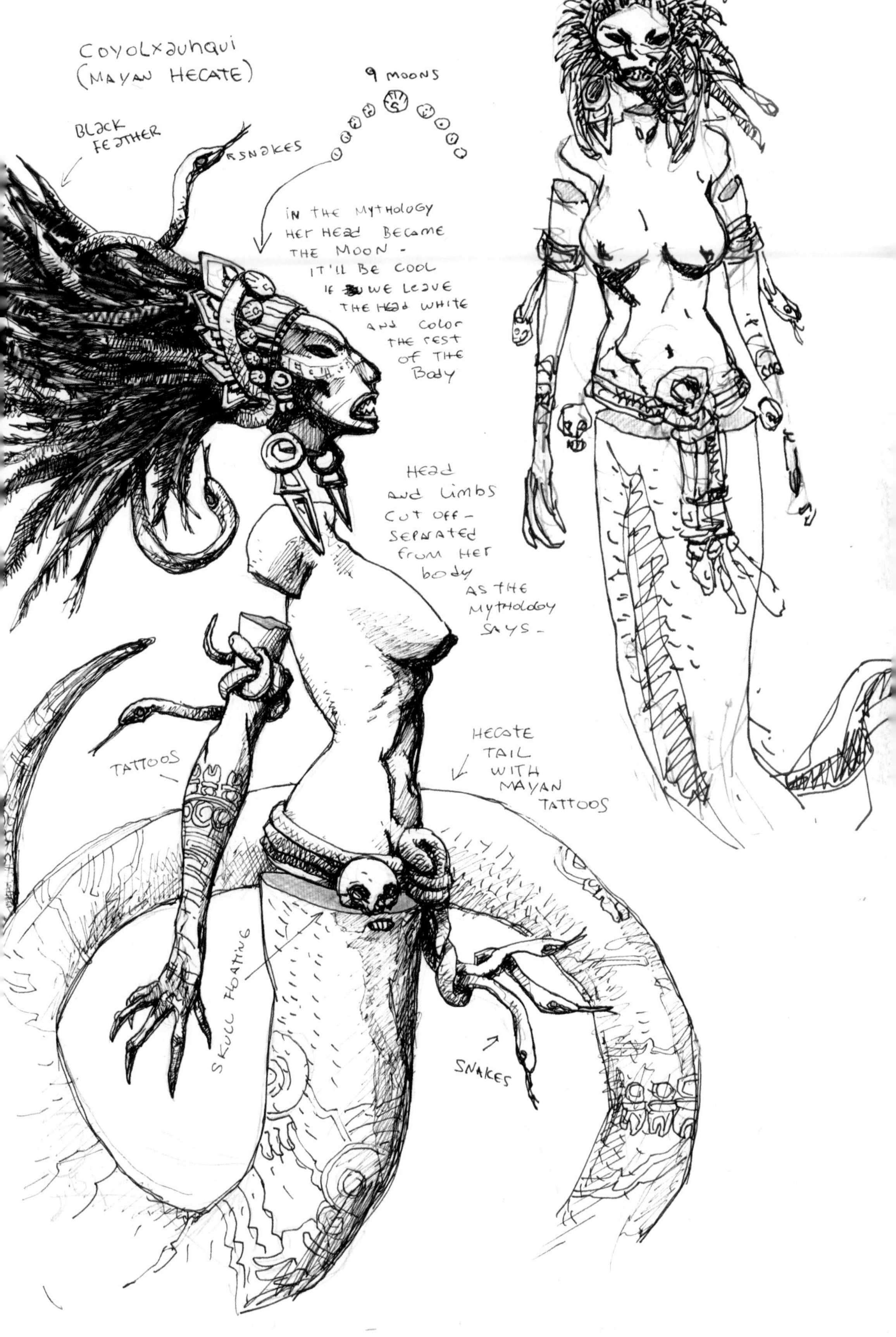
COYOLXAUHQUI
(MAYAN HECATE)
9 MOONS
BLACK FEATHER
SNAKES
IN THE MYTHOLOGY HER HEAD BECAME THE MOON - IT'LL BE COOL IF WE LEAVE THE HEAD WHITE AND COLOR THE REST OF THE BODY
HEAD AND LIMBS CUT OFF - SEPARATED FROM HER BODY AS THE MYTHOLOGY SAYS -
TATTOOS
HECATE TAIL WITH MAYAN TATTOOS
SKULL FLOATING
SNAKES

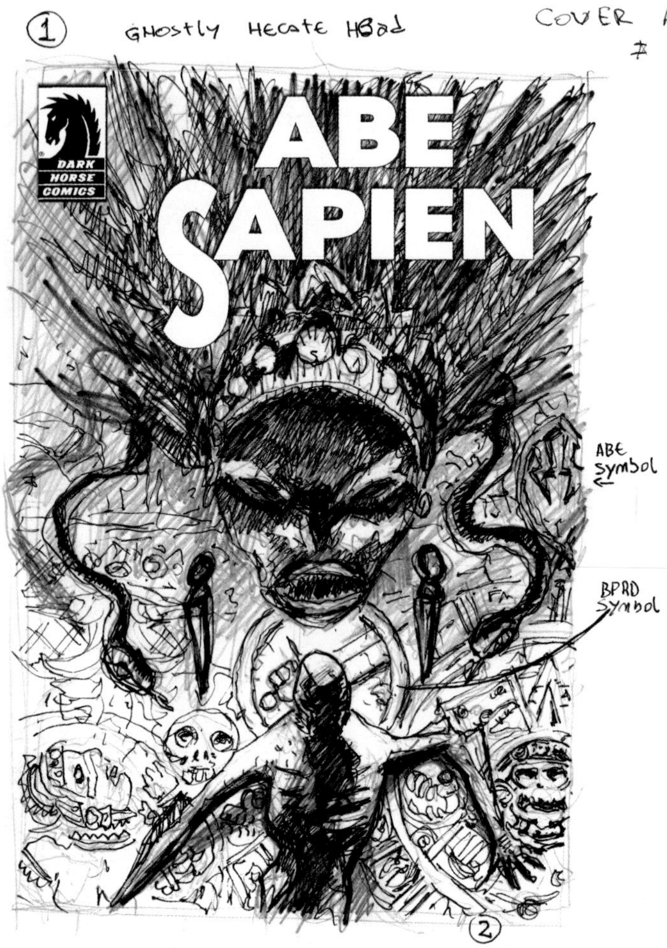
1
GHOSTLY HECATE HEAD
COVER ABE
DARK HORSE COMICS
ABE SAPIEN
ABE symbol
BPRD symbol

Max's cover sketches for issue #6. We immediately loved the one below.

Facing: A raw scan of his line art for the cover, seen in color (by Dave Stewart) on the chapter break for *The Shape of Things to Come* on page 5.

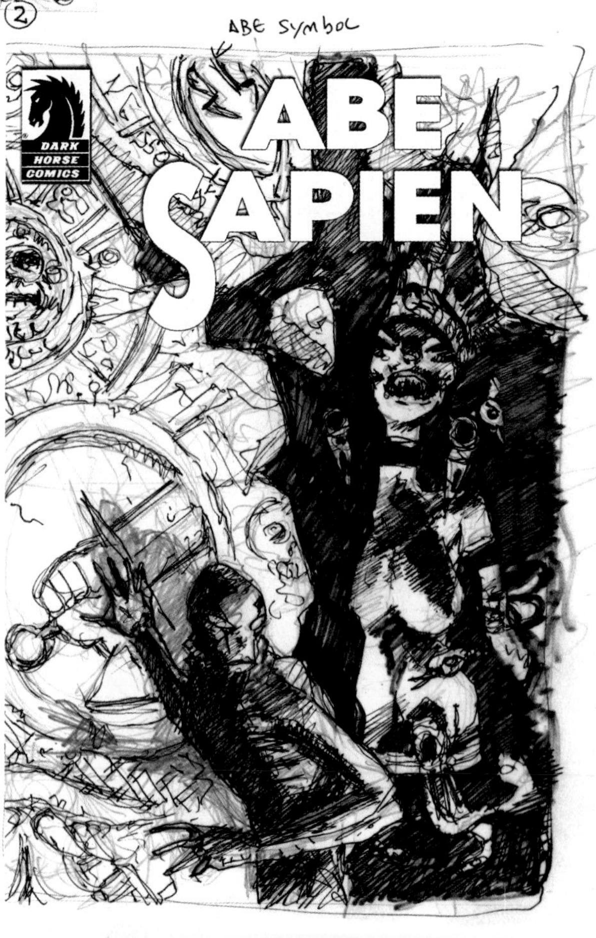
2
ABE symbol
DARK HORSE COMICS
ABE SAPIEN

When Max penciled the final art, he didn't place Abe's hand on the B.P.R.D. symbol, as he had in the sketch. We asked him to move the hand onto the symbol, giving the suggestion that he's holding the sword—turned out Max hadn't noticed he'd put it there on the sketch, but agreed that it was a nice touch.

ABE (#6) COVER MAX FIUMARA

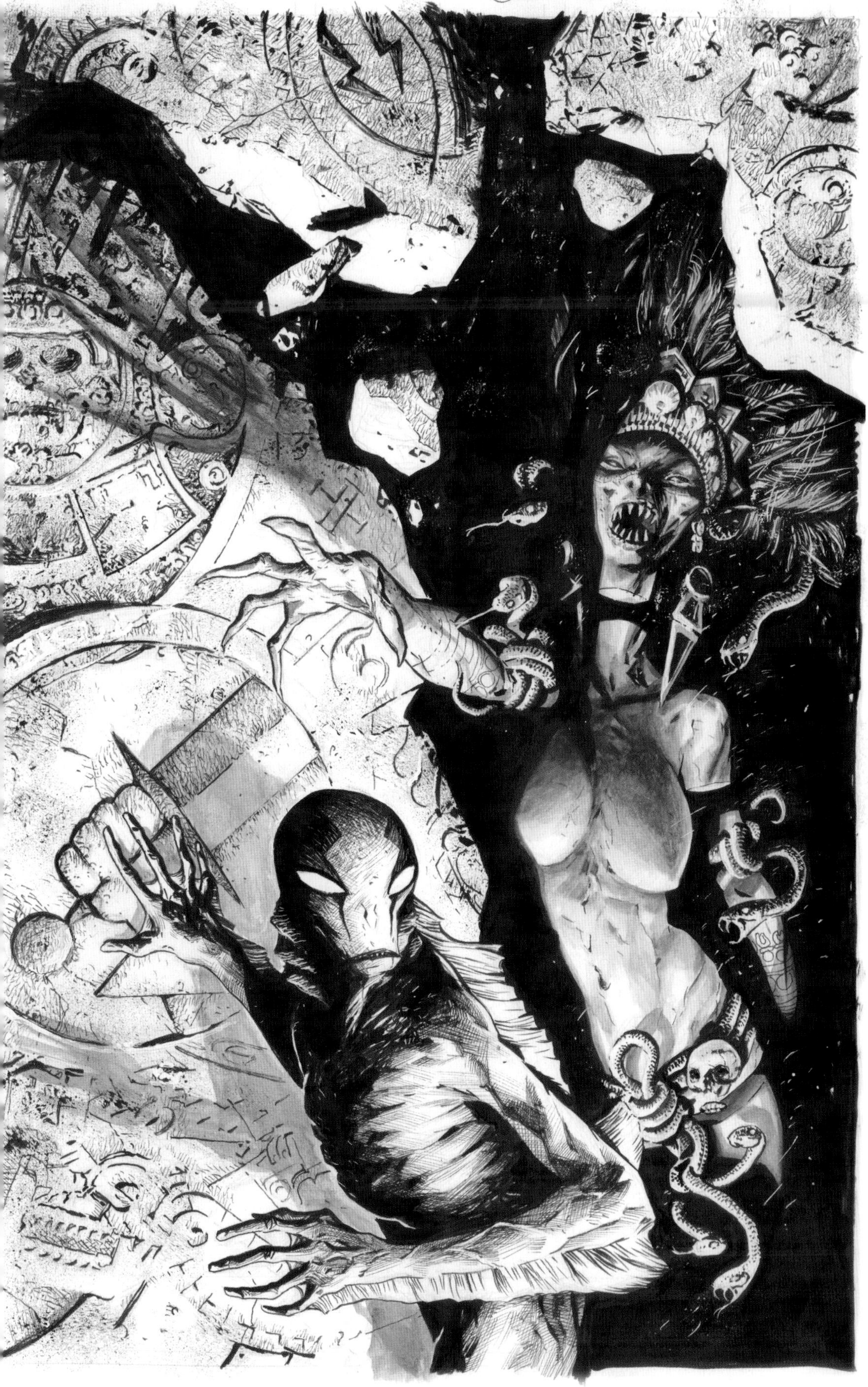

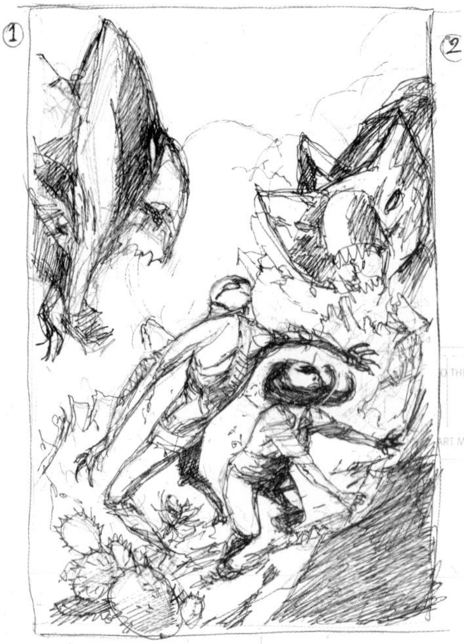
1

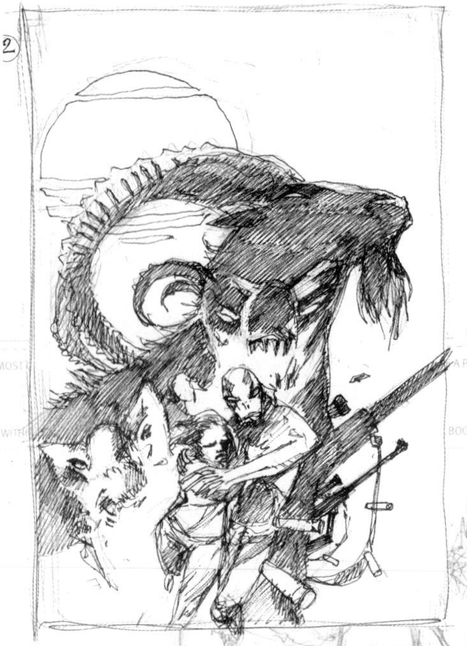
2
2

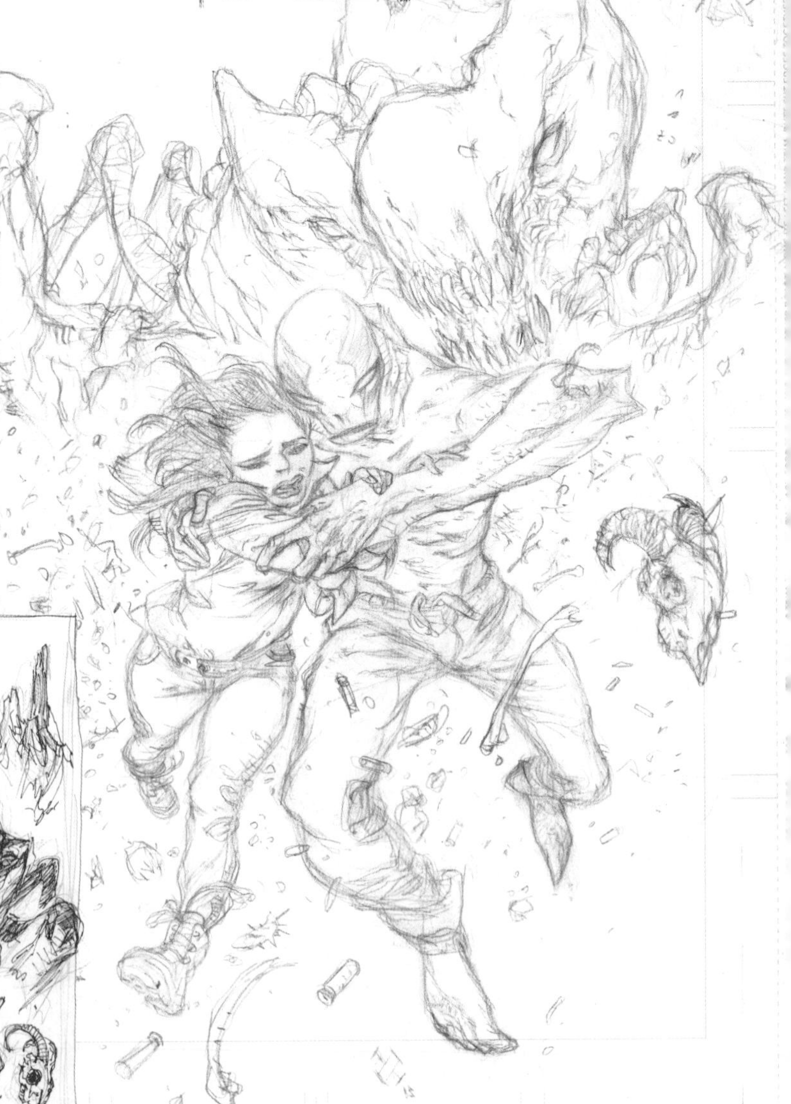
PAGE:
A PAGE IS CUT TO SIZE
BOOK PAGE
PENCIL ONLY, DRAW ON THE REVERSE SIDE OF THIS BOARD AND INK IN TRIM MARKS IN BLACK.

Max's cover sketches, pencils, and final colors (by Dave) for the issue #7 cover.

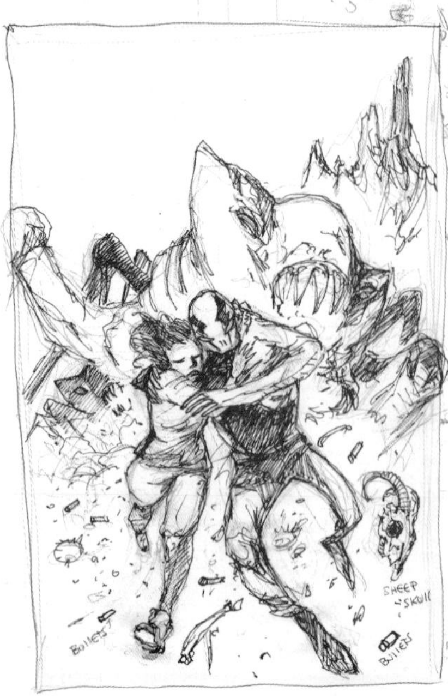
SHEEP SKULL
Bullets
Bullets

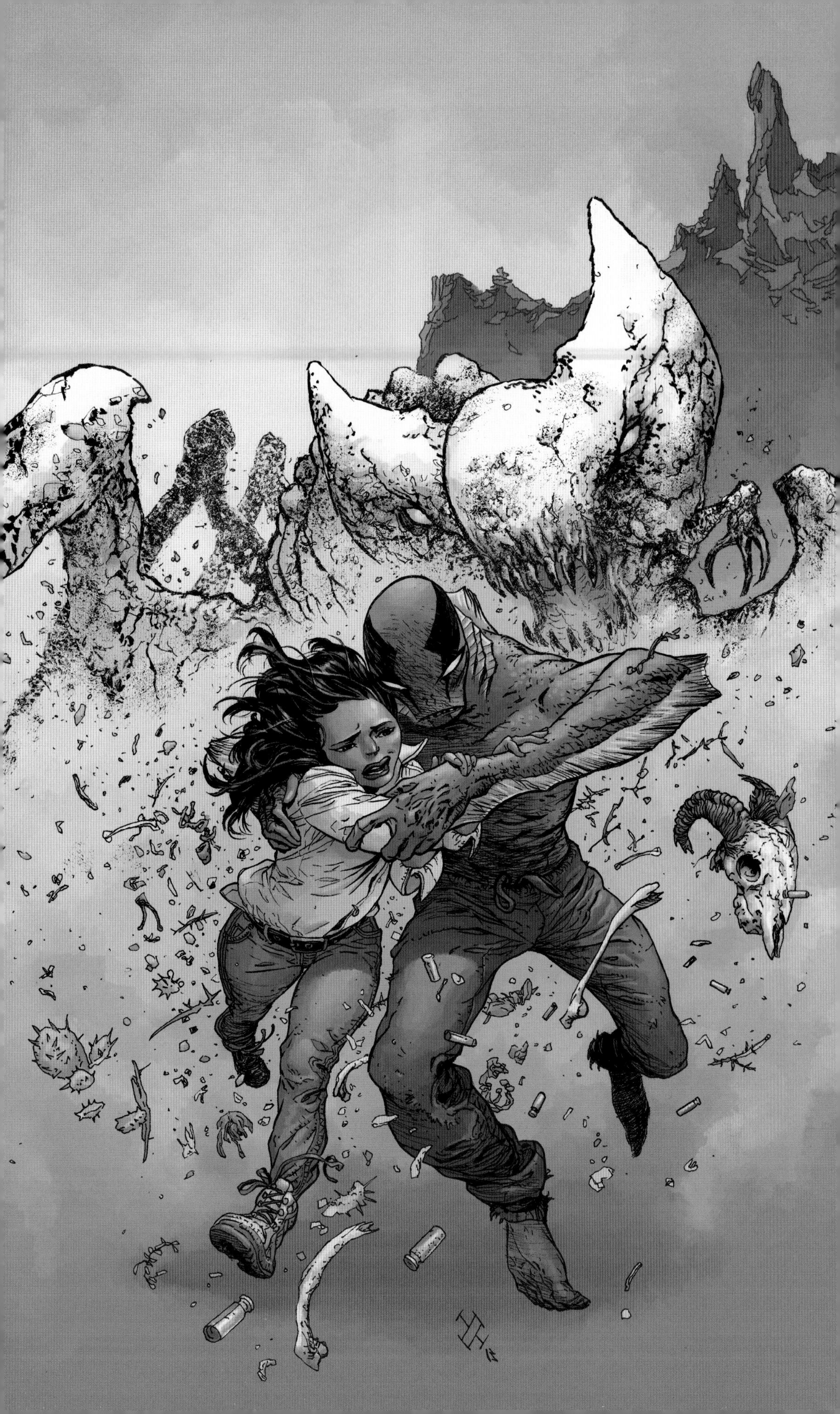

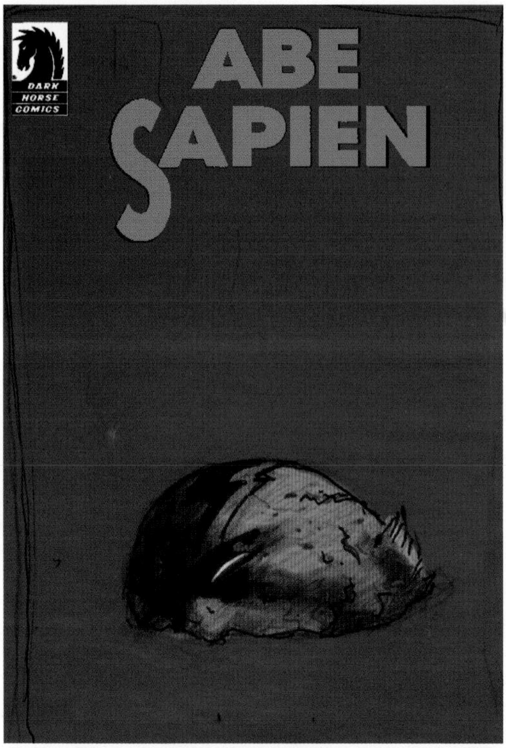
ABE
SAPIEN
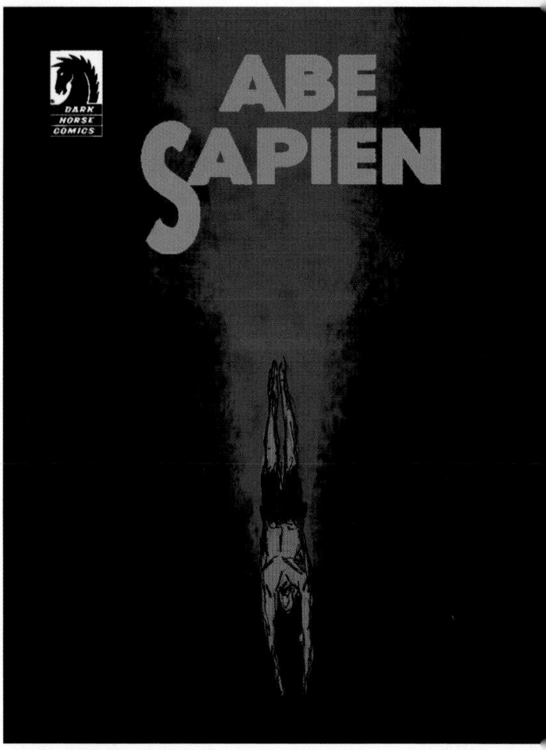
ABE
SAPIEN
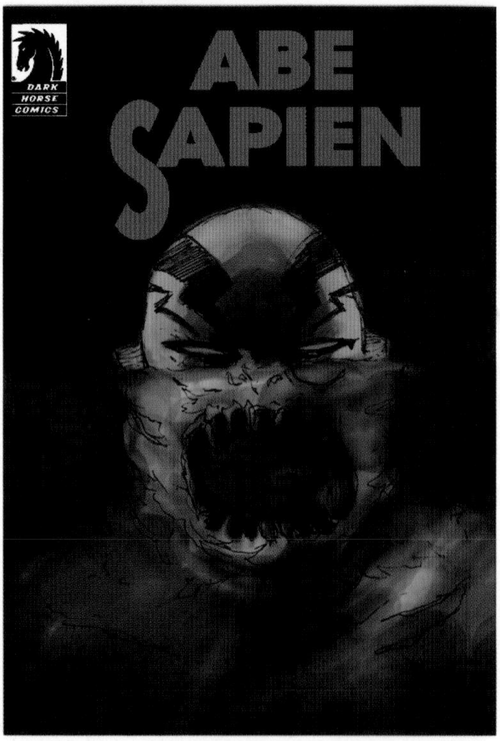
ABE
SAPIEN
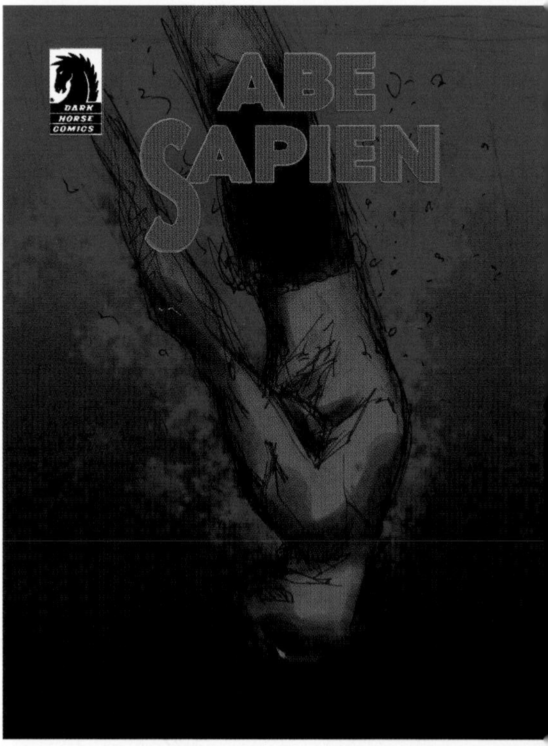
ABE
SAPIEN

Mike Oeming did a fill-in story for issue #8, not collected here.
These are Max's cover sketches and the raw inks for the issue #8 cover.

DARK HORSE COMICS ART BOARD

TITLE: ABE SAPIEN ISSUE: #08 ARTIST: MAX FIUMARA PAGE: Cover

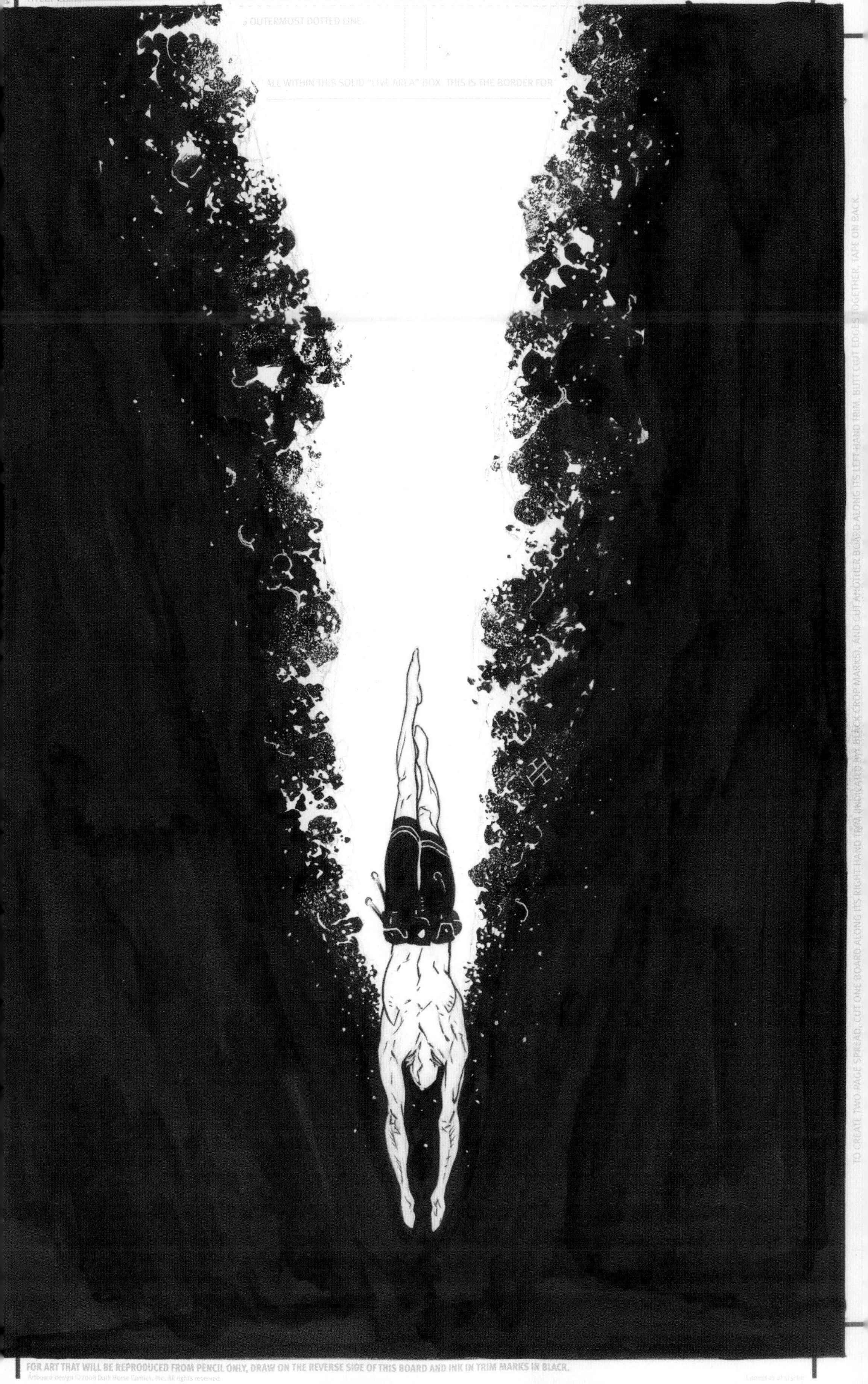

FOR ART THAT WILL BE REPRODUCED FROM PENCIL ONLY, DRAW ON THE REVERSE SIDE OF THIS BOARD AND INK IN TRIM MARKS IN BLACK.

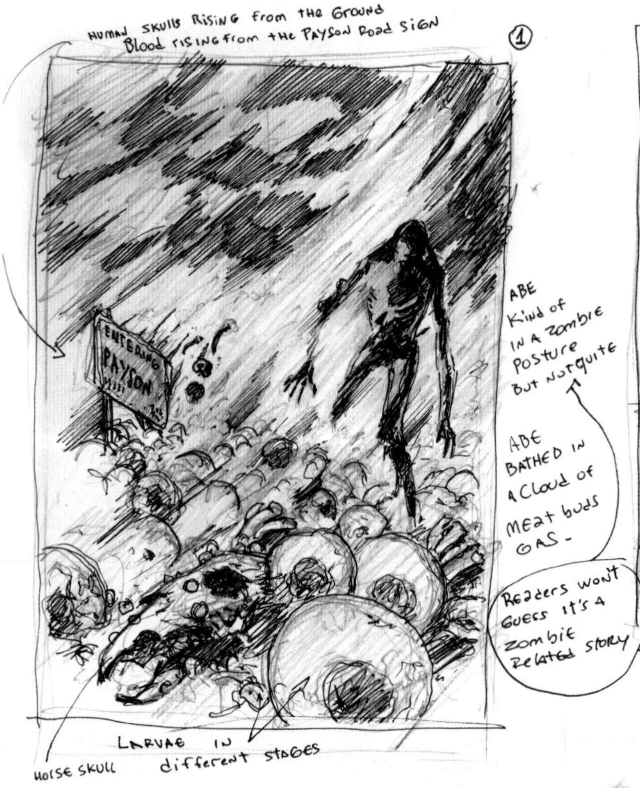

HUMAN SKULLS RISING FROM THE GROUND
Blood rising from the PAYSON Road SIGN
1
ENTERING
PAYSON
ABE
Kind of in a zombie posture but not quite
ABE BATHED IN A Cloud of MEAT buds GAS -
Readers won't guess it's a zombie related story
LARVAE IN different STAGES
HORSE SKULL

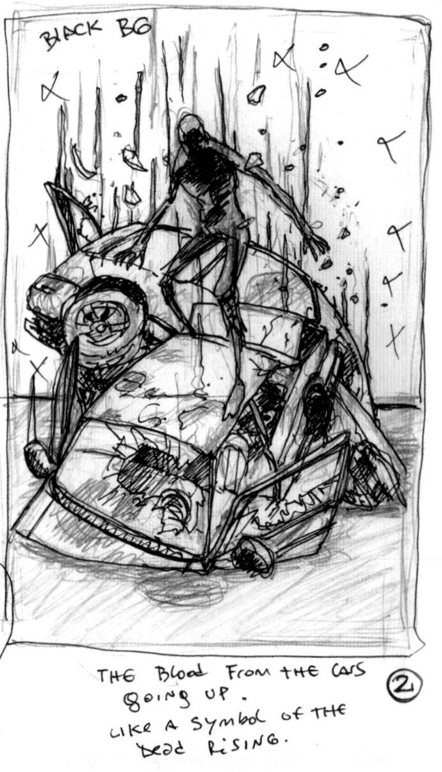

BLACK BG
THE Blood From the cars going up.
Like a symbol of the Dead rising.
2

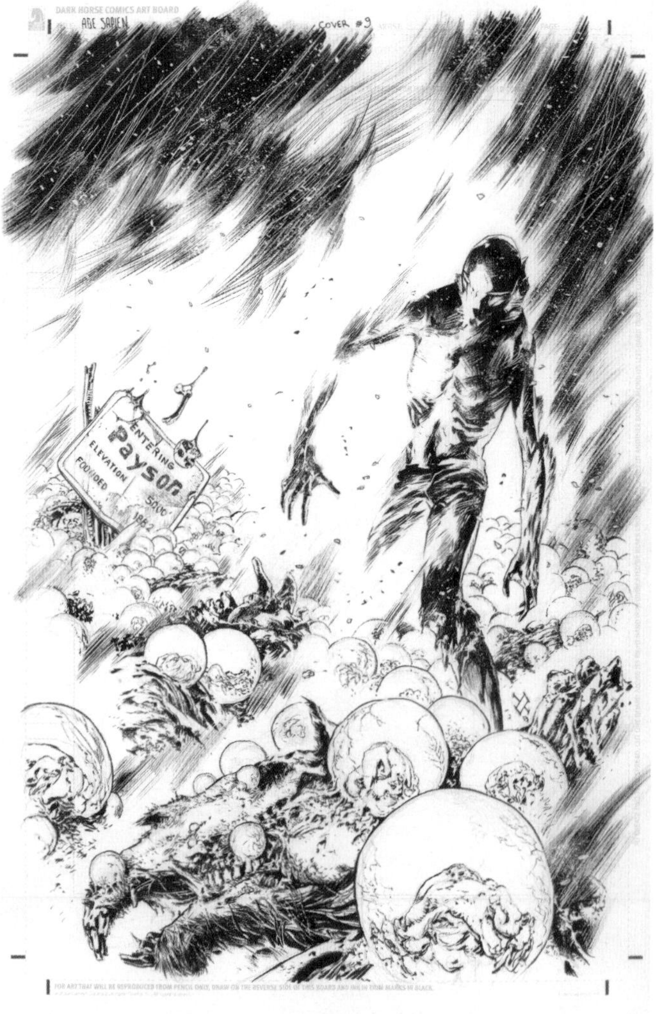

DARK HORSE COMICS ART BOARD
ABE SAPIEN
COVER #9
ENTERING
Payson
ELEVATION
FOUNDED

Max's sketches, raw inks, and final art (colored by Dave) for the issue #9 cover. Payson, Arizona, is a real town, and some people in the town were very helpful in our attempt to re-create the town in a comic, only to wreck it.

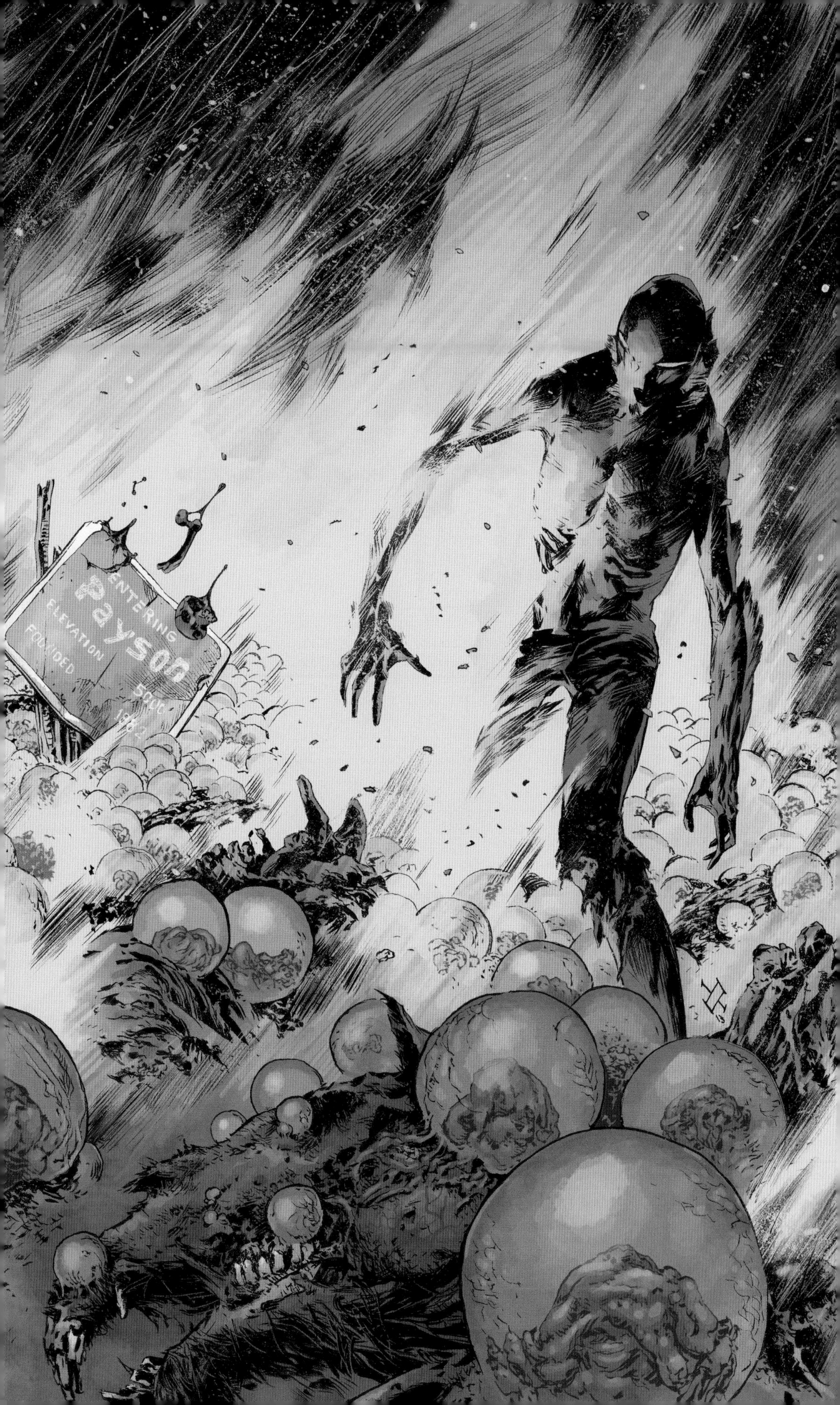
ENTERING
Payson
ELEVATION
5000
FOUNDED

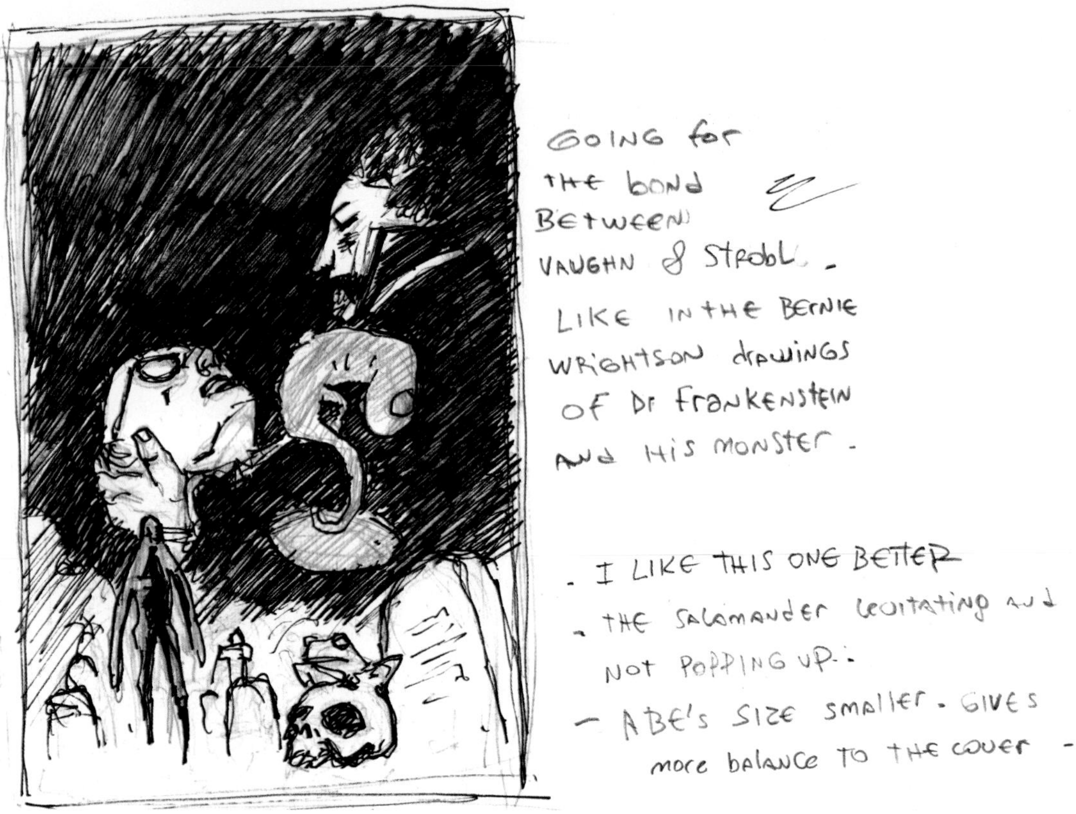
GOING for THE bond BETWEEN VAUGHN & STROBL. - LIKE IN THE BERNIE WRIGHTSON drawings OF Dr Frankenstein AND HIS MONSTER.
- I LIKE THIS ONE BETTER
- THE SALAMANDER LEVITATING AND NOT POPPING UP.
- ABE'S SIZE SMALLER. GIVES more balance TO THE COVER -

Max's cover sketches for our issue #10 cover, featuring Vaughn and Strobl. The final art can be seen on the *To the Last Man* chapter break on page 51. Max had done this cover right before I visited them in Argentina, and while talking about the cover there, we decided we loved Abe's pose so much, we'd use an event in issue #12 to alter his posture for the foreseeable future.

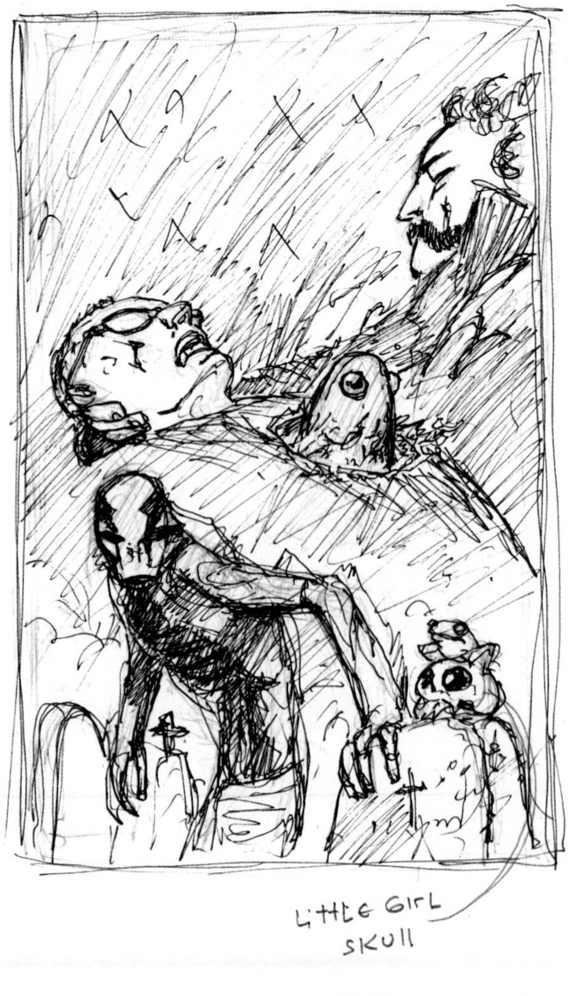
LITTLE GIRL SKULL

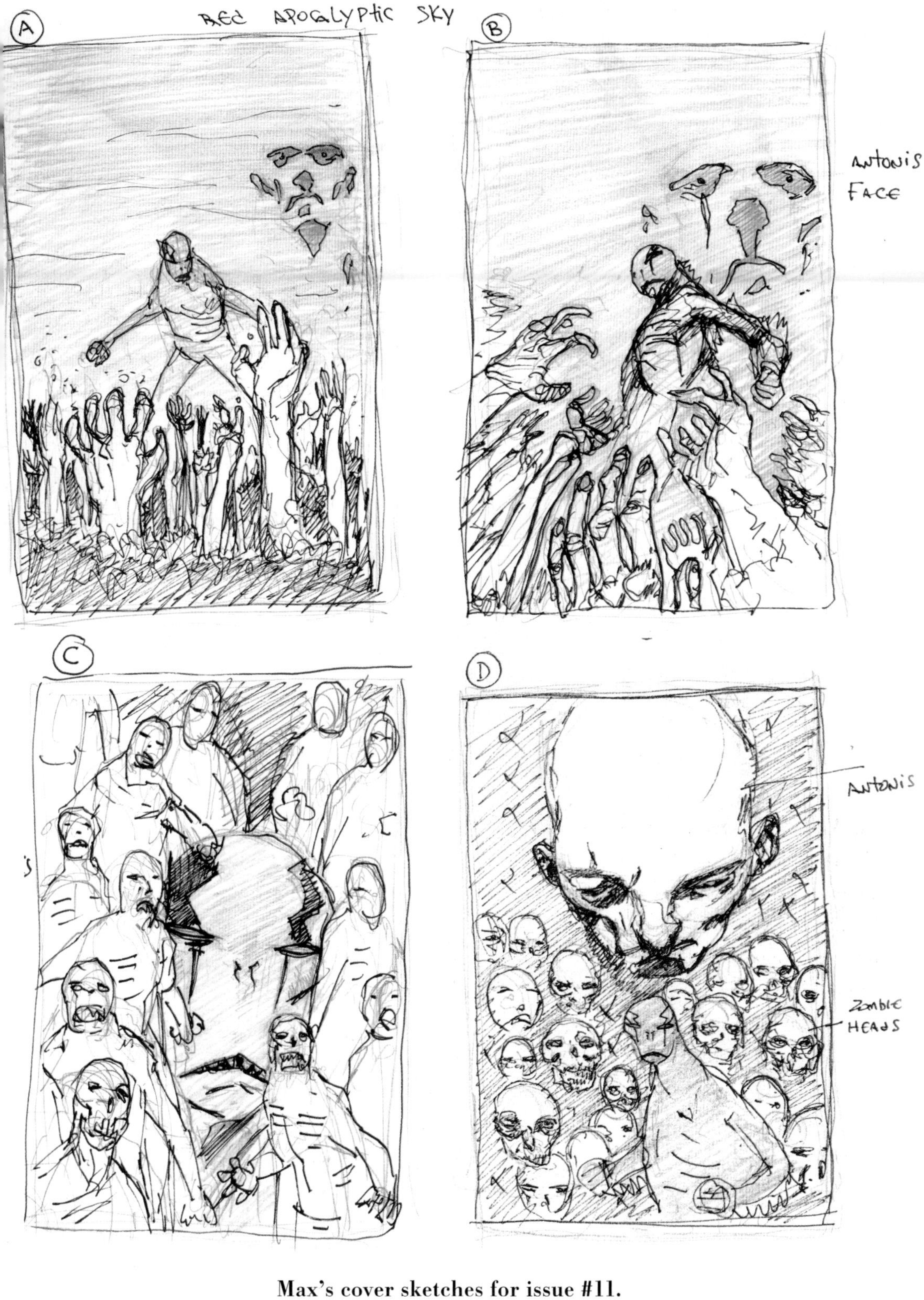
A
RED APOCALYPTIC SKY
B
ANTONIS FACE
C
D
ANTONIS
ZOMBIE HEADS

Max's cover sketches for issue #11.

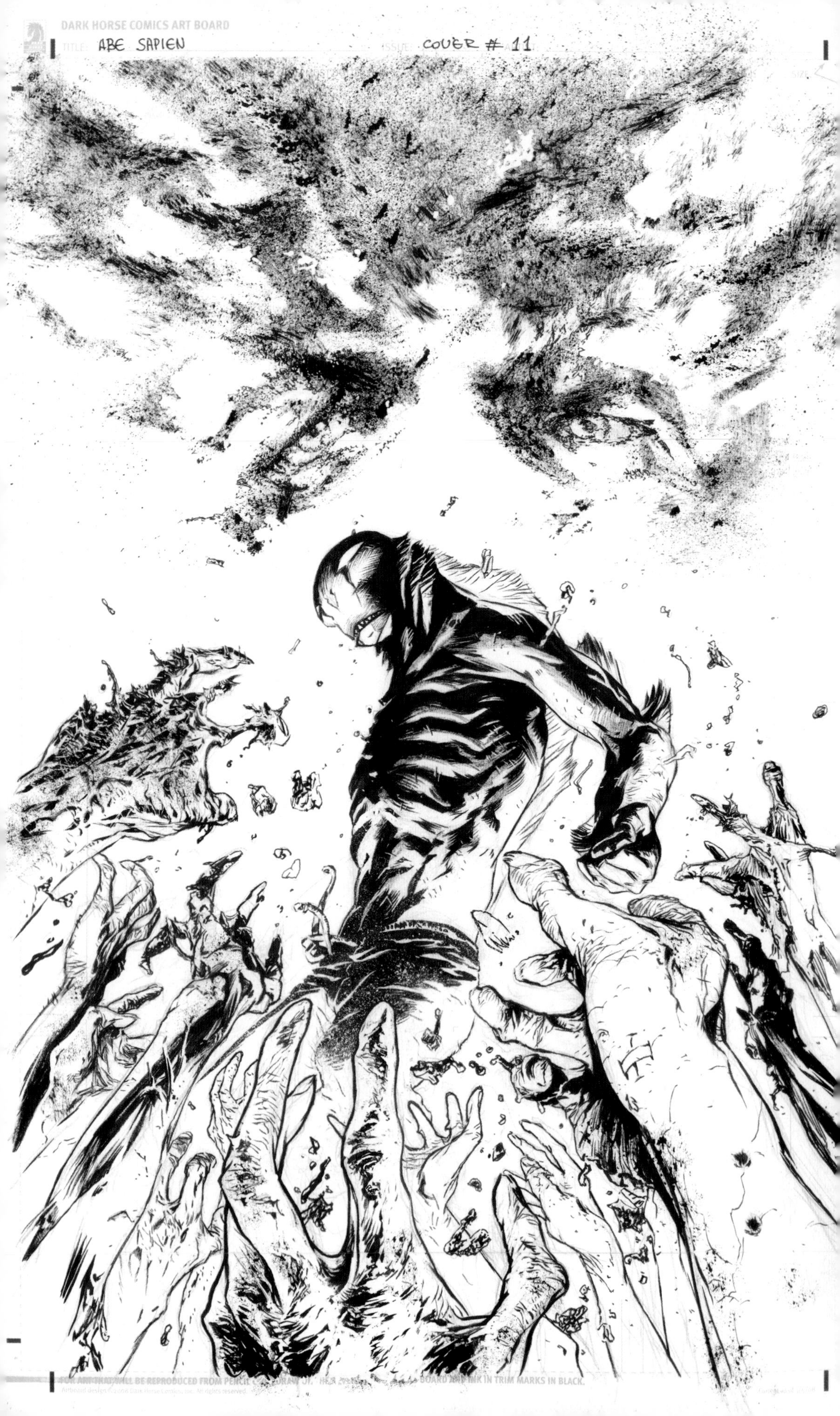
DARK HORSE COMICS ART BOARD
TITLE: ABE SAPIEN
ISSUE: COVER # 11

Max's designs for Antonis, Strobl's mentor turned foe.

Facing: Raw scan of Max's cover for issue #11.

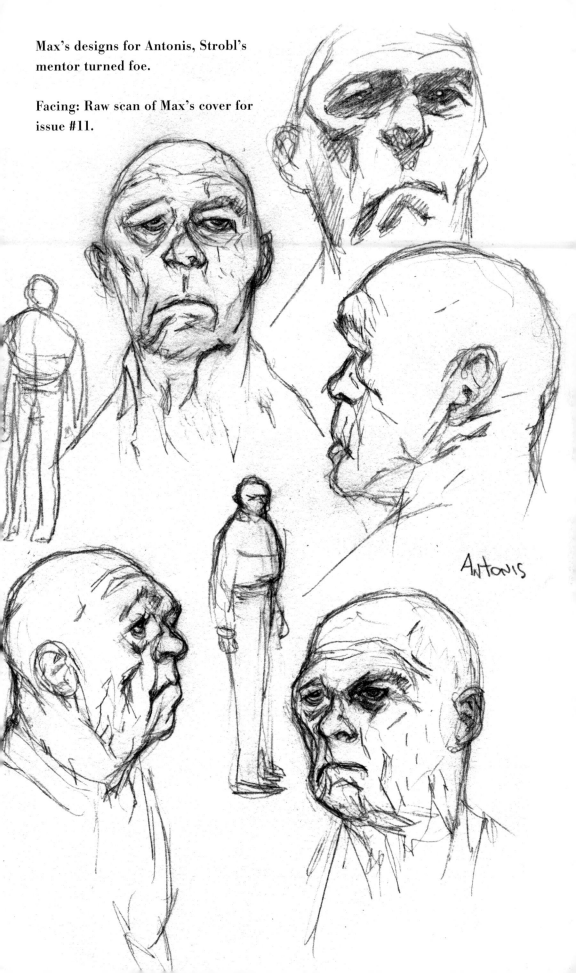

ANTONIS

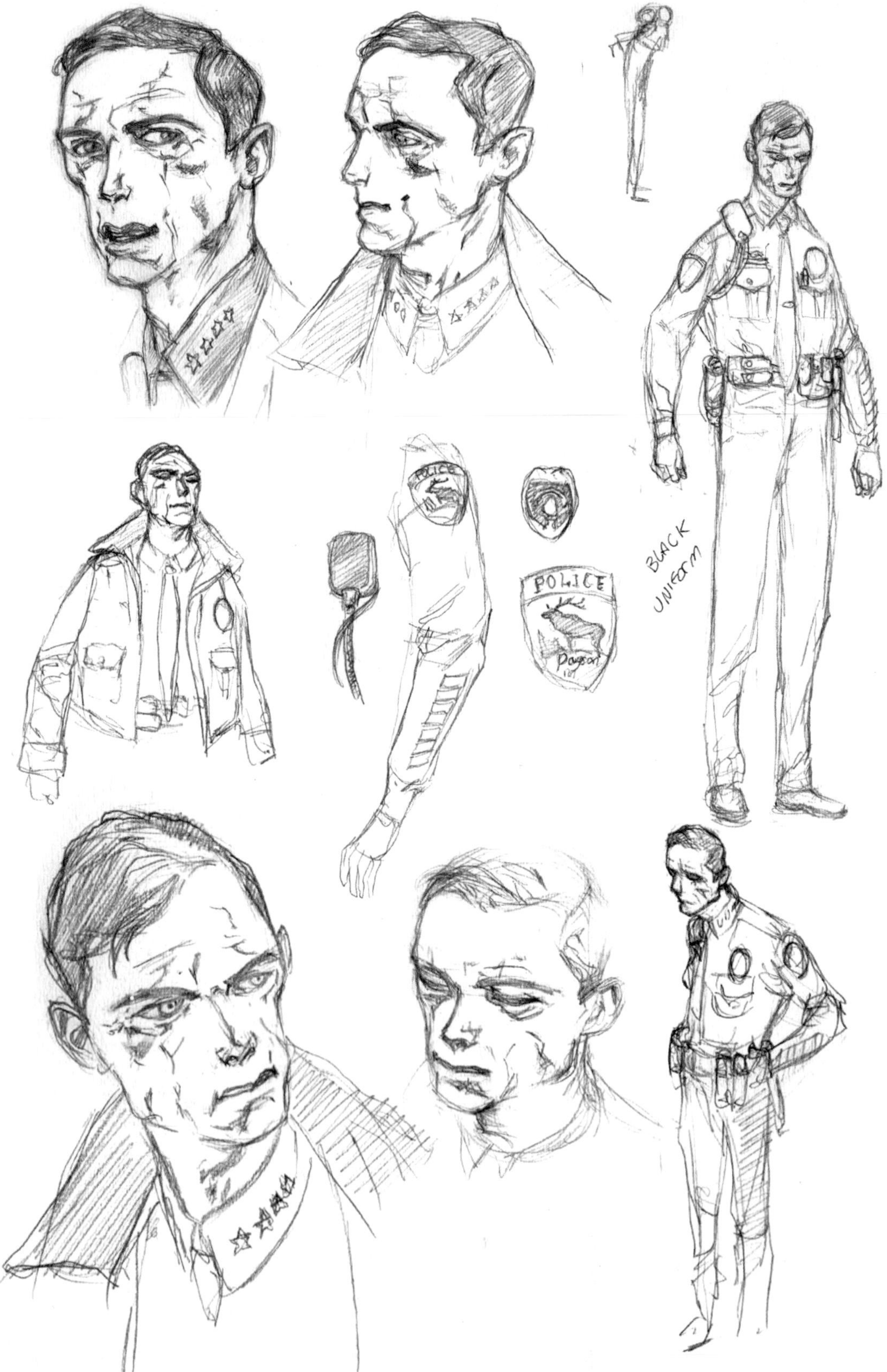
POLICE
Payson
BLACK UNIFORM

Max's designs for the denizens of Payson, and, following, the cult members.

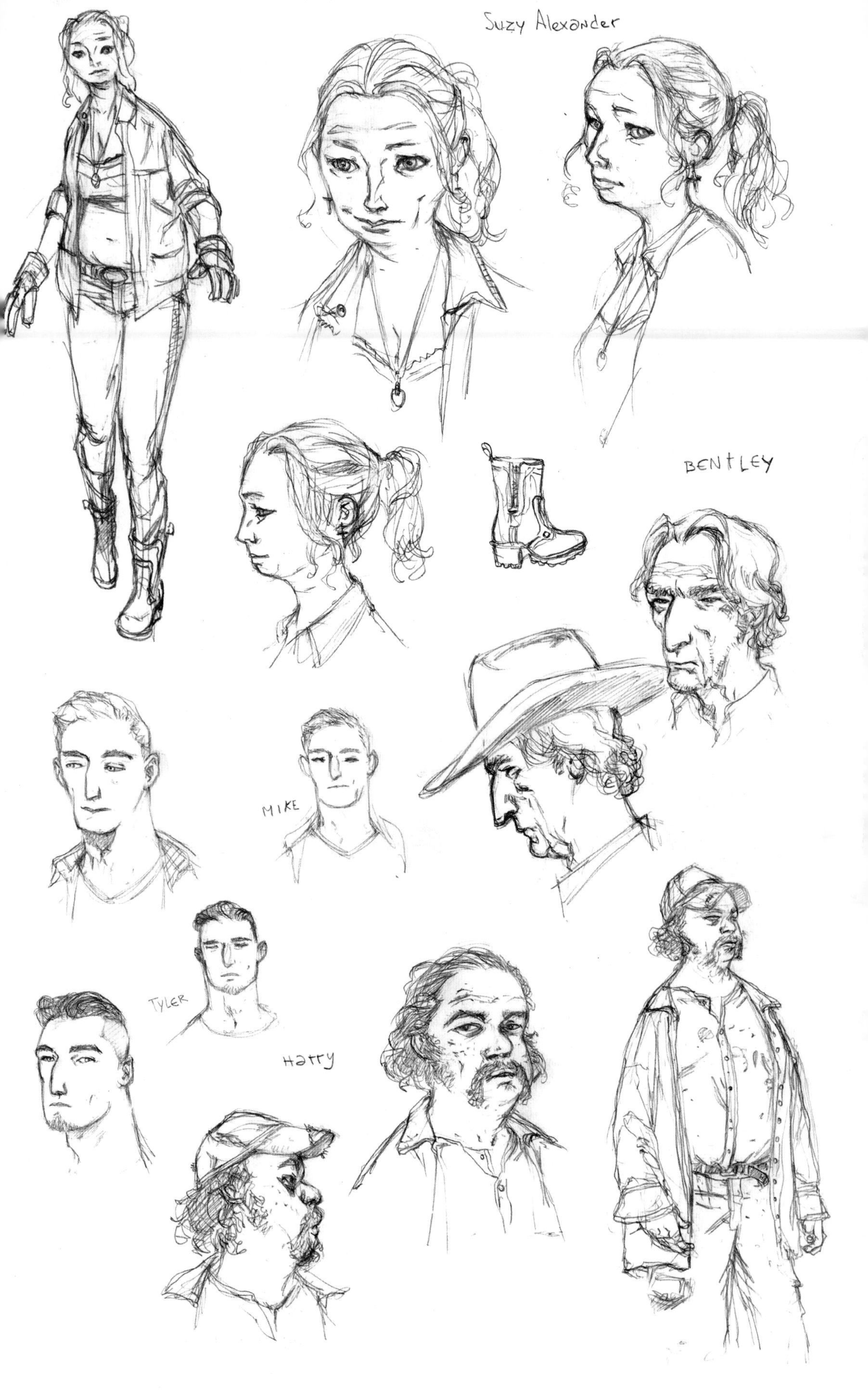
Suzy Alexander
BENTLEY
MIKE
TYLER
Harry

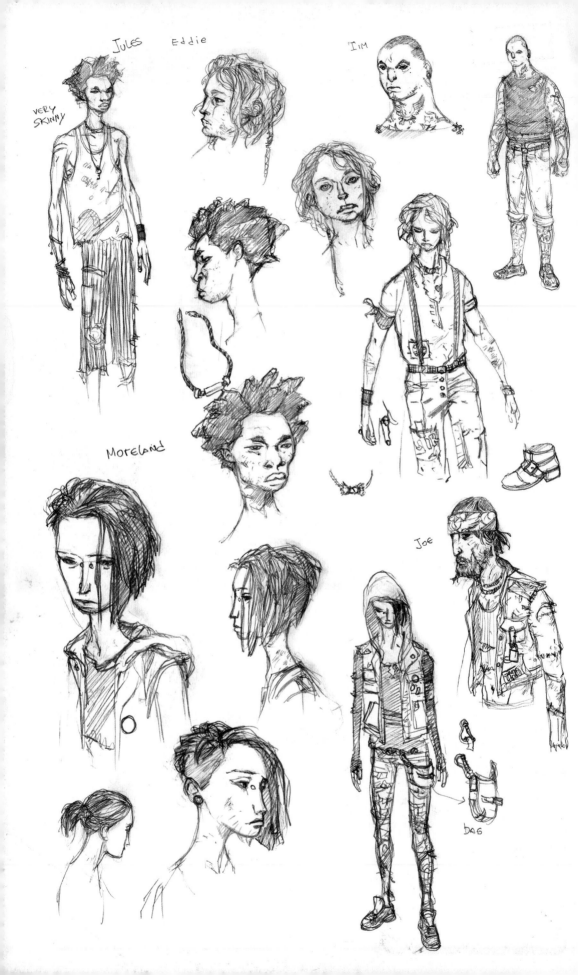

Jules   Eddie

very
skinny

Moreland

Joe

bag

Also by MIKE MIGNOLA

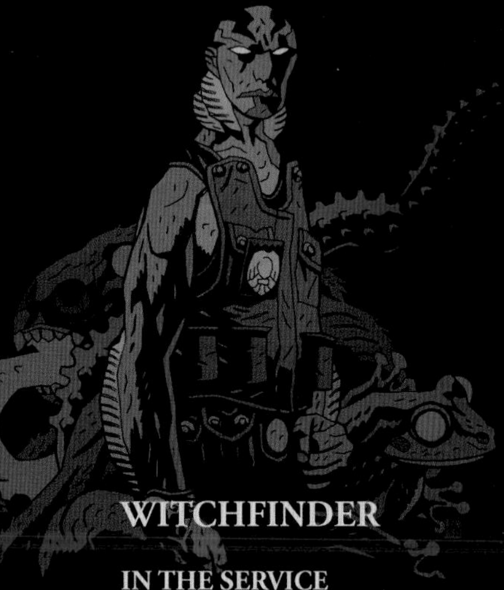

B.P.R.D.

PLAGUE OF FROGS
Volume 1
with Chris Golden, Guy Davis,
and others
ISBN 978-1-59582-609-1 | $34.99
Volume 2
with John Arcudi, Davis,
and others
ISBN 978-1-59582-672-5 | $34.99
Volume 3
with Arcudi, and Davis
ISBN 978-1-59582-860-6 | $34.99
Volume 4
with Arcudi and Davis
ISBN 978-1-59582-974-0 | $34.99

1946
with Joshua Dysart and Paul
Azaceta
ISBN 978-1-59582-191-1 | $17.99

1947
with Dysart, Fábio Moon, and
Gabriel Bá
ISBN 978-1-59582-478-3 | $17.99

1948
with Arcudi and Max Fiumara
ISBN 978-1-61655-183-4 | $17.99

BEING HUMAN
with Arcudi, Davis, and others
ISBN 978-1-59582-756-2 | $17.99

VAMPIRE
with Moon and Bá
ISBN 978-1-61655-196-4 | $19.99

B.P.R.D. HELL ON EARTH

NEW WORLD
with Arcudi and Davis
ISBN 978-1-59582-707-4 | $19.99

GODS AND MONSTERS
with Arcudi, Davis, and Crook
ISBN 978-1-59582-822-4 | $19.99

RUSSIA
with Arcudi, Crook, and
Duncan Fegredo
ISBN 978-1-59582-946-7 | $19.9

**THE DEVIL'S ENGINE AND
THE LONG DEATH**
with Arcudi, Crook, and
James Harren
ISBN 978-1-59582-981-8 | $19.99

**THE PICKENS COUNTY
HORROR AND OTHERS**
with Scott Allie, Jason Latour,
Harren, Max Fiumara, and
Becky Cloonan
ISBN 978-1-61655-140-7 | $19.99

**THE RETURN OF
THE MASTER**
with Arcudi and Crook
ISBN 978-1-61655-193-3 | $19.99

A COLD DAY IN HELL
with Arcudi, Peter Snejbjerg, and
Laurence Campbell
ISBN 978-1-61655-199-5 | $19.99

ABE SAPIEN

THE DROWNING
with Jason Shawn Alexander
ISBN 978-1-59582-185-0 | $17.99

**THE DEVIL DOES NOT JEST
AND OTHER STORIES**
with Arcudi, Harren, and others
ISBN 978-1-59582-925-2 | $17.99

**DARK AND TERRIBLE AND
THE NEW RACE OF MAN**
with Allie, Arcudi, Sebastián
Fiumara, and Max Fiumara
ISBN 978-1-61655-284-8 | $19.99

LOBSTER JOHNSON

THE IRON PROMETHEUS
with Jason Armstrong
ISBN 978-1-59307-975-8 | $17.99

THE BURNING HAND
with Arcudi and Tonci Zonjic
ISBN 978-1-61655-031-8 | $17.99

SATAN SMELLS A RAT
with Arcudi, Fiumara, Joe
Querio, Wilfredo Torres, and
Kevin Nowlan
ISBN 978-1-61655-203-9 | $18.99

WITCHFINDER

**IN THE SERVICE
OF ANGELS**
with Ben Stenbeck
ISBN 978-1-59582-483-7 | $17.99

LOST AND GONE FOREVER
with Arcudi and John Severin
ISBN 978-1-59582-794-4 | $17.99

THE AMAZING SCREW-ON HEAD AND OTHER CURIOUS OBJECTS
ISBN 978-1-59582-501-8 | $17.99

BALTIMORE

THE PLAGUE SHIPS
with Golden and Stenbeck
ISBN 978-1-59582-677-0 | $24.99

THE CURSE BELLS
with Golden and Stenbeck
ISBN 978-1-59582-674-9 | $24.99

**A PASSING STRANGER
AND OTHER STORIES**
with Golden and Stenbeck
ISBN 978-1-61655-182-7 | $24.99

CHAPEL OF BONES
with Golden and Stenbeck
ISBN 978-1-61655-328-9 | $24.99

NOVELS

**LOBSTER JOHNSON:
THE SATAN FACTORY**
with Thomas E. Sniegoski
ISBN 978-1-59582-203-1 | $12.95

**JOE GOLEM AND THE
DROWNING CITY**
with Golden
ISBN 978-1-59582-971-9 | $99.99

HELLBOY *by* MIKE MIGNOLA

HELLBOY LIBRARY
EDITION VOLUME 1:
Seed of Destruction
and Wake the Devil
ISBN 978-1-59307-910-9 | $49.99

HELLBOY LIBRARY
EDITION VOLUME 2:
The Chained Coffin
and The Right Hand of Doom
ISBN 978-1-59307-989-5 | $49.99

HELLBOY LIBRARY
EDITION VOLUME 3:
Conqueror Worm
and Strange Places
ISBN 978-1-59582-352-6 | $49.99

HELLBOY LIBRARY
EDITION VOLUME 4:
The Crooked Man and The Troll Witch
with Richard Corben and others
ISBN 978-1-59582-658-9 | $49.99

HELLBOY LIBRARY
EDITION VOLUME 5:
Darkness Calls and the Wild Hunt
with Duncan Fegredo
ISBN 978-1-59582-886-6 | $49.99

HELLBOY LIBRARY
EDITION VOLUME 6:
The Storm and the Fury
and The Bride of Hell
with Duncan Fegredo, Richard Corben, Kevin
Nowlan, and Scott Hampton
ISBN 978-1-61655-133-9 | $49.99

SEED OF DESTRUCTION
with John Byrne
ISBN 978-1-59307-094-6 | $17.99

WAKE THE DEVIL
ISBN 978-1-59307-095-3 | $17.99

THE CHAINED COFFIN AND OTHERS
ISBN 978-1-59307-091-5 | $17.99

THE RIGHT HAND OF DOOM
ISBN 978-1-59307-093-9 | $17.99

CONQUEROR WORM
ISBN 978-1-59307-092-2 | $17.99

STRANGE PLACES
ISBN 978-1-59307-475-3 | $17.99

THE TROLL WITCH
AND OTHERS
ISBN 978-1-59307-860-7 | $17.99

DARKNESS CALLS
with Duncan Fegredo
ISBN 978-1-59307-896-6 | $19.99

THE WILD HUNT
with Duncan Fegredo
ISBN 978-1-59582-352-6 | $19.99

THE CROOKED MAN
AND OTHERS
with Richard Corben
ISBN 978-1-59582-477-6 | $17.99

THE BRIDE OF HELL AND OTHERS
with Richard Corben, Kevin Nowlan,
and Scott Hampton
ISBN 978-1-59582-740-1 | $19.99

THE STORM AND THE FURY
with Duncan Fegredo
ISBN 978-1-59582-827-9 | $19.99

HOUSE OF THE LIVING DEAD
with Richard Corben
ISBN 978-1-59582-757-9 | $14.99

THE MIDNIGHT CIRCUS
with Duncan Fegredo
ISBN 978-1-61655-238-1 | $14.99

HELLBOY: THE FIRST 20 YEARS
ISBN 978-1-61655-353-1 | $19.99

THE ART OF HELLBOY
ISBN 978-1-59307-089-2 | $29.99

HELLBOY II:
THE ART OF THE MOVIE
ISBN 978-1-59307-964-2 | $24.99

HELLBOY: THE COMPANION
ISBN 978-1-59307-655-9 | $14.99

HELLBOY: WEIRD TALES
VOLUME 1
ISBN 978-1-56971-622-9 | $17.99
VOLUME 2
ISBN 978-1-56971-953-4 | $17.99

HELLBOY: MASKS AND MONSTERS
with James Robinson and Scott Benefiel
ISBN 978-1-59582-567-4 | $17.99

NOVELS

HELLBOY: EMERALD HELL
By Tom Piccirilli
ISBN 978-1-59582-141-6 | $12.99

HELLBOY: THE ALL-SEEING EYE
By Mark Morris
ISBN 978-1-59582-141-6 | $12.99

HELLBOY: THE FIRE WOLVES
By Tim Lebbon
ISBN 978-1-59582-204-8 | $12.99

HELLBOY: THE ICE WOLVES
By Mark Chadbourn
ISBN 978-1-59582-205-5 | $12.99

SHORT STORIES
Illustrated by Mike Mignola

HELLBOY: ODD JOBS
By Poppy Z. Brite, Greg Rucka,
and others
ISBN 978-1-56971-440-9 | $14.99

HELLBOY: ODDER JOBS
By Frank Darabont, Guillermo del Toro,
and others
ISBN 978-1-59307-226-1 | $14.99

HELLBOY: ODDEST JOBS
By Joe R. Lansdale, China Miéville,
and others
ISBN 978-1-59307-944-4 | $14.99